79

7

217

15

360

301

355

344

365 THINGS TO DO WITH LEGO® BRICKS

WRITTEN BY
SIMON HUGO

MODELS BY
**JOSHUA BERRY,
JASON BRISCOE,
STUART CRAWSHAW,
NAOMI FARR, ALICE FINCH,
ROD GILLIES, KEVIN HALL,
BARNEY MAIN
AND DREW MAUGHAN**

Pick an activity...

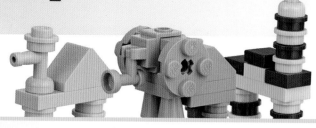

ANIMALS AND OTHER CREATURES

TRICKS AND PRANKS

CREEPY THINGS

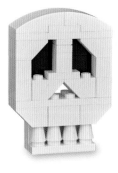

FOR SPORTS LOVERS

MULTI-PLAYER GAMES

ONE-PLAYER GAMES

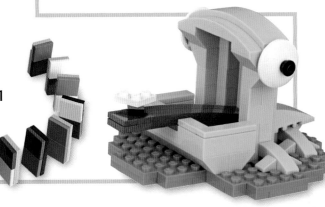

GROUP CHALLENGES

SOLO CHALLENGES

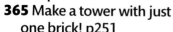

DISCOVER WITH LEGO BRICKS

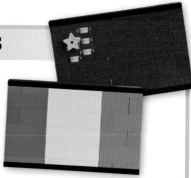

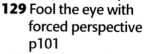
HOW-TOS

GIVE A GIFT

GET ARTY

MAKE A DISPLAY

PUZZLES AND BRAINTEASERS

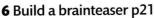

PUT ON A SHOW

BUILD IN MICRO-SCALE

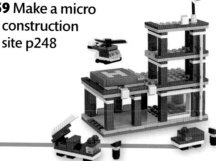

BE ORGANISED

FUN THINGS TO DO WITH YOUR MINIFIGURES

GET SNAP HAPPY

MAKE IT ALL ABOUT YOU

ON THE MOVE

EYE CAUTION
For models with shooting functions, do not aim the shooter at eyes.

LET ME HELP YOU DECIDE WHAT TO DO TODAY!

Sometimes it can be hard to know where to begin! Ask yourself a few simple questions and discover some amazing activities to get you started.

What will you do today?

HOW MUCH TIME DO YOU HAVE?

UNDER 15 MINUTES

Look for this time symbol around the activity numbers for activities that take less than 15 minutes.

15

Make a start with:
9 Create tower dudes (p22);
33 Make a micro bot (p38);
43 Mix up your minifigures (p42).

WHAT BRICKS DO YOU HAVE?

ONLY A FEW BRICKS

Try an activity with small and simple builds, like these:
116 Take the 20-to-1 challenge (p93); **167** Bring back the dinosaurs (p125); **284** Build a micro zoo (p201).

LOTS OF THE SAME COLOUR

Take on an activity with models in almost all one colour, such as these: **34** Build a useful giant brick (p39); **256** Build a single colour scene (p183); **355** Penguin parade (p246).

LOTS OF THE SAME TYPE

Look for activities with models with lots of similar sections and pieces. Try one of these: **87** Build a super-bendy snake (p73); **162** Pick-a-brick challenge (p121); **254** Topple a trail of LEGO dominoes (p182).

LOTS OF TIME

Look for this time symbol for activities that take more than one hour for an all-day or weekend project.

 60

Take on one of these: **85** Mix things up with a sliding square puzzle (p72); **192** Make your own LEGO® movie (p140); **200** Make an amazing drawing machine (p146–147).

UNDER AN HOUR

For activities that take longer than 15 minutes but less than one hour, look for this time symbol.

45

Try one of the following:
109 Spot the difference (p88);
155 Recreate a creepy-crawly (p118);
358 Make a pencil pot (p247).

ARE YOU UP FOR A SOLO CHALLENGE?

YES

Building alone? Take on one of the following: **235** Create your coat of arms (p170); **291** Go to the movies (p205); **304** Make a model of your home (p214).

NO

Playing with friends? Try one of these:
90 Start a chain of creativity (p75);
114 Hunt for the hidden pirate (p92);
211 Play a game of sinking ships (p155).

WHAT KIND OF TIMED CHALLENGE WOULD YOU LIKE TO TAKE ON?

I WANT TO RACE AGAINST THE CLOCK
Beat the clock with one of the following: **58** Balance a brick tower (p53); **201** Take the five-by-five challenge (p147); **237** Escape from a LEGO maze (p171).

I WANT TO BEAT MY PERSONAL BEST
Try to set a new record with one of these: **24** Give your bricks a spin (p32-33); **110** Take aim in tin-can alley (p89); **242** Put together a puzzle cube (p174).

WHAT ARE YOU IN THE MOOD FOR?

BEING ACTIVE
Break a sweat doing one of these: **66** Play a game of crazy golf (p58); **80** Run an egg-and-spoon race (p68); **184** Run a LEGO relay race (p135).

PLAYING A PRANK
Trick your friends with one of the following: **1** Play a mouse trick (p18); **224** Play a TV remote prank (p163); **301** Play a pencil prank (p212).

IMPRESSING MY FRIENDS
Wow your friends with a more complicated project, like these: **83** Build a 3-D butterfly picture (p70–71); (p85); **119** Play a little pinball (p95); **134** Build a ship in a bottle (p104).

WHO ARE YOU BUILDING FOR?

MYSELF
Take on a fun solo project, like one of these: **10** Build a family tree (p23); **146** Play a game of peg solitaire (p113); **273** Make your own name (p194–195).

BEING DRAMATIC
Put on a showstopping performance. Try: **26** Be a singing star (p34); **91** Put on a LEGO magic show (p76); **263** Start a skiffle band (p188).

GETTING ORGANISED
Take on one of these and get things in order: **105** Sort your LEGO bricks (p85); **199** Keep track with a weekly planner (p144–145); **279** Grow a jewellery tree (p198).

FOR SOMEONE ELSE
Make someone's day with a LEGO gift, like one of the following: **5** Give some LEGO love (p20); **123** Give a 3-D greetings card (p164); **169** Give a beautiful bunch of flowers (p126).

DISCOVERING SOMETHING NEW
Learn more with one of these activities: **55** Explore the human body (p51); **56** Build curves with straight bricks (p52); **183** How tall are you in LEGO bricks? (p135).

IT'S TIME TO LEARN SOME TECHNICAL KNOW-HOW!

No one needs to be told how to build with LEGO® bricks! Their simple but brilliant design makes it obvious how they fit together. But the best LEGO models are made by people who follow a few simple guidelines. Read on to learn their building secrets!

Build basics

Make connections

Every single LEGO element can fit onto another in at least one way. Play around with a few unusual parts and you might be surprised by the ways you are able to connect them! Just because you've always used a piece in a certain way in the past, doesn't mean you can't do something completely different with it today!

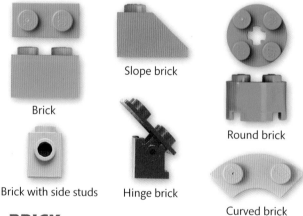

Croissants fit onto this owl as feathers (see page 87), and can also fit onto parts with clips

Speak the lingo

When you are building, it's often enough to point and say, "Pass me that piece, please!" But knowing the names of key LEGO elements will help you get more from a book like this one. Here are the main terms you will find on these pages.

Brick

Slope brick

Round brick

Brick with side studs

Hinge brick

Curved brick

TILE
Tiles are the same thickness as plates, but have smooth tops with no studs at all. They are very useful for builds with sliding parts, and for making models look more realistic by covering up large areas of exposed studs.

Tile

Printed tile

Long tile

BRICK
Bricks are the regular, rectangular pieces that form the basis of most builds, and which have round studs on top for fixing them to other pieces. Some special bricks are not a standard block shape, and have other descriptive names.

LEGO bricks and plates come in lots of different sizes, and you will sometimes see them given names based on how many studs they have on top. For example, a 2x4 brick has two studs on its short side and four studs on its long side, while a 4x4 plate is a square shape. Some special bricks have names with three numbers, such as a 1x2x5 brick. The third number is the piece's height in standard bricks.

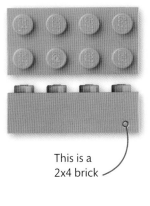

This is a 2x4 brick

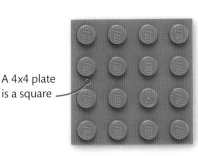

A 4x4 plate is a square

A 1x10 brick is long and thin

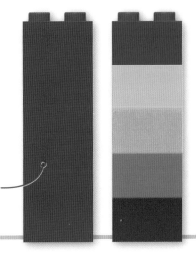

This 1x2x5 brick is the same size as five 1x2 bricks

PLATE

Plates are just like bricks, only flatter. A stack of three plates is exactly the same height as one brick. One special kind of plate is a jumper plate, which has just one central stud, so whatever is built onto it can "jump" the regular pattern of studs. It shifts the bricks placed on top of it by half a stud.

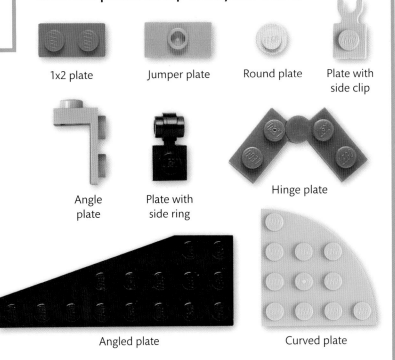

1x2 plate

Jumper plate

Round plate

Plate with side clip

Angle plate

Plate with side ring

Hinge plate

Angled plate

Curved plate

Hold it together

A strong LEGO build contains lots of overlapping pieces at different sizes to hold everything together. Long bricks and plates are useful for locking smaller ones in place, while smaller pieces can lock themselves together if they are staggered (so that their sides do not line up). Corner bricks and plates make a strong connection where walls meet up, but again, only if they are overlapped with other parts.

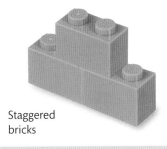

Staggered bricks

2x2 corner plate

Keep it steady

If you want your model to stand up, it will need a stable base. Most freestanding builds start with a large plate to stop them from tipping over, while others stand on several bricks spread out like feet. As you build upward, try not to put all the pieces on one side of the model. Spread the weight evenly and it won't wobble or fall.

Build a stable base to stop your models from tipping over!

Building this robot on a base plate makes it much more stable (see page 64)

A broad base and balanced sides stop this jewellery tree from tipping over (see page 198)

Think big – or small!

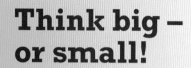

Lots of LEGO builds are made to match the size of a LEGO minifigure, with doors they can fit through and seats they can sit in. But LEGO models can be built at any scale, from micro to mega! Micro-scale makes a few bricks go a long way, and uses small, unusual pieces in whole new ways. Building at life-size – or larger – makes a great challenge, and can lead to things you can really use!

This DNA helix (on page 217) is millions of times bigger than the real thing!

THIS MINI FAN IS PERFECT FOR ME!

You can really cool off with a life-sized fan (see page 84)

Get technical

Lots of LEGO sets include pieces that were originally designed to function in LEGO® Technic creations. Don't be afraid to use special LEGO Technic pieces and connecting parts in your builds. They can be very useful for adding strength, movement or just cool-looking details!

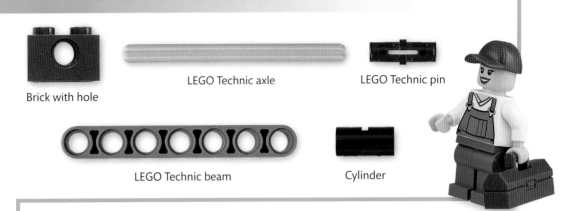

Brick with hole

LEGO Technic axle

LEGO Technic pin

LEGO Technic beam

Cylinder

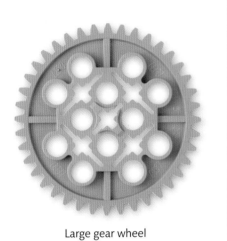

Large gear wheel

A telescope can become a tree trunk in a micro-scale build (see page 41)

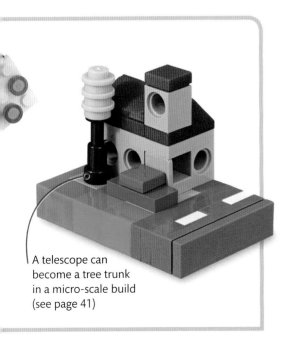

Think sideways

The bowl of this sink (on page 195) is built sideways and connects to bricks with side studs

Brick with two side studs

Brick with four side studs

Whatever you want to build, think about whether it might look better if some or all of the parts were used on their sides – or even upside down! Angle plates and bricks with side studs offer ways to build in more than one direction. Even without these, you could make an entire model using only bricks laid down on their sides.

Create a large flat surface by laying bricks on their side (see page 47)

Build upwards, too, by connecting pieces to bricks with side studs

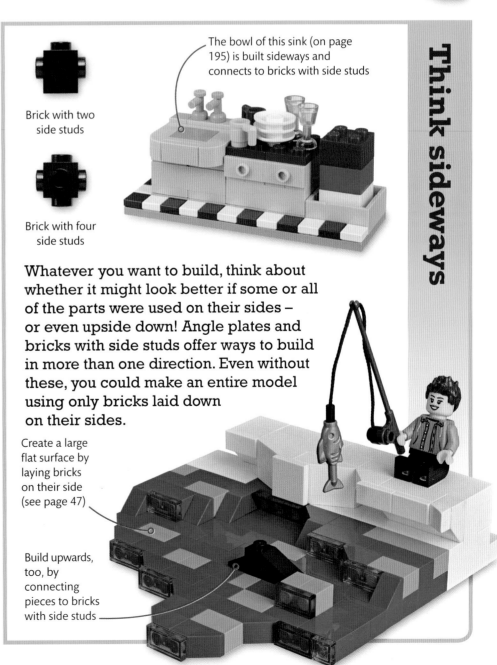

There are far more than 365 things to do with LEGO® bricks – this book is just the tip of the iceberg! Use the ideas on these pages as a starting point for your own creations, and don't be put off if you don't have all the pieces shown. No one else has the exact mix of LEGO bricks that you have – so try to make something unique!

Be inspired

Look to all areas of your life for building ideas: unusual bricks in your LEGO collection, cool buildings in your neighbourhood, or things you have read about in books. Even maths homework can inspire ways to build exciting shapes!

Find out how to make amazing 3-D shapes like this 12-sided dodecahedron on page 233

Plan ahead

The awesome mechanical parrot on page 218 requires careful planning

Sometimes an amazing build just happens, but many ideas take time to form. Before you start on a big building project, you might find it helps to draw a picture of how you want it to look, and then think about the bricks you will use to bring it to life.

These four flowers are all built in different ways

Test out your creativity and build a bunch of flowers on page 126

You can build anything with a handful of LEGO bricks and enough imagination. Don't let the lack of a certain piece or colour stop you in your tracks – look for a clever way to make what you need from what you have!

Look for solutions

Take it further

A finished build is just the start of your LEGO adventure! How will you use it? Will you film or photograph it? What could you add to it? How would you build it differently next time? What does it make you want to build next?

Think about how you will play with or use the models you build.

Keep an open mind

Don't worry if your build doesn't go the way you imagined it would – keep going and it might turn into something completely different and even better than you expected. The fun part is finding out where your bricks will take you!

UM... I'M NOT SURE WHAT THIS IS!

If your model isn't working out, simply change it into something else!

DISCOVER MORE BUILDING TIPS THROUGHOUT THE BOOK!

1 Play a mouse trick

Eek! A mouse! Push this four-wheeled frightener past your friends or family to give them a start! Look for pieces in your collection that might work as a nose, tail, ears and eyes.

I'M WHEELY SCARED!

Ears made from radar dishes

Nose is a LEGO® Technic ball

Wheels slot onto long LEGO Technic pins

ON THE DANCE FLOOR
A smooth disco dance floor for smooth disco dancers can be made from multicoloured tiles. You don't have to build a dance floor, though. You could build a stage with a LEGO® version of your favourite band, or even a mini concert hall – build whatever you like!

Smooth tiles cover the speaker top and sides

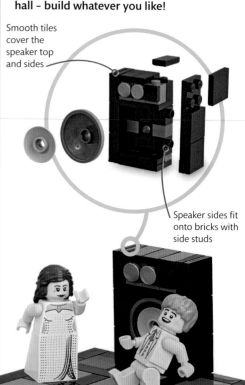

Speaker sides fit onto bricks with side studs

Get the party started with a dance floor that doubles as a stand for your MP3 player. It won't just put you in the mood to dance – it also lets you easily see what song is playing, or watch the music video that goes with it.

Make sure the build is tall enough for your music player to lean against

Make a cradle for your music player using smooth pieces

A broad base stops the build from tipping over

2 Make a music stand

Climb a mountain

3

Want to be a mountaineer? Start small by scaling this LEGO mountain in a fun two-player game! All you need is six minifigures (three for each player) and enough bricks to build a mountaintop that has the same number of steps on each side.

SPINNER

You can make your own spinner for working out the number of steps to move on each turn. This one has sections numbered one to four, held together with plates in the middle and at the edges. Use a LEGO Technic axle on the top to spin it on a smooth, flat surface.

HOW TO PLAY

1 Each player lines up their three minifigures at the base of the mountain.

2 Players take turns spinning the spinner and move any one of their minifigures the number of steps up the mountain shown on the spinner.

3 If one of your climbers lands in a space directly opposite a minifigure on the other side (excluding the very top level), the other player has to send that minifigure back to the bottom!

4 The winner is the first player to get all three of their minifigures to the top of the mountain.

The spinner moves on a slide plate underneath

Plates with bars stop the spinner from landing between two numbers

LEGO Technic axle

The spinner has landed on four – a minifigure can move four steps up!

Your mountain can be any size, but this one has seven steps up from the bottom

I CAN SEE MY HOUSE FROM HERE!

I WISH I'D REMEMBERED MY GLOVES!

Differently angled slopes make realistic rocky sides

Starting level

④ Strike a pose

What do minifigures get up to when they think no one is looking? Why not grab your camera and find out! You can create all kinds of funny and interesting scenes with just one or two minifigures and some everyday household objects – all of which will seem giant-sized to a minifigure!

THIS WATER LOOKS FUNNY...

A box full of cotton wool makes a bubbly swimming bath for a minifigure diver

I'M HAVING A BALL!

Pose your minifigures in a way that tells a story

A tennis ball becomes a giant boulder

SETTING THE SCENE

Play up the size difference between the real world and the LEGO one. A minifigure would need mountain-climbing gear to reach the top of a real chair, and a team of friends just to pick up a pencil! Look for items around your home that could form the basis of a fun scene.

Climber's rope can be fixed to a chair with adhesive putty

I MUST BE NEARLY THERE!

Share a heart with your best friend on page 177.

Show someone how much you care with a LEGO heart! There are lots of different ways to make them. Be sure to build with care – or your LEGO heart might just break!

Curved brick makes a rounded corner

Two curved red plates overlap to make this heart

Sloped bricks form the bottom of the heart

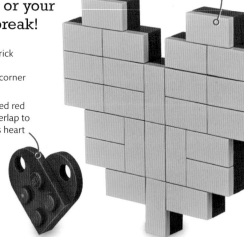

Pink tiles go on top of two layers of red plates

⑤ Give some LEGO® love

6 Build a brainteaser

Each shape has a corner that isn't linked by studs.

Each side is made of two plates and a top layer of tiles

The two parts of the puzzle are exactly the same shape

These sides touch but aren't linked by studs – which is the key to solving the puzzle!

Use smooth tiles to cover the studs

Layers of overlapping plates connect the sides

It looks as if the only way to separate these shapes is to break off some of the bricks, but there is a clever way to slide them apart without breaking them or changing their shape. Challenge your friends to see who can solve it in the quickest time!

Save your pennies

7

Start saving with a LEGO piggy bank. Your piggy bank doesn't need to be piggy-shaped, but it will need a hollow middle, a slot to put money in and a way to get your money out again!

Make sure the slot is big enough for coins to fit through

A layer of smooth plates makes it easy to lift the lid off

Snout is a brick with two holes and a tile on top

Open mouth is created with a slope brick

OPEN UP!
Build the top of your piggy bank separately so it can lift off easily and let you get at your savings. Or why not try adding a plug to the bottom of your build instead?

8 Show how you feel today

IT'S NOT RUDE TO MAKE FACES!

Eyebrows can be very expressive

Express your mood with LEGO bricks! Build a face with just eyes and a nose and you can easily add details that change as often as your moods. How many different looks can your LEGO face make?

Life belt is an open mouth

Plates attach to base plate underneath

Radar dishes for eyes

Pink pieces for rosy cheeks

See how much character you can squeeze into tiny brick towers. These groups of tower dudes have just enough clues to give away who they are meant to be! Build your own teams of tower dudes – and quiz your friends to see who can name them in the quickest time!

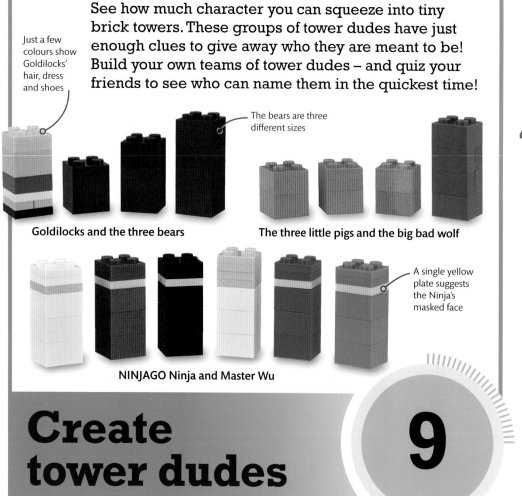

Just a few colours show Goldilocks' hair, dress and shoes

The bears are three different sizes

Goldilocks and the three bears

The three little pigs and the big bad wolf

A single yellow plate suggests the Ninja's masked face

NINJAGO Ninja and Master Wu

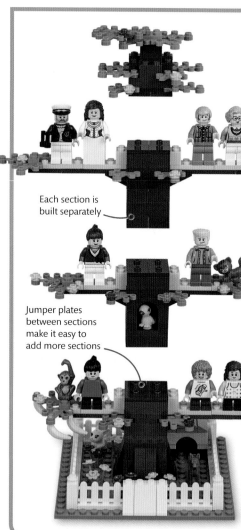

Each section is built separately

Jumper plates between sections make it easy to add more sections

Create tower dudes 9

Build a family tree

10

Grandparents fill this top level – great-grandparents would go even higher!

BRANCHING OUT
Fill your tree with the minifigures that look most like your family members, or which best reflect their personalities, hobbies or jobs. If you want to keep building your tree higher, ask your parents or grandparents to tell you more about their relatives. If your family is very small, why not build a tree featuring all your friends?

2x2 brick is built into the trunk

Long plates are sandwiched into the middle of each section

Slope bricks support each branch

This level is for parents – aunts and uncles can go here too

Add extra details, such as your relative's favourite animal

Children line up on the lowest branches

Create your very own LEGO family tree! The branches show the different parts of your family. Begin with yourself and your brothers, sisters or cousins at the bottom and put your oldest relatives at the top. You could even add your pets too!

Even the family dog gets a place in the garden!

11 Make a gift box

Design a gift box that is so pretty, you might not want to give it away. If that is the case, you could also use it as a seasonal decoration, or as a secret place where you and your best friend can leave messages for each other!

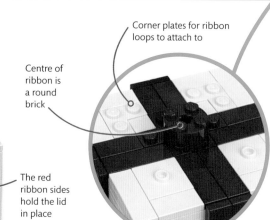

Corner plates for ribbon loops to attach to

Centre of ribbon is a round brick

The red ribbon sides hold the lid in place

ALL WRAPPED UP

The ribbon is what makes this box really special. At the sides, it is made with smooth tiles fixed to bricks with side studs. The loops of the bow on top are made from four curved bricks, with two single bricks at the pointed ends.

HOW TO PLAY

1. Set a timer to two minutes. Players take turns rolling the two sheep onto a soft surface, scoring points depending on how they land.

2. A sheep on its side is worth one point; a sheep on its back is worth two points; a sheep with its face down is worth three points; and a sheep standing on its feet is worth four points.

3. The winner is the player who gets the most points in two minutes.

The sheep should be small enough to fit in your hand

Baa-nish boredom with this fun and easy-to-play game. Any number of players can take part: all you need is two LEGO sheep and a soft surface, such as a carpet.

This slope brick allows the sheep to come to rest face down

Play the sheep roll game

12

13 Take a trip to Miniland

Click hinges allow the arms to move

Head attaches to a jumper plate (plate with a single stud)

Chin is a jumper plate

A SMALL WORLD
You can add lots of detail and variation to your Miniland figures, so you can build both adults and children in all sorts of action poses. Begin your build with the torso and use a 2x3 brick as your starting point.

Each hand is a plate with clip

Thigh is a slope brick

Miniland is the amazingly realistic part of LEGOLAND® Parks, where lifelike LEGO people live among detailed models of real-world places. Bring a piece of Miniland home by building a figure in Miniland scale, which is bigger than a minifigure but smaller than you!

I THINK I TOOK A WRONG TURN...

It is easier to use bricks that are all the same size

Challenge your friends to see how many LEGO bricks they can stack in 30 seconds. The trick is to always be picking up the next brick with your spare hand! The winner is the person with the tallest tower. If your tower collapses before the time is up, you have to start again!

STOP MONKEYING AROUND!

Each player should start with the same number of bricks

You could use two bricks to create a more stable base

14 Build the tallest tower

15 Feed the frog

A fly can be a single brick

Tub piece – you could make a brick-built container instead

Build the mouth big enough for lots of flies to fit inside!

Fly's wings are made from a white corner plate

Press down to launch a fly

Use curved tiles for the frog's round head

Radar dishes for eyes

Lily pads are made from different-sized stacked plates

Catapult pivots on LEGO Technic pins

MOVABLE FEAST

Build your fly-firing catapult on its own lily pad so you can try it at different distances from the frog's mouth. Use your smallest bricks as flies or build your own from other small pieces.

BUILDER'S TIP

Make sure the catapult's pivot is closer to the end you press down on for a bigger swing at the other end.

This frog loves to eat flies – especially when they are flung into its massive mouth from a distance! Try building your own frog and catapult feeder, and see how many flies you can flip into the frog's mouth in one minute.

16

Black borders make the colours really stand out

Details like the veins on this leaf don't need a border

Flower is a flat, 2-D design

17 Decorate your door

Let everyone know how much you love LEGO bricks with a sign to hang from your door handle. You can slide different messages inside it, so that people know when you are too busy building to be disturbed!

DESIGN A SIGN
Remember to check the size of your door handle before you start building, and make the hook of the sign big enough and strong enough to hang securely. Write a fun message on thin cardboard and slot it inside the LEGO frame.

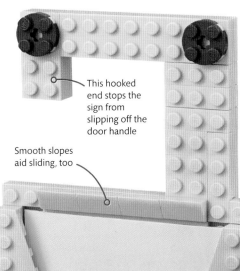

Raised plates make a frame that overlaps the edges of the cardboard sign

Smooth tiles help the cardboard slide in and out

Write a different message on the other side of the card.

This hooked end stops the sign from slipping off the door handle

Smooth slopes aid sliding, too

Knock if you love LEGO bricks!

Take on a pixel power challenge

Make your building all about the blocks! With thick black outlines and no curved bricks, these flowers look like old-fashioned computer graphics. What is the blockiest flower you can build that still looks like a flower?

18 Design a dream home

A LEGO house can look like anything! Think of the strangest house you can and try to build it using your LEGO bricks. Be inspired by objects around your home. Or why not build a home for one of your favourite minifigures?

Add regular home details like a chimney stack, windows and doors to make any object look more like a house.

There is room for minifigures to sit and eat inside

Smooth tiles top the walls so the roof can lift off easily

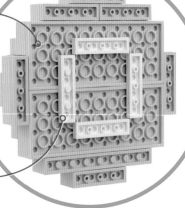

Two large plates form the base of the roof

This square of plates holds the roof in place

Small round plates make great salad leaves

Tomato slices are red slope bricks

THEY DO SAY YOU ARE WHAT YOU EAT!

BURGER HOUSE
This house has lots of layers but only one room! The different colours and shapes look like burger patties, cheese slices and salad, all contained within a sesame seed bun. The domed roof lifts off for easy access to the dining room inside.

Alarm ringers are radar dishes

Slope bricks create the round shape of the door

Door swings open on a pair of hinge plates

Room for a comfy bed!

Clock hands are made from a spanner and a holder piece

I ALWAYS GET TO BED IN TIME!

ALARM-CLOCK HOUSE

It is not obvious that this clock is also a home until the door swings open to reveal a bedroom with another, smaller, alarm clock inside! The clues are there though, with windows and brickwork details on the side and overhanging red roof slope bricks on top.

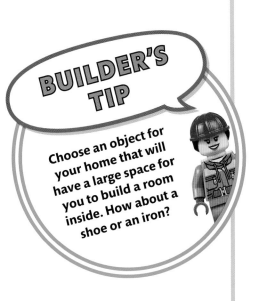

BUILDER'S TIP

Choose an object for your home that will have a large space for you to build a room inside. How about a shoe or an iron?

Build anything but...

19

Challenge your friends' creativity! Give each player the same selection of bricks and ask them to build anything they want in two minutes. There is just one catch: their creations must not resemble one particular object of your choosing, such as a duck. It is amazing how difficult it is to think of something different to build!

A beak-like slope brick will make it harder to avoid a build that resembles a duck!

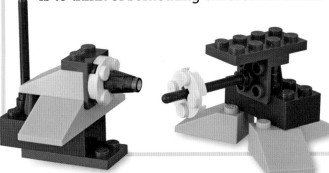

Pile up a totem pole

20

Build up a stack of creatures and faces to make a magnificent totem pole! Traditional totem poles are carved from wood and use animal symbols to represent people, events and stories. Make each part of your pole symbolise something important to you.

Each section has a jumper plate (a plate with just one stud) on top

Look at real-life totem poles in books or online to get more building ideas.

The single-stud connection makes it easy to rearrange the sections

Mix made-up creatures with real ones

Build much bigger letters on pages 60–61.

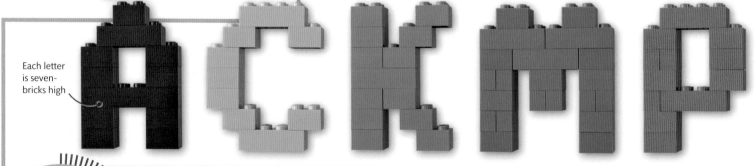

Each letter is seven-bricks high

21

Spell it out with a LEGO alphabet

Don't pick the clown trousers!

22

Use this game of chance to decide who gets to do a task you don't want to do! Everyone selects one minifigure from the line-up, and then the front sections are flipped down. Whoever has chosen the minifigure in the clown trousers is the person who has to do the chore! The person who places the minifigures can't take part!

You could change the game so the person who finds the clown trousers wins a prize!

The diver is the one wearing clown trousers!

Pull down to reveal the legs

DON'T LOOK AT ME. I'M INNOCENT!

The folding front sections open on hinge bricks

A transparent round brick connects the tail

Form the letters by stacking and overlapping bricks

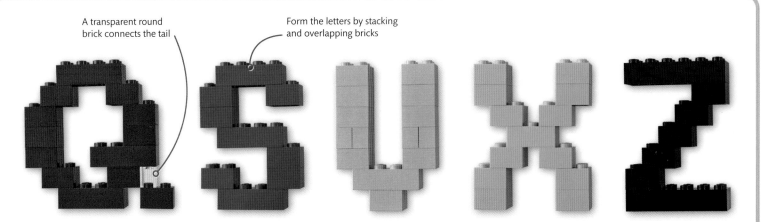

Make a statement with words built out of colourful LEGO letters! Spell out messages as a decoration, or find funny anagrams by mixing up all the letters in your name. For a freestanding display, fit the letters together to make them stronger, or build them into a wall of bricks to make a flat, upright sign.

Capital letters are easiest to build and display as they don't have low-hanging parts.

23

Make a lot with a little

"ABANDON SHIP!"

Head is attached to brick with side stud

Tentacle parts slot into bricks with holes

You don't need lots of bricks to make this tentacled monster! A few pieces are spaced out to let your imagination fill in the blanks. What else could you build? How about eyes peeping over a wall, or an elephant trunk peeking through trees?

Brick with side stud holds boat in place

The base is a wall of blue bricks on its side

The rowing boat is all one piece

Give your bricks a spin

24

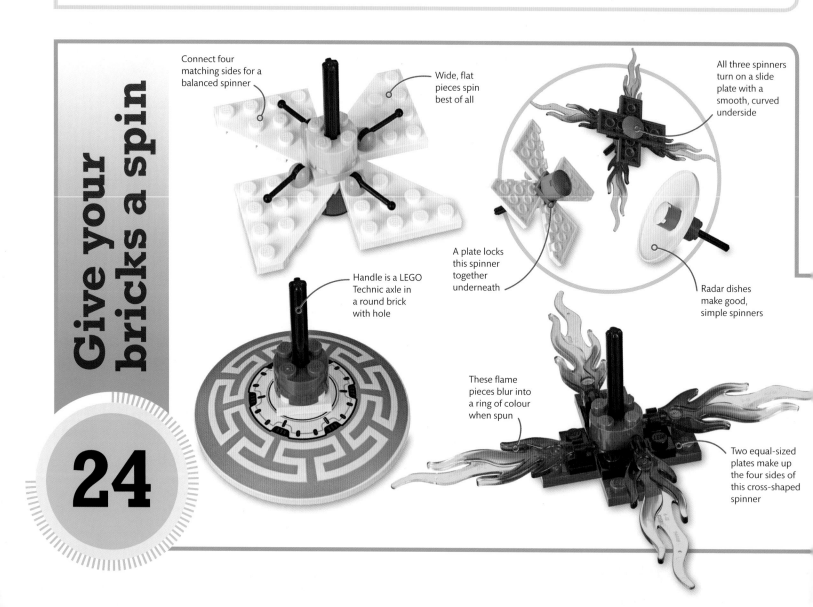

Connect four matching sides for a balanced spinner

Wide, flat pieces spin best of all

All three spinners turn on a slide plate with a smooth, curved underside

A plate locks this spinner together underneath

Radar dishes make good, simple spinners

Handle is a LEGO Technic axle in a round brick with hole

These flame pieces blur into a ring of colour when spun

Two equal-sized plates make up the four sides of this cross-shaped spinner

25 Build a monster truck

There's nowhere this monster truck can't go! Grab the biggest wheels in your LEGO collection and build them onto a sturdy frame. Then put them to the test with an off-road challenge across books or piles of bricks!

Huge grille is made from four grille pieces

Make sure the wheel arches do not obstruct the tyres

Small round bricks look like monster truck suspension

THE SPECIAL BRICK

LEGO Technic plates with a ring beneath (or bearing plates) are useful for connecting wheels to vehicles. Axles fit into the rings.

Use hardback books to make ramps and jumps

Wheel is held in place by a LEGO Technic axle

Plate with ring beneath connects wheel and axle to the frame

Make a LEGO spinning top with just a handful of pieces. You can then add more details by building out from the centre. Any extra details should be added to all sides to ensure it spins properly. Time your builds to see which one spins the longest, then see if you can beat your best time!

THE WHEEL DEAL
The body of the car can be as simple or detailed as you like. Don't worry if your biggest LEGO wheels are on the small side – just make the vehicle on top even smaller!

Create an illusion

The front stack of bricks supports the top brick alone

How can this top brick be at the front and the back?

Minifigure is midway between the front and back stacks

From the front, these studs are hidden behind the top, horizontal brick

Rear stack of bricks is not attached to anything at the top

DOORWAY DECEPTION
At first glance it looks as though the adventurer is about to pass through the door. But look at the bottom right of the doorway, and it is already behind him! Turning the model to the side reveals that it isn't a doorway at all, but two separate structures.

26 Build a bofflejot

What is a bofflejot? Anything you want it to be! This game starts with making up a brand-new word, and then asking the players to build what they think it is in three minutes. There is no right or wrong answer, so you can use any bricks to play.

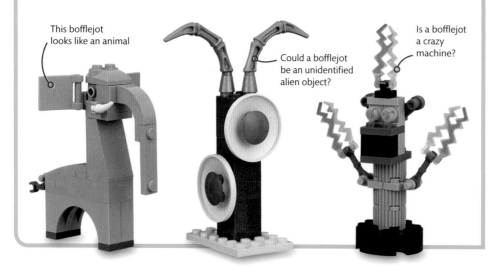

This bofflejot looks like an animal

Could a bofflejot be an unidentified alien object?

Is a bofflejot a crazy machine?

Rotate this build clockwise to reveal this isn't a triangle after all!

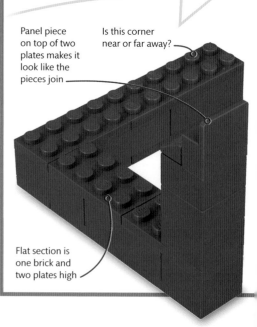

Panel piece on top of two plates makes it look like the pieces join

Is this corner near or far away?

Flat section is one brick and two plates high

27

Baffle your friends with LEGO builds that will trick their minds! Both of these models are optical illusions – they confuse the brain into thinking it is seeing something it is not. Simply look at the models from a different angle and everything becomes clear! Recreate these optical illusions, or have fun coming up with your very own!

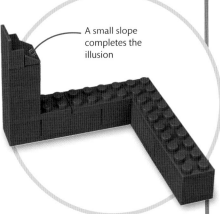

A small slope completes the illusion

TRICKY TRIANGLE
If the shape on the left looks normal to you, try running your finger around the picture and thinking about how it fits together. It just can't tell its front from its back, or its top from its bottom! Seen from another angle, it clearly isn't a triangle at all.

28

Be a singing star

Put on a pop-star performance with a life-sized model microphone. It won't improve your singing, but it will make you look the part! Then all you have to do is sing your heart out!

All the bricks in this build are upside down.

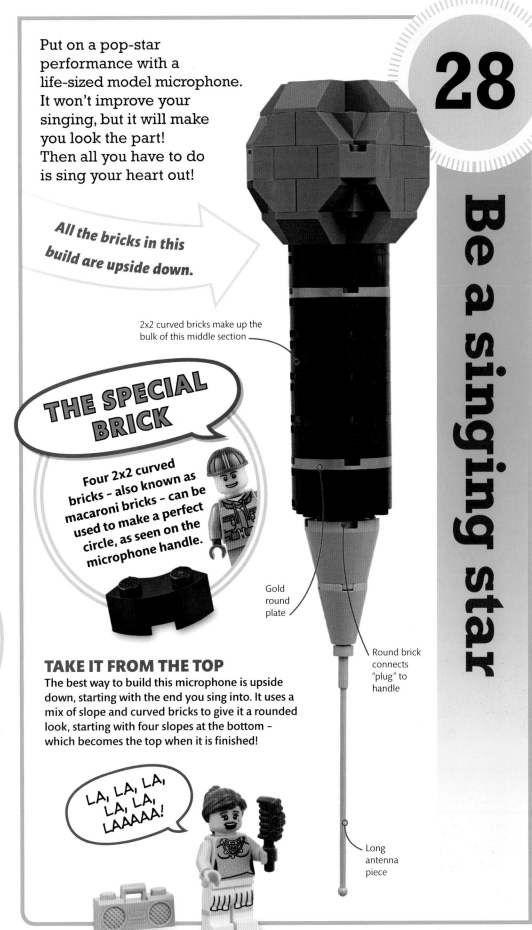

2x2 curved bricks make up the bulk of this middle section

THE SPECIAL BRICK
Four 2x2 curved bricks – also known as macaroni bricks – can be used to make a perfect circle, as seen on the microphone handle.

Gold round plate

Round brick connects "plug" to handle

TAKE IT FROM THE TOP
The best way to build this microphone is upside down, starting with the end you sing into. It uses a mix of slope and curved bricks to give it a rounded look, starting with four slopes at the bottom – which becomes the top when it is finished!

LA, LA, LA, LA, LA, LAAAAA!

Long antenna piece

29 Play the mirror match game

Can you spot which butterfly wing on the right is the mirror image of the one on the left? Make your own mirror-image models and test your friends to see who can match them up in the quickest time!

The more details you add, the harder the game will be!

The differences can be in the body as well as the wings

Use whichever pieces you have a lot of, so that you can make copies

There's no end to the stunts and tricks you can do when you make your own skate park. If you build it, these minifigures will jump it, grind it or slide it in style. With your fingers out of the way thanks to long handles, you can even capture their moves on camera!

Railings are good for jumping over and onto

Smooth tiles are best for skateboards to run over

Steps and different kinds of slopes are a challenge for skaters

Handle is a plate with long bar

Handle fits onto underside of skateboard

1x1 cone connects to neck bracket

Green shoots without flowers look like grass or weeds

Ramp is a mix of steep and shallow slope bricks

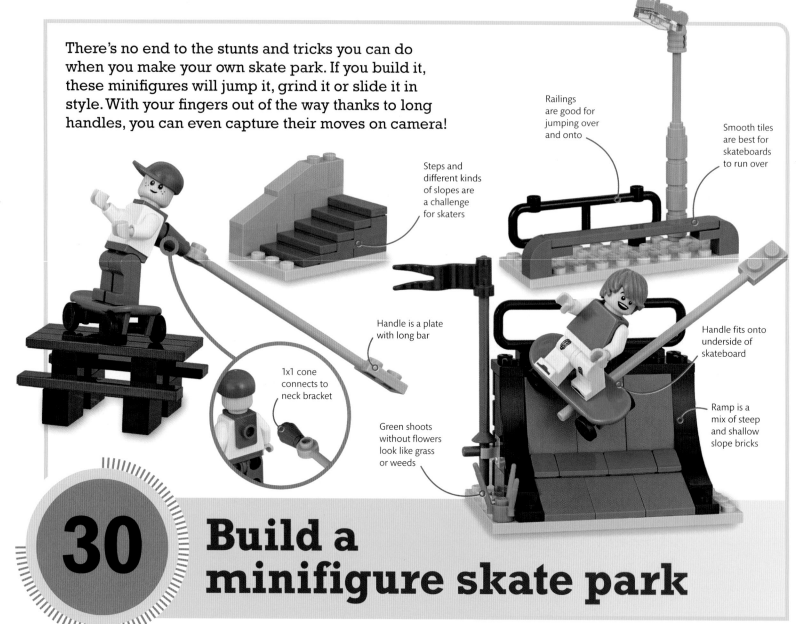

30 Build a minifigure skate park

It's time to get organised! This stationery organiser looks super stylish and makes great use of space. It has lots of useful compartments, including sections that swing out on hinges, so you'll always have room for your favourite pens and pencils. You could even add a hidden compartment for extra secret stuff!

THINK INSIDE THE BOX

Start by thinking about what needs to fit in your organiser. It needs to be tall enough for pens to stand up in, and the smaller sections should be big enough for things like erasers, binder clips and USB drives.

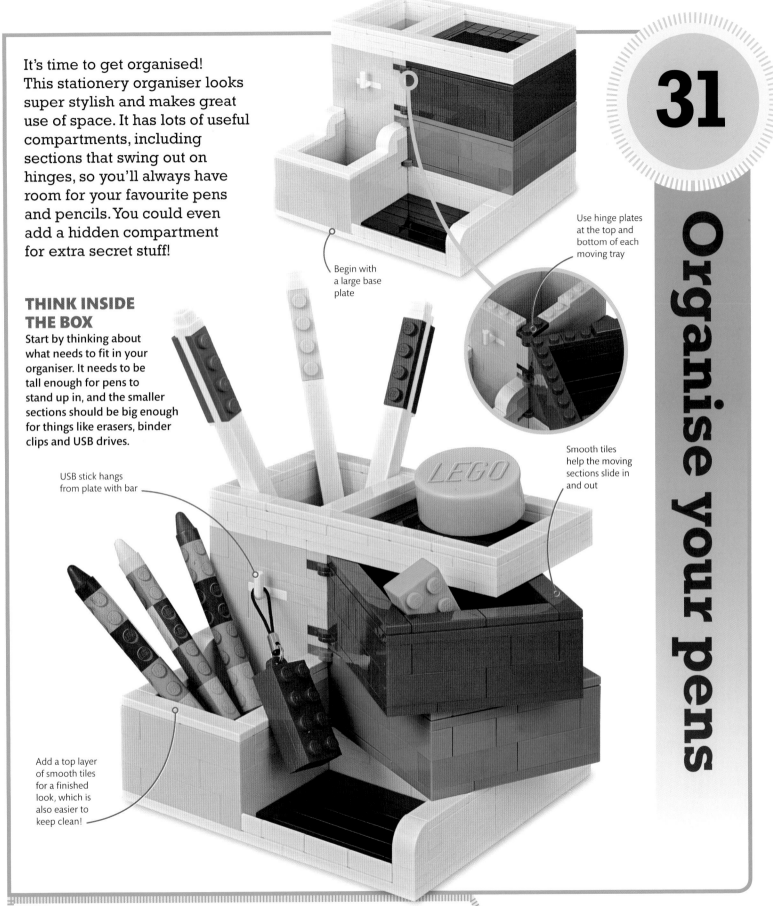

31 Organise your pens

Begin with a large base plate

Use hinge plates at the top and bottom of each moving tray

Smooth tiles help the moving sections slide in and out

USB stick hangs from plate with bar

Add a top layer of smooth tiles for a finished look, which is also easier to keep clean!

Set sail for a pirate pencil pot on page 247.

32 Start a super spy tool kit

Pay attention, secret agents! These are the gadgets you need to complete your undercover mission. One is a pen with a secret compartment, the other is a dart shooter in disguise. You must set up the portable movement sensors without getting caught. Good luck!

Laser beam receiver is a grey radar dish

Laser beam transmitter is a red radar dish

Portable movement sensors

Tiles are mirrors to reflect laser beam around corners

Tile for pocket clip

Attach pointed end of pen with an angle plate

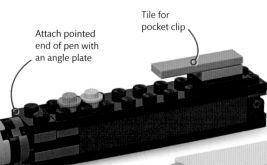

Pen with secret compartment

FOR SPIES' EYES ONLY!

Push to fire the nib missile

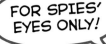

KITTED OUT

If someone passes through the movement sensors' invisible laser beams, they won't know about it – but you will! What else will you include in your spy tool kit? A listening device? A miniature camera? A radar tracker?

Dart shooter pen

Hinge brick allows top to lift open

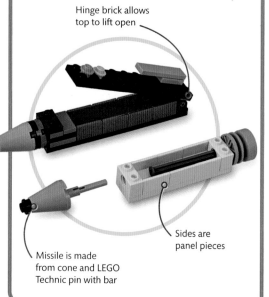

Sides are panel pieces

Missile is made from cone and LEGO Technic pin with bar

Make a micro-bot 33

You don't need a lot of bricks to make a brilliant robot! This one is made from just 12 pieces. Can you make one with even fewer? See how many micro-bots you can make in 10 minutes.

Eyes are a binoculars piece

Robot body is small brick with side studs

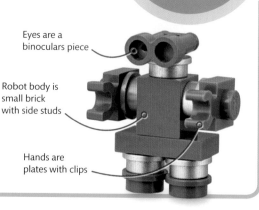

Hands are plates with clips

Build a useful giant brick

34

What could you do with a giant LEGO brick? Build a pot for your pencils? Or a stand for a photo or postcard? Or a huge money box? This money box is exactly the same shape as a standard 2x4 brick, but more than 200 times bigger in volume. Put all your pennies inside to make your savings grow too!

Building a slot that lifts out makes it easier to get to your savings.

Smooth tiles fit onto bricks with side studs

Each stud is made from four curved bricks around a 2x2 round brick

Slot part is built separately

Slope bricks create slot shape

Stack bricks to create box shape

Smooth tiles hide most of the studs

SCALING UP

Building a giant brick at this scale works because the curved bricks are the right size to recreate the studs. If you don't have enough pieces to build a 2x4 brick, try a 2x2 brick. Keep it at the same scale, so that each side is six times as long and tall as the original brick (216 times bigger in volume overall).

BUILDER'S TIP

Although you will display your money box on its side, build it with the studs (real and giant!) facing upwards.

Find out how to make a piggy bank on page 21.

35 Get a hold on your chopsticks

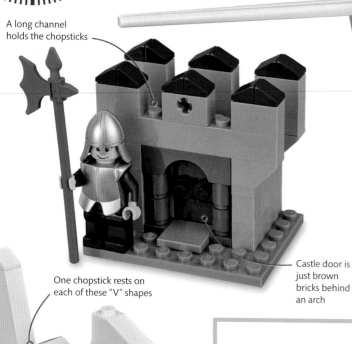

A long channel holds the chopsticks

Two "hands" hold the chopsticks above this ogre's head

Castle door is just brown bricks behind an arch

Feet are spread apart for stability

Add a special ingredient to dinner by making your own chopstick holders! They do not just decorate the table, they are useful, too – and you can make them look like absolutely anything you want! Why not make one for everyone at the table?

One chopstick rests on each of these "V" shapes

All-white design looks like a folded paper crane

Start the crane with plates in a cross shape

DESIGNING YOUR HOLDERS

Most chopsticks are about one LEGO stud wide, so a two-stud space should be big enough to hold a pair. Alternatively, you could lean individual chopsticks in two smaller slots, as with the paper crane design above.

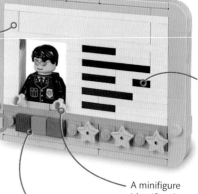

Why not add a sticker to the front with your name on it?

Bricks with studs on the top and side attach beneath a long grey plate

Black plates look like identification information

Give your secret club an extra level of security with LEGO membership cards. Anyone who doesn't have the right colour combination on the front can't get in!

The secret colour code can be changed as often as you like

A minifigure identifies the holder

Identify yourself! 36

37 Transform a tangram

What can you make with seven shapes? A tangram, an ancient Chinese puzzle that starts as a square, can be rearranged in hundreds of different ways! The rules are simple: use all seven pieces, and make sure they don't overlap.

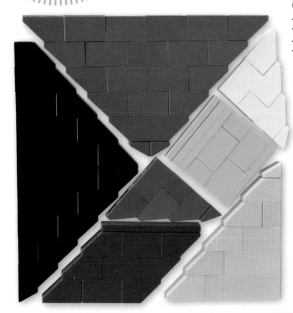

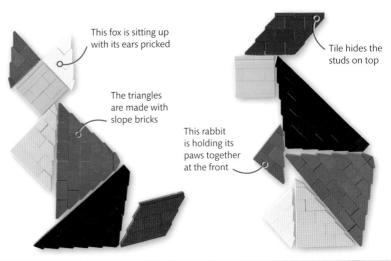

This fox is sitting up with its ears pricked

The triangles are made with slope bricks

Tile hides the studs on top

This rabbit is holding its paws together at the front

Create a micro-scale house

38

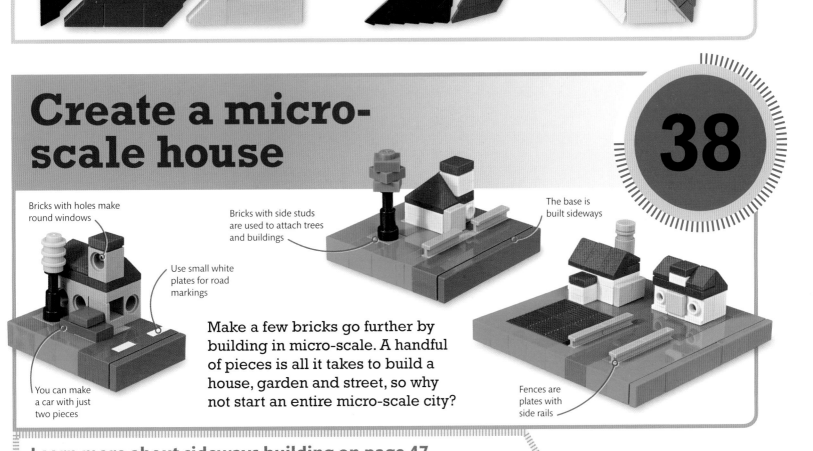

Bricks with holes make round windows

Bricks with side studs are used to attach trees and buildings

Use small white plates for road markings

You can make a car with just two pieces

The base is built sideways

Make a few bricks go further by building in micro-scale. A handful of pieces is all it takes to build a house, garden and street, so why not start an entire micro-scale city?

Fences are plates with side rails

Learn more about sideways building on page 47.

39

Take great photos of your LEGO models

Arrange soft lighting all around your model

Drape a white bedsheet over a chair to create a clean, white background

Share your creativity with professional-looking photos of your models. Use a stand to keep your camera steady and choose a well-lit space to work in. Focus your lens directly on your model rather than the background to ensure you get sharp images. Don't use the camera flash or point lights directly at your model, as this will create shiny areas on the bricks.

Make a date

40

A hook with a ball plugs into a plate with a socket

A curved plate with hole and a curved tile hold the numbers in place

Build a LEGO calendar, and you'll never need another one! After 12 months, all you have to do is change the year, and it's ready to use all over again!

Build a deep base for stability

ADDING THE NUMBERS

Each digit is built separately on a small plate. To make all the day and month combinations, you will need two of each digit, plus an extra number two and two extra number ones – but it is just as easy to adapt digits as you go.

The number eight uses the most parts, so all other numbers can be made from an eight

Change challenge

41

Play a fun observation game with any LEGO scene. Everyone takes a close look at the build, and then one person secretly changes something about it. Whoever spots the difference first gets to make the next change.

There's something different about this juggler display...

Who would notice if you moved this minifigure?

MUSEUM PIECE
This detailed museum scene is perfect for a change challenge. There is a lot going on, so you could add a piece, move a piece or take a piece away and it wouldn't be obvious straight away. Why not time your friends to see how long it takes for each change to be spotted?

Mix up your minifigures

42

I'D REALLY LIKE SOME LONGER LEGS!

What adventures would a skateboarding clown or an American football-playing Aztec warrior have? There's only one way to find out! Mix up the heads, torsos and accessories of your minifigures to create some cool new characters. To make it really random, match up the parts without looking!

Animate a bear

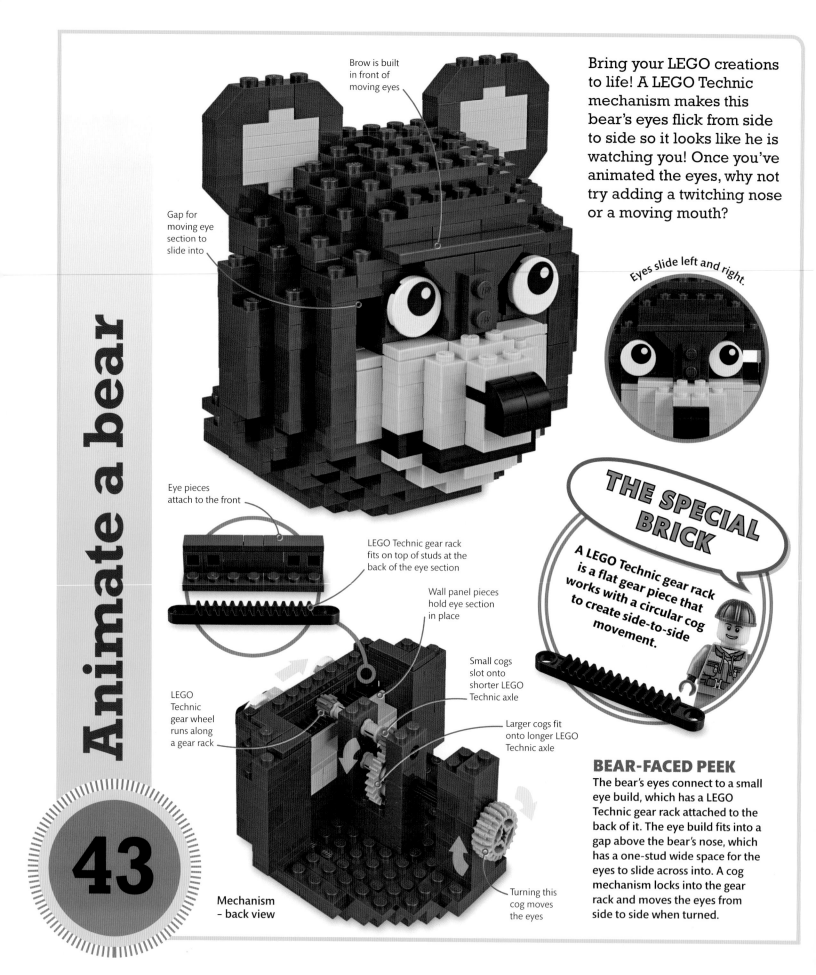

Brow is built in front of moving eyes

Gap for moving eye section to slide into

Bring your LEGO creations to life! A LEGO Technic mechanism makes this bear's eyes flick from side to side so it looks like he is watching you! Once you've animated the eyes, why not try adding a twitching nose or a moving mouth?

Eyes slide left and right.

Eye pieces attach to the front

LEGO Technic gear rack fits on top of studs at the back of the eye section

Wall panel pieces hold eye section in place

Small cogs slot onto shorter LEGO Technic axle

LEGO Technic gear wheel runs along a gear rack

Larger cogs fit onto longer LEGO Technic axle

THE SPECIAL BRICK

A LEGO Technic gear rack is a flat gear piece that works with a circular cog to create side-to-side movement.

BEAR-FACED PEEK

The bear's eyes connect to a small eye build, which has a LEGO Technic gear rack attached to the back of it. The eye build fits into a gap above the bear's nose, which has a one-stud wide space for the eyes to slide across into. A cog mechanism locks into the gear rack and moves the eyes from side to side when turned.

Mechanism – back view

Turning this cog moves the eyes

43

Make a memory challenge

Each pattern is completely flat so it can be turned face down

Make sure the pairs are exactly identical

A plain border stops each design from being recognisable face down

All the bases need to be the same size and colour

Build a set of matching pairs and play this brain-teasing memory game for any number of players! Build at least 10 pairs, place them face down and shuffle them. Take turns turning over two at random. If you find two that match, keep hold of them. If you turn over a pair that do not match, place them face down where they came from. The winner is the player with the most pairs at the end.

LEGO die has six coloured sides

Each player starts with this built base

Body

One of two antennae

One of two eyes

Head

Compete to build your own LEGO beetle, adding pieces according to the roll of a coloured die. Can you be the first to build your bug? If you do not have a coloured die, use a regular one and assign numbers to each colour (e.g. 1 = red, 2 = blue).

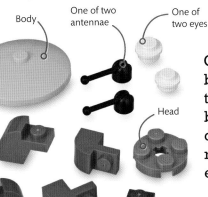

One of four legs

Tail

It takes 11 pieces to build a beetle

HOW TO PLAY

1 Each player starts with a base onto which the beetle parts can be added (see left), and all the pieces to make one beetle.

2 Players take turns rolling the die, and can add one beetle part of the colour rolled on each turn.

3 Each player must add the central body part before they can add any other parts, so must roll the colour of that part first of all. They must also add the head before they can add eyes or antennae.

4 The winner is the first player to add all pieces and shout "BEETLE!"

Play a beetle building game

46 Make the most of the weather

Transparent-blue bar pieces look like pouring rain

White plates alternate with clear plates to resemble snow

Small parts make a miniature landscape of trees and hills

Clear elements make the sun appear to float

Taller, thinner pins are easier to knock down than short, wide ones

These pins are made from turkey legs, bottles and coconuts as big as minifigure heads!

Microfigure skeletons are the perfect size for pins

Pins are placed on smooth tiles equal distances apart

I'LL KNOCK THEM ALL DOWN!

Cannon blasts 1x1 round bricks

Turntable piece allows you to move the cannon from side to side

Line up lots of 1x1 round bricks to use as ammunition

Swap bowling balls for cannonballs with a knockdown game that makes perfect target practice for budding pirates! Build defenses around your cannon and add two opposing teams of pirates and soldiers. Create a set of pins and ready, aim, fire!

47 Build a pirate bowling alley

Each of the weather builds attaches to one green landscape.

Create a weather station to let everyone know whether they should grab shades or snowshoes before they go out! Simply check the forecast, then add the matching part to your model. Come rain or shine, this ever-changing landscape will keep everyone updated on the local weather.

HOW TO PLAY

1 Position your pins 15cm (6 inches) away from your cannon.

2 Each player has 60 seconds to use their five cannonballs to knock down as many pins as they can. Keep score of the number of pins knocked down in the five goes before setting the pins back up for the next player's turn.

3 Repeat step three another four times each, keeping a note of the scores.

4 The player who knocks over the most pins in total wins the game.

Add details such as a turret or a cannon tower

THIS WAY AND THAT

Surfaces such as ice and water are perfect subjects for sideways building. Slope bricks angled differently can create the smooth yet irregular look of waves and frozen landscapes. Don't forget that you can also attach a sideways build to an upright one using bricks with side studs or bracket pieces.

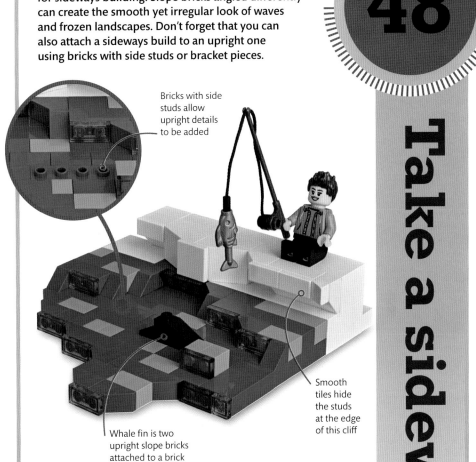

Bricks with side studs allow upright details to be added

Smooth tiles hide the studs at the edge of this cliff

Whale fin is two upright slope bricks attached to a brick with side studs

Flowers fit onto bricks with side studs

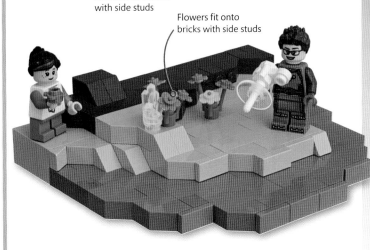

Take a sideways look

Sometimes, the best way to approach a build is from the side! Laying bricks down so that their studs are not on top allows you to make large flat surfaces without the need for lots of smooth tile pieces. What will you create with sideways building?

Create a micro-scale space base

Micro-scale building can make your bricks go a long way – even all the way into space! This rocket and moon buggy are made from just nine pieces each and would easily fit in the palm of your hand.

49

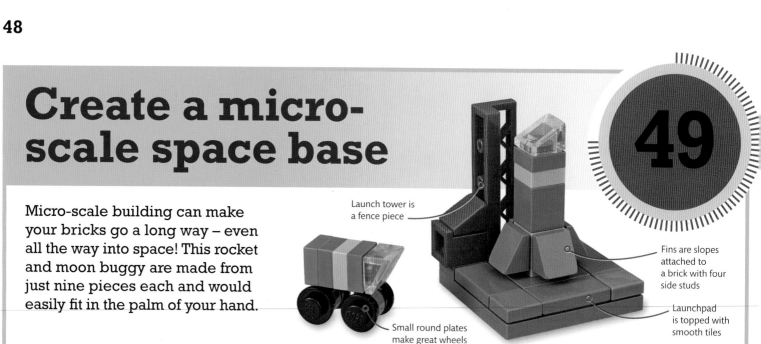

Launch tower is a fence piece

Fins are slopes attached to a brick with four side studs

Launchpad is topped with smooth tiles

Small round plates make great wheels

50 Perk up your pencils

Use a pencil pot to create a work of art – without drawing anything! Make some fun characters to sit on top of your pens and pencils when you are not using them, and they will become a designer decoration in their own right!

Base of head is a 2x2 plate centred on top stud of body

Zebra stripes are made from layers of plates

A barrel piece is a good fit for many pens

The clown's hair is made from grey slope bricks

The entire clown head is built upside down, starting with this round plate

Yellow cone pieces make for a zany bow tie

WORK IT OUT WITH A PENCIL

Most pencils are about the same width as a 1x1 LEGO brick. Both the zebra and the squid have square slots in the bottom that fit the end of a pencil, while the clown uses an upside-down barrel piece. Before you start to build, check the width of your pens and pencils against different LEGO pieces.

51 Build a sports tactics board

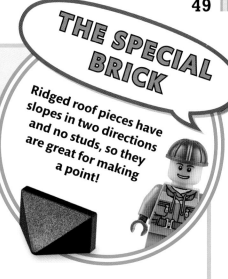

THE SPECIAL BRICK

Ridged roof pieces have slopes in two directions and no studs, so they are great for making a point!

Round bricks are the players on this football pitch

Mark out the pitch lines with thin white plates

Instead of round bricks, you could use minifigures

Small round bricks show opposing players on this basketball court

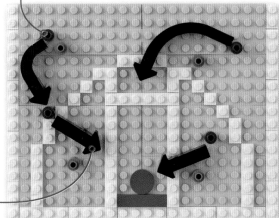

The pointers are ridged roof pieces

Give your side a sporting advantage with a tactics board built out of LEGO bricks. Using different-coloured bricks to show the positions of the players, your sports team can plan its winning moves and replay its victories!

Cactus branches are made from small half arch bricks

Deserts often contain lots of animal bones

LET'S SHAKE THINGS UP!

LEGO minifigures are full of character, so it's easy to imagine the adventures they might have and the places they might live in. This Maraca Man seems right at home in the desert. What mini worlds can you build for your favourite characters to inhabit?

Start by thinking up a life story for your minifigure.

52 Make your minifigures feel at home

53 Go panning for gold

Finding one small brick in a sea of big ones can be like panning for gold – slow, but worth it when you uncover the treasure! Make a filter system as a fun way to speed up the process, and separate smaller LEGO parts from larger ones with a little gentle shaking.

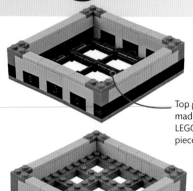

Top grid is made from LEGO Technic pieces

Studs in the corners hold the different layers together

SHAKE AND SIZE

Gently shaking bricks on a grid separates those that are small enough to fall through the holes from the bigger ones, which remain on the top. Combining grids with different-sized holes – biggest at the top and smallest at the bottom – will filter bricks into layers sorted by size.

Only pieces that are one stud wide fit through the smallest grid

Create your own photo props

54

Build fun photobooth props, then capture your and your friends' new looks with some selfies! Your accessories can be as glamorous or as weird as you like. If you hold small models in front of your face, closer to the camera, they will look like they are the perfect fit!

Hold each prop at the very edge for the best photo effects.

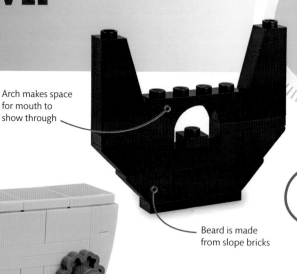

Arch makes space for mouth to show through

Beard is made from slope bricks

Use small pieces, like this flower, as inspiration

HATS AND BEARDS ARE COOL!

55 Explore the human body

There is more going on inside the human body than in the biggest LEGO creation! Scientists and doctors use anatomical models like this to learn how people work underneath their skin. Build your own and then go online to find out what all the different parts are for!

Pink slopes create a brain inside the skull

Bone is bar piece clipped onto a plate

Ribs are curved half arch bricks and smooth tiles

BUILDER'S TIP

Smooth tiles lift the main arm and leg pieces above the base studs so they can be angled diagonally.

Textured piece for intestines

Dark-red parts are tendons and muscle

Elbow and shoulder joints are made from hinge plates with tiles on top

INSIDE STORY

This model shows bones and organs on one half of the body and muscles and organs on the other. It might look a little grisly, but it is a great way to learn more about human anatomy! What other kinds of anatomical models could you build? Try a horse or a dog, or even a dinosaur!

Fingers and toes are grille pieces

Meet a spooky standing skeleton on page 213.

56 Build curves with straight bricks

Don't go round in circles when trying to create a LEGO curve! Cylinders, snake-like shapes and even spirals are all possible when you get to grips with a few basic tips and tricks. Take a look at the examples below and try to create your own circular builds.

Circles are perfectly symmetrical, so the same pieces are used on the opposite sides of each ring

BECOME A RING MASTER

Once you've mastered the art of making a flat LEGO circle, there is no end to the round things you can build! Layering circles of different sizes on top of each other can create cone shapes and domes – and two domes back-to-back can be combined to make a ball!

Domed roof is made from smaller and smaller circles

Use these rings as a template for your circular buildings

The bigger the ring, the longer the straight edge at the top, bottom and sides

Each row of this wall alternates rectangular bricks and small round bricks

Walls built in this way can curve in one direction and then the other!

This shorter wall uses rectangular plates and small round plates instead of bricks

BUILDER'S TIP

Laying a round object such as a drinks coaster on a base plate can act as a template when starting to build a circle.

This lighthouse has round levels in three sizes, using similar shapes to the rings above

RIPPLE EFFECT

The round elements in these walls make them flexible so that they can curve back and forth like a snake! Making them all one colour gives the differently shaped parts a unified appearance. Try using one colour for the round pieces and another for the rectangular pieces to create an interesting look!

Discover how to build spheres on pages 62–63.

Play the four-in-a-row game

57

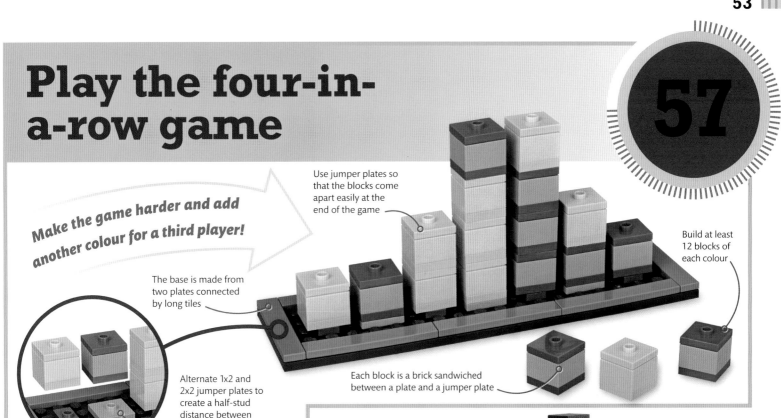

Make the game harder and add another colour for a third player!

Use jumper plates so that the blocks come apart easily at the end of the game

Build at least 12 blocks of each colour

The base is made from two plates connected by long tiles

Each block is a brick sandwiched between a plate and a jumper plate

Alternate 1x2 and 2x2 jumper plates to create a half-stud distance between each column

This great game for two players can go on forever if the players are good enough – and have enough bricks! The two players compete to get four blocks in a row. It sounds easy, but watch out! Your opponent will try to block you!

HOW TO PLAY

1. Play starts with no blocks on the board. Both players choose a colour and take turns to add blocks of that colour to the board.

2. Blocks can be added to any of the seven columns no matter how many blocks are already in that column.

3. The aim of the game is to create an uninterrupted row of four blocks in your colour – and to stop your opponent from doing the same in their colour. Rows can be horizontal, vertical or diagonal.

4. The winner is the first person to create a row of four. If the blocks run out before a winner is declared, all the blocks are removed and play begins again.

Here's a brick-stacking challenge with a difference – the bricks were never meant to be stacked this way! Balancing bricks on their side makes a very unstable, slipping, sliding tower. It's no good for building, but it makes a fun game! See how many you can stack in 30 seconds!

58

Balance a brick tower

Wider bricks are easier to stack sideways than narrow ones

WE CAN DO THIS!

59 Go bird-watching

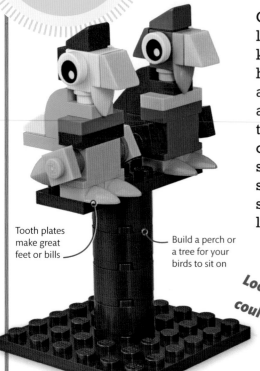

Create a 3-D bird-watching log! Many bird-watchers keep notes on the birds they have seen, and sometimes add drawings. Go one better and use LEGO bricks to build the birds you see in the wild or at the zoo. They won't stand still while you build them, so make your own notes and sketches, then refer to them later to build your birds.

Bricks with side studs hold the wings in place

Big, stubby bill made from a sideways bow piece

Tooth plates make great feet or bills

Build a perch or a tree for your birds to sit on

Tooth plates also work as feather tips on wings and tails

Look in your collection for pieces that could work for wings, beaks and feet.

Each leg is a stack of round plates

Can you solve this LEGO brainteaser? Instead of numbers, this sudoku puzzle is made up of colours. Build it exactly as shown, then see if you can fill in the blanks!

HOW TO PLAY

1. The aim of the game is to fill the grid using just six colours so that no colour repeats in any row, column or rectangular section.

2. When complete, each row, column and rectangular section should contain one brick of each colour.

3. The bricks already shown cannot be moved. So you don't get confused, use square bricks for the ones you add in.

A yellow piece must go here. Can you see why?

With a yellow piece added above, can you work out where the yellow piece goes in this section?

Time yourself to see how quickly you can fill the blanks

60 Solve a LEGO sudoku

You can find the solution on page 253 ▶

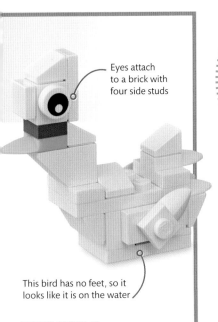

Eyes attach to a brick with four side studs

This bird has no feet, so it looks like it is on the water

BUILDING A FLOCK

Curved and sloping pieces are some of the most important when it comes to building birds, and bricks with side studs are useful for adding wings. Make your models small and you will have enough bricks to build all the birds you see. Soon you will build up an entire flock!

61 Hold on to your post

Make the thumb the shortest part and the middle finger longest.

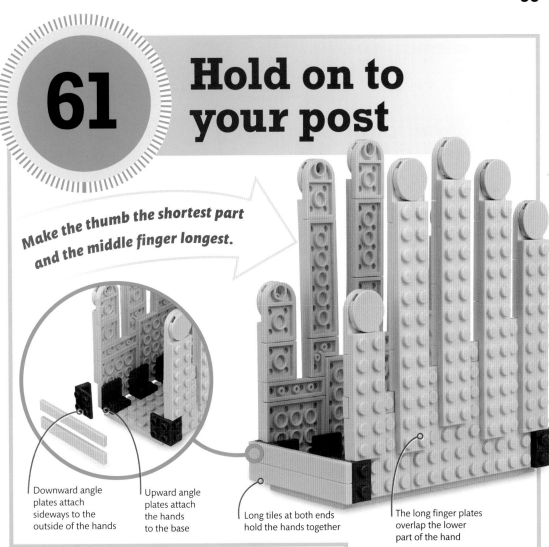

Downward angle plates attach sideways to the outside of the hands

Upward angle plates attach the hands to the base

Long tiles at both ends hold the hands together

The long finger plates overlap the lower part of the hand

Get a grip on your cards and letters! If you are lucky enough to get lots of post, this handy, hand-shaped letter rack will help you keep it all tidy.

Make a mini zip line

62

LEGO slide handle piece

A faucet piece hooks over the wire

A handle piece acts as a stopper

The minifigure holds onto a LEGO Technic pin with bar

Watch your minifigures race along a zip line made from string or cotton thread. Use a LEGO slide handle piece, or build your own slide handle.

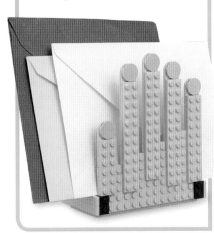

63 Make a lucky dip machine

Windows are transparent wall pieces

Round plates on the sides stop the drawer from being pulled out too far

Build a LEGO lucky dip machine that looks like a classic sweet dispenser! Push the drawer in to catch a LEGO piece and then pull it out again to see what piece you've got. What else could you put inside your lucky dip machine?

Slopes channel pieces into the drawer

Smooth tiles let the drawer slide

Pieces are a mix of small round bricks, balls and plates

TEST OF DRAWERS

Make the items in your lucky dip machine roughly the same size, and the drawer just big enough to hold one of whatever it dispenses. If the drawer is too big, extra items might fall in and poke out over the top, which will stop it from sliding open.

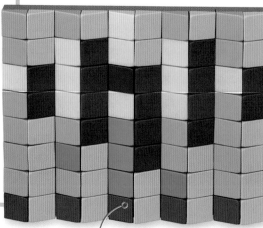

Build one picture first, with slopes facing left on every other stud across

Build another picture in the gaps with slopes facing right

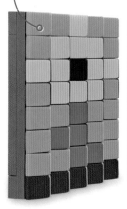

Turn this LEGO build to the left and a heart appears. Turn it to the right, and the heart becomes a flower! Can you work out how the magic happens?

The base plate is 10 studs across, but each picture is only five slopes wide

Build a magic mosaic

64

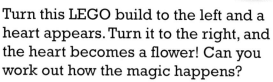

65 Tell a tale in six scenes

THIS MAP WILL LEAD ME TO THE PRINCESS!

Bulrushes are single round bricks on antennae

Make sure your brave hero is equipped for an adventure

All three of these scenes fit onto same-sized base plates

Part 1

The princess has been trapped in this high tower!

DON'T COME UP, I'LL COME DOWN!

SMALL SCENES, BIG ADVENTURES

Remember to keep your scenes small and to leave out excess detail so that it is always clear what is happening. Focus on one or two characters who go to lots of different places, and be sure to finish with a happy ending!

Why not photograph your scenes to show your friends?

Stone details are made using differently coloured tiles

Part 2

This string has stud attachments at both ends

Just the head is enough to suggest an entire dragon in this small scene

Who knew that a dragon was guarding the tower?

THESE ADVENTURES DO TEND TO DRAG-ON!

Swap minifigure faces to show a range of expressions in different scenes

Add drama with some scary bones and skulls

Part 3

Can you tell a story without using words? Put your building skills to the test by making six small scenes that tell an entire tale. Start your story from scratch or build the final three scenes of the adventure shown here. Our hero has saved the princess from the tower, but can she save him from the fire-breathing dragon?

Create a thrilling comic strip on page 230.

66 Play a game of crazy golf

ON THE COURSE

Build as many obstacles as you can and spread them out across a room. Use your fingers to flick a LEGO ball around the course, or blow it along using a drinking straw. Time how long it takes you to get around the course and then try to beat your record!

Rotor blade pieces fit onto plates with clip hinges

This plate with pin beneath slots into a brick with hole on the front of the windmill, and allows the sails to turn

Can you guide a ball under, over and through a range of obstacles? Put your skills to the test with a crazy golfing challenge! Putt through a series of miniature builds, like this windmill and winding racetrack. For a big finale, build a steep ramp and a tricky final target.

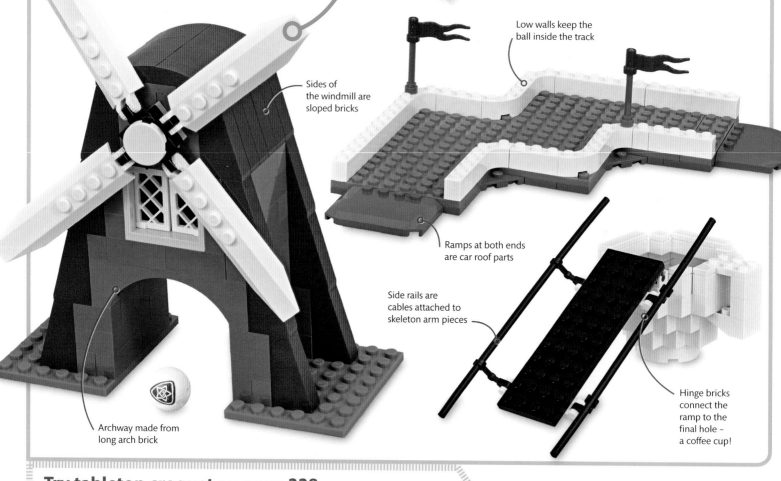

Low walls keep the ball inside the track

Sides of the windmill are sloped bricks

Ramps at both ends are car roof parts

Side rails are cables attached to skeleton arm pieces

Archway made from long arch brick

Hinge bricks connect the ramp to the final hole – a coffee cup!

Try tabletop croquet on page 228.

67 Make a moving monster picture

The picture looks strange when you can see both red and blue parts

Bone held on by black plate with clip

You can bring this dinosaur back to life when you look at it through 3-D glasses! Switching between a pair of coloured filters makes the dinosaur's huge jaws open and shut! What other moving pictures could you build?

LOOK LEFT, THEN RIGHT

Because red and blue appear through different sides of 3-D glasses with red and blue filters, looking through a pair with just your left eye and then your right eye animates the image. If you don't have 3-D glasses like this, you can make your own colour filters using transparent coloured LEGO pieces or see-through sweet wrappers.

How many different-coloured parts do you have in your LEGO collection? It's probably more than you think! Why not put together a palette showing all the different colours you can find? Ask your friends to do the same, and then compare to find out who has the most colours, and which ones are the rarest.

Show your true colours

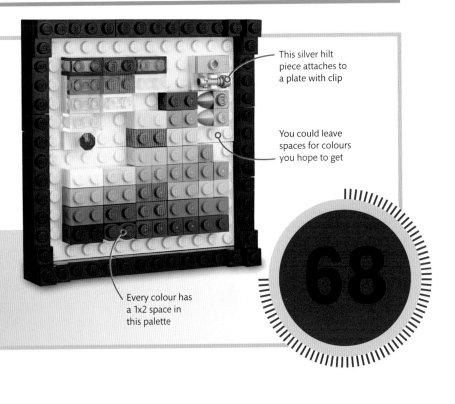

This silver hilt piece attaches to a plate with clip

You could leave spaces for colours you hope to get

Every colour has a 1x2 space in this palette

68

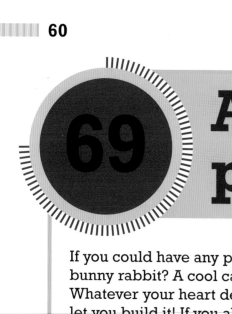

Adopt your perfect pet

Don't forget the tail – a small white plate

Sloped corner bricks make the rabbit's big back legs

Bunny whiskers are made from plates with side clips

If you could have any pet, what would it be? A big-eared bunny rabbit? A cool cat? Or a devoted dog? Whatever your heart desires, LEGO bricks let you build it! If you already have your perfect pet, why not make a LEGO model version of it instead.

Cat ears are small slopes

THE PET SET
Your LEGO pet won't need to be house-trained, but you might want to build it a food bowl and somewhere to sleep. One of the best things about LEGO pets is that they can be any size – so you could even build your own pony, or a pet elephant!

Nose is an upside-down small round plate

Droopy ears are angled plates

Make a fabulous fish tank on page 176.

CAPITAL GROWTH
This letter A has an outdoor theme, with flowers and greenery growing all over it. Unlike the other two letters, it is built sideways with its studs pointing toward the front. This method has the advantage that the whole front of the letter can easily be covered with decorations.

Make the letter 3-D by adding decorations to the sides

This big flower is eight angled plates joined together

A spider lurks in the undergrowth

Add bricks to the base to make it wide and stable

The middle of the A is a plate attached by hinge plates at the sides

This pink flower is made from small round plates

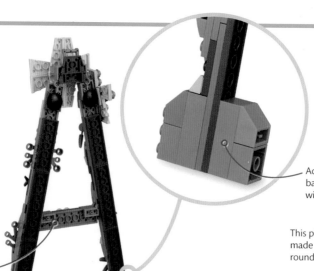

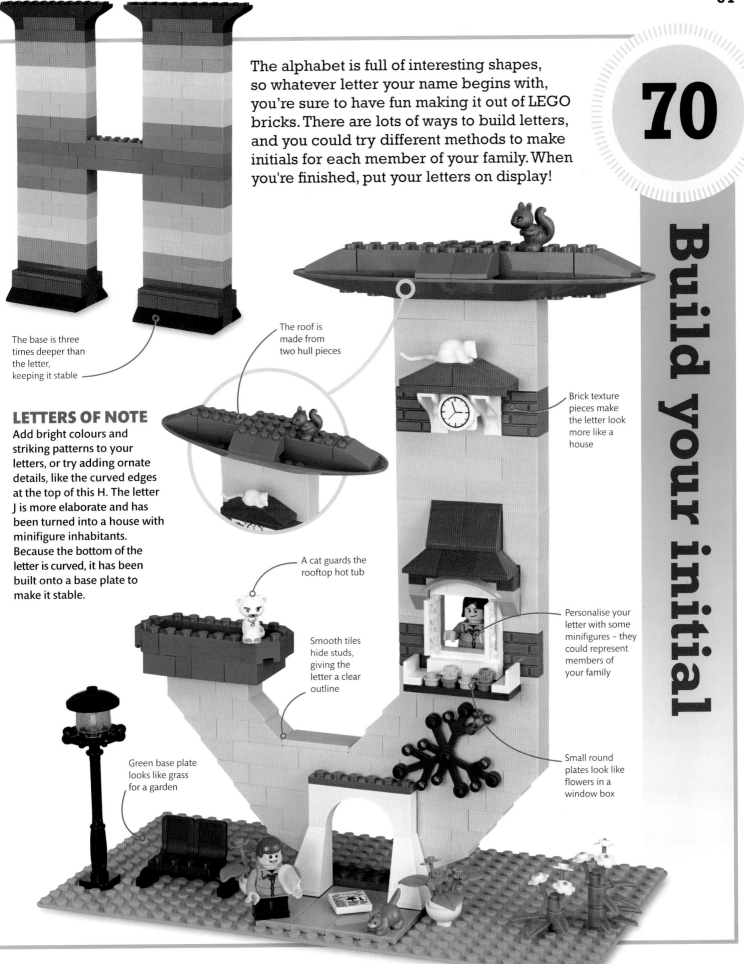

The alphabet is full of interesting shapes, so whatever letter your name begins with, you're sure to have fun making it out of LEGO bricks. There are lots of ways to build letters, and you could try different methods to make initials for each member of your family. When you're finished, put your letters on display!

70

Build your initial

The base is three times deeper than the letter, keeping it stable

The roof is made from two hull pieces

Brick texture pieces make the letter look more like a house

LETTERS OF NOTE

Add bright colours and striking patterns to your letters, or try adding ornate details, like the curved edges at the top of this H. The letter J is more elaborate and has been turned into a house with minifigure inhabitants. Because the bottom of the letter is curved, it has been built onto a base plate to make it stable.

A cat guards the rooftop hot tub

Smooth tiles hide studs, giving the letter a clear outline

Personalise your letter with some minifigures – they could represent members of your family

Green base plate looks like grass for a garden

Small round plates look like flowers in a window box

Create a pecking woodpecker

Let go of this woodpecker at the top of his pole and he will peck all the way down to the bottom! He doesn't fall because he weighs just enough to flex the springy pole into a slight curve, vibrating him back and forth – just like a real woodpecker.

Foot is a LEGO Technic axle connector with a cross hole, which attaches the bird to the pole

Connecting the foot in two places stops the bird from tipping to one side

PECKING ORDERS

The woodpecker has to be the right size and weight for the pecking effect to work, so keep on experimenting if it doesn't work straightaway. Copy the bird in the picture as closely as possible using whatever parts you have. Make it any colour you like.

Long LEGO Technic axle

A round brick connects the axle to the base plate

Saturn is surrounded by rings of ice and rock

1x2 plates surround a 2x2 plate at the base of this globe

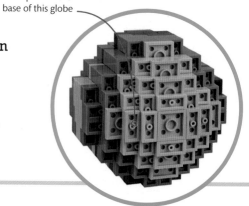

Set course for space with your very own model solar system. The planets that orbit the sun are different colours and sizes, so making them all will look out of this world! Build globe shapes for a challenge, but flat planets on a black base plate will look great too.

73 Make a micro movie set

The car is just two tiny bricks!

Look for pieces with ridges and holes to create realistic micro-buildings

Use computer software to add effects to your movie poster

Play around with scale by putting a small monster into an even smaller setting and making it look huge! Take a close-up photo of the action and turn it into a movie poster – or even a mini movie!

BRICKZILLA

ATTACK ON   BRICK CITY

"UNMISSABLE" - THE NEWS

Explore the solar system

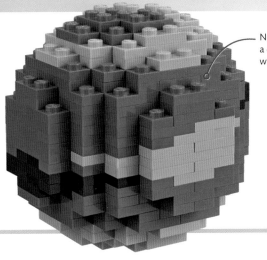

Neptune is a cold, blue world

WORLD BUILDING

Building a sphere is like building a stack of flat round shapes. The round layers get bigger from the bottom up to the middle, and then smaller again toward the top. To make a planet look more realistic, use plates of similar colours to create sideways bands of weather across its surface.

Mars is a small, reddish-brown planet

WHICH WAY IS HOME?

74 Make a life-sized postbox

A LEGO postbox is really something to write home about! It makes a great place to collect cards in the run-up to your birthday, and it can be a fun way for family members to send messages to each other – with you as the delivery service! Use it to pass notes back and forth with a friend, or make it a suggestion box for LEGO building ideas!

Make a canopy with curved half arch bricks

Large half arch bricks give the slot its shape

BIRTHDAY CARDS FOR BEN

Build a reminder robot

75

Wouldn't it be great to have a robot that remembers things for you? This mini messenger may not have his own memory banks, but he will hold on to any important notes you make and pass on the data to anyone who sees him!

Look for unusual pieces to create distinctive robot parts

Each arm is made from three sections linked by LEGO Technic pieces

Use black LEGO Technic pins for a stiff arm connection

Hands are upside-down tap pieces attached to LEGO Technic half pins

Write your message on a card the robot can hold

DON'T FORGET TO BUY ROBOT OIL

76

Follow the teams on their way to the final with a flowchart for any sports league or tournament! Use different-coloured minifigures to represent each team, and advance the winners along the chart at every stage of the contest.

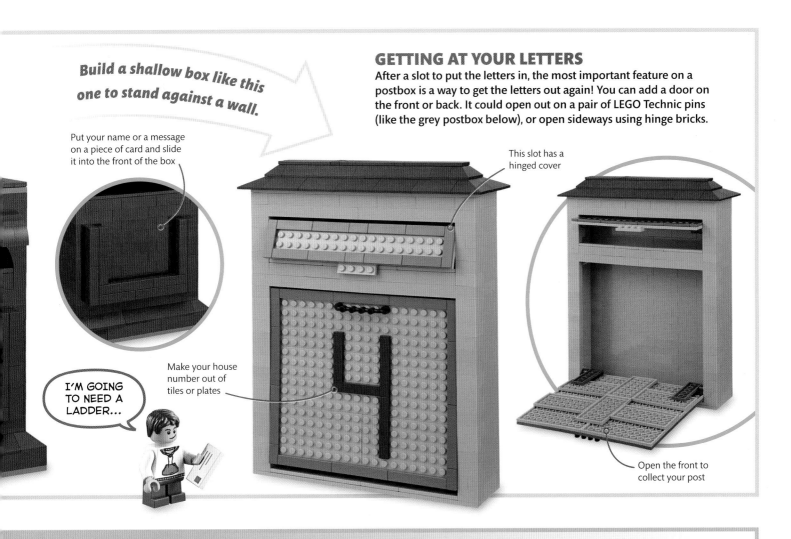

Build a shallow box like this one to stand against a wall.

Put your name or a message on a piece of card and slide it into the front of the box

GETTING AT YOUR LETTERS
After a slot to put the letters in, the most important feature on a postbox is a way to get the letters out again! You can add a door on the front or back. It could open out on a pair of LEGO Technic pins (like the grey postbox below), or open sideways using hinge bricks.

This slot has a hinged cover

Make your house number out of tiles or plates

I'M GOING TO NEED A LADDER...

Open the front to collect your post

Go with the flow of your favourite sport

The Blues were one of eight teams in the quarter-finals

Blues went through to play the Reds in the semi-finals

The Blue player's face gets happier at each stage of the contest!

WE ARE THE CHAMPIONS!

The Blues beat the Orange team to take the trophy in the final

77 Go ten-pin ghouling

Ten-pin ghouling is just like ten-pin bowling, only spookier! A ghostly figure lurks at the end of this dark alley, and the pins are a gang of scary creatures. Try not to shake as you roll the ball, and aim for a strike – if you dare!

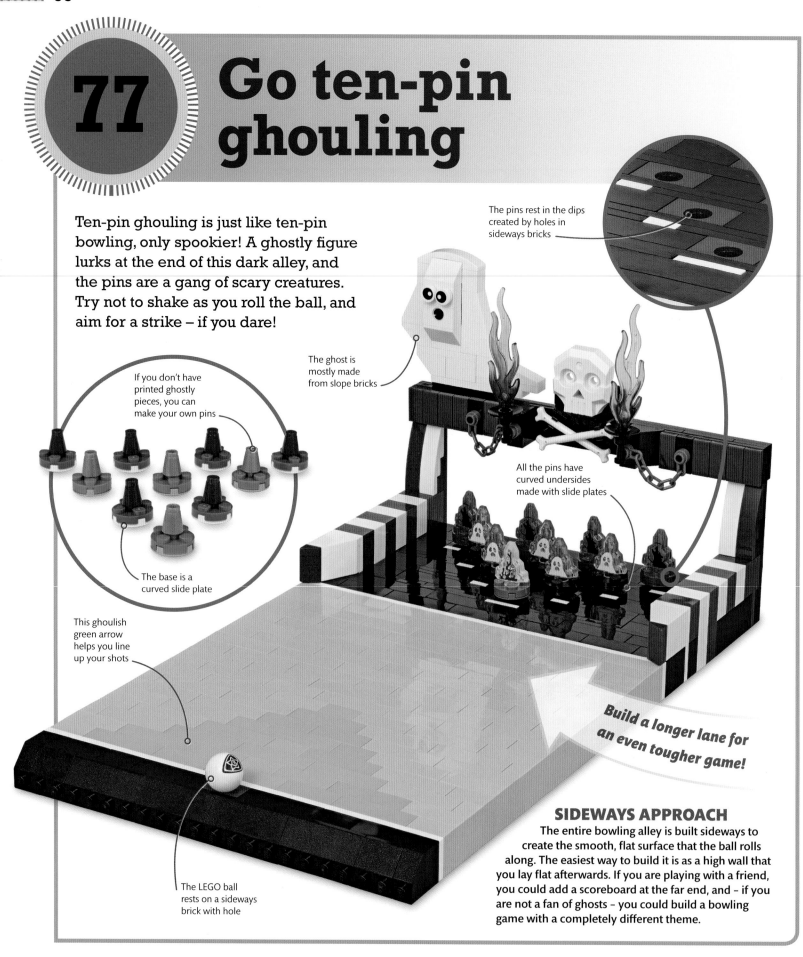

The pins rest in the dips created by holes in sideways bricks

The ghost is mostly made from slope bricks

If you don't have printed ghostly pieces, you can make your own pins

All the pins have curved undersides made with slide plates

The base is a curved slide plate

This ghoulish green arrow helps you line up your shots

The LEGO ball rests on a sideways brick with hole

Build a longer lane for an even tougher game!

SIDEWAYS APPROACH
The entire bowling alley is built sideways to create the smooth, flat surface that the ball rolls along. The easiest way to build it is as a high wall that you lay flat afterwards. If you are playing with a friend, you could add a scoreboard at the far end, and – if you are not a fan of ghosts – you could build a bowling game with a completely different theme.

Take your pick with a spinner

The spinner turns on a 1x1 cone

Twist bar to spin the wheel

Don't get in a spin when making a decision – let one of these handy gadgets help you out! First decide what each colour represents (such as yes, no, maybe, not yet). You could even make some outcomes more likely than others.

The spinner is more likely to land on the larger corner sections

Two layers of LEGO Technic half beams overlap to make the sides of the hexagon

Coloured tiles attach to LEGO Technic half beams

LEGO Technic angle connector spins on a plate with pin

Celebrate with a Chinese dragon

In China, people see in the New Year and other important events by dancing with life-sized dragon puppets. Mark a special occasion of your own by building a miniature dragon.

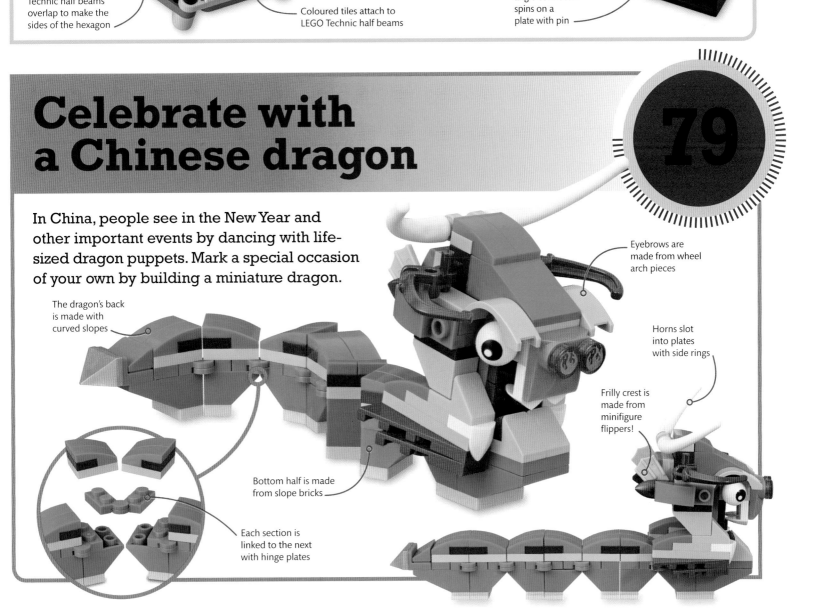

The dragon's back is made with curved slopes

Eyebrows are made from wheel arch pieces

Horns slot into plates with side rings

Frilly crest is made from minifigure flippers!

Bottom half is made from slope bricks

Each section is linked to the next with hinge plates

80 Run an egg-and-spoon race

See how far you can run before your LEGO egg falls from the LEGO spoon! Build two eggs and spoons for a race, or take turns to see who can run the furthest.

Just two studs hold the top and bottom of the egg together

Add a yolk and white inside your egg

Hold the handle part of the spoon only

DO YOU WANT BACON WITH THAT?

Overlap long plates to make a sturdy spoon handle

End of the spoon is a large radar dish

What would the LEGO® Friends Heartlake Food Market look like if it was a LEGO® Pirates set? Maybe something like this! Using the instructions for one of your sets as a starting point, see if you can build it as if it belonged to a different play theme, with different colours and fun details.

BUILDER'S TIP

Plan ahead! Think about what kinds of themed pieces you have before you start building.

Pirates prefer plain benches to pink ones!

The upper level is a jail, rather than a pretty apartment

THE SAME, BUT DIFFERENT

This pirate blacksmith shop is the same size and shape as the Friends set it is based on, but it looks completely different. What would a LEGO® NINJAGO® fire station look like? Or a LEGO Friends spaceship?

Food for sale, just like at the Friends market

BACK

LEGO Friends Heartlake Food Market

A parrot is
a pirate's
best friend

FRONT

A robot arm and
a shield make an
old-fashioned sign

They don't dress
like this in
Heartlake City!

Defensive spikes
replace flowers
at this window

Heavy wooden
door instead of a
modern glass one

Base plate is the
same size as in the
Friends set, but in
an earthy tan colour

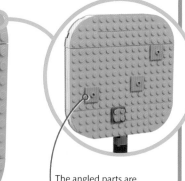

The angled parts are attached using jumper plates and turntables

Create the butterfly first, then build the white background around it

Cast your vote

Front view shows tick on a bright-blue background

Are you a yes or a no? Let everyone know with your very own voting paddle! With a tick on one side and a cross on the other, it is perfect for judging your own talent contests with friends, or simply putting your opinion across in no uncertain terms!

SPREAD YOUR WINGS

Start by building the middle part of the butterfly from round bricks, and add plates coming out in two directions to form an "L" shape. Each wing should look like a mirror image of the other, and both are built in the same way – just at different angles.

Back view is a cross on a dull-coloured background

This wing is made more realistic by having one section slightly higher than the other

A frame makes the build look more like a work of art

CHOOSING SIDES

As well as the one shown here, you could also make a paddle with a smiling face on one side and an unhappy face on the other – or with sides that spell out "YES" and "NO". For a strong handle, thread a long LEGO Technic axle through the round bricks to hold them together.

82

83

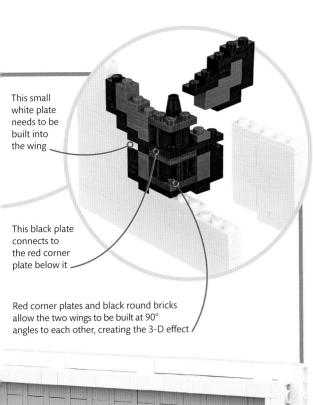

This small white plate needs to be built into the wing

This black plate connects to the red corner plate below it

Red corner plates and black round bricks allow the two wings to be built at 90° angles to each other, creating the 3-D effect

Photograph a UFO

84

Amaze your friends with photos of unidentified flying objects soaring through the sky! Use a transparent antenna or bar to hold a micro-scale model in front of your camera.

Dome pieces make a hot-air balloon shape

Transparent radar dish piece

Use unusually shaped parts like this axe to make your UFOs look less like LEGO builds

Transparent antenna piece

Blue bricks make it look like this butterfly is flying in a clear blue sky

Wow! These butterflies really fly out at you! They would be great builds all by themselves, but by building them into a larger flat background they look like pictures that have come to life. Be sure to show yours off before it flies away!

Build a 3-D butterfly picture

85 Mix things up with a sliding puzzle

When does a pattern become a puzzle? When you split it up into sliding shapes! Each part of this design is made from a plate that moves on hidden grooves and rails, so that you can mix it up and make a game. Time yourself to see how long it takes to put the pattern back together again!

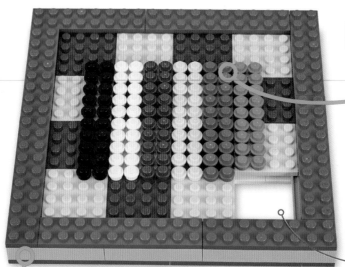

Each puzzle piece has two rails created by overhanging jumper plates

There are grooves along the opposite sides, which the other pieces slot into

Each piece slots into the pieces above and to the left, or into the outer frame

Leave one free square so that the puzzle pieces can move around

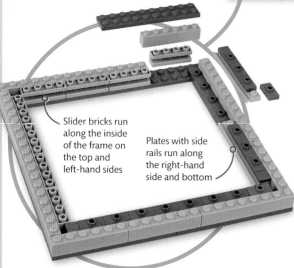

Slider bricks run along the inside of the frame on the top and left-hand sides

Plates with side rails run along the right-hand side and bottom

PIECING IT ALL TOGETHER

Start by building 12 puzzle pieces, but don't decorate the tops yet. Slot the 12 puzzle pieces into the frame in three columns, and then build three more puzzle pieces inside the frame. When all 15 puzzle pieces are in, decorate the tops with round plates. Scramble the pieces to create the puzzle! Make sure you take a photo of the completed puzzle first or refer to this page when putting the pattern back together again.

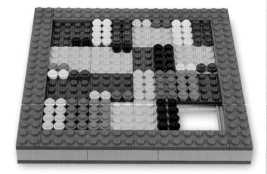

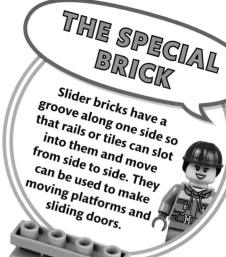

THE SPECIAL BRICK

Slider bricks have a groove along one side so that rails or tiles can slot into them and move from side to side. They can be used to make moving platforms and sliding doors.

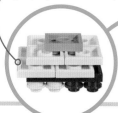

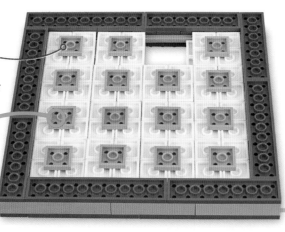

The bottom of each puzzle piece is held together with a 2x2 plate

Four 2x2 jumper plates are sandwiched between another layer of jumper plates and a 4x4 plate

86 Play a game of LEGO bingo

HOW TO PLAY

1 Once you have made the grids, nominate someone to be the bingo caller, who will pull random LEGO pieces out of a box.

2 Whenever a piece matches the shape of one on a player's grid (don't worry about the colour), the player can mark it off.

3 The first player to mark off a row of three (in any direction) on their grid shouts "Bingo!" – and is the winner!

It is very important to use pieces that you have more than one of!

Mark off pieces you have matched with round bricks in the corner of the section

To play, make a grid with nine sections, and place a different LEGO piece in each one. You can make grids for any number of players, but no two grids should have exactly the same bricks. Who will be the first to shout "Bingo!"?

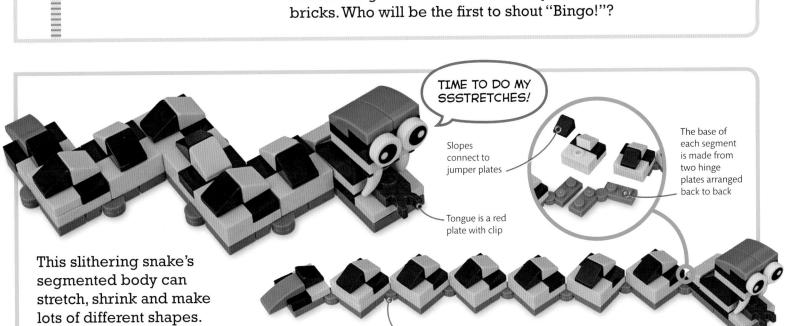

TIME TO DO MY SSSTRETCHES!

Slopes connect to jumper plates

The base of each segment is made from two hinge plates arranged back to back

Tongue is a red plate with clip

This slithering snake's segmented body can stretch, shrink and make lots of different shapes. It might just get away if you're not too careful!

This snake is made with seven hinge plates, but you could use more for a longer snake!

Build a super-bendy snake

87

88 Play a LEGO logo game

The world is full of logos – on storefronts, billboards and even LEGO sets! See how many logos you can build from LEGO bricks, and then quiz your friends to see which ones they can name.

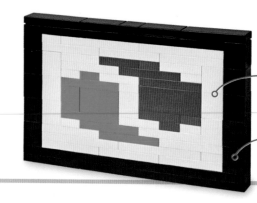

This LEGO Exploriens logo (a 1990s LEGO® Space subtheme) is built flat using plates

The Octan logo has been used in LEGO® Town and City sets since 1992

This logo is built upright, using layers of bricks and plates

89 Celebrate spring

The cute bunny ears are slope bricks mounted on single bricks

Both arms are half arch bricks

The carrot is built around a plate with a ring that looks like a clutching paw

Spring is a lovely time of year. When it comes around, why not make some LEGO models to mark the occasion? If it seems a long way off, you can build something that reminds you of it! The rabbit, chick and egg are all symbols of spring. How would you represent it?

Slope bricks make wide bunny cheeks

Fluffy tail is a large flower

Each leg connects to a LEGO Technic pin with an axle end

LEGO Technic pin sits inside 1x6 brick with holes

Start a chain of creativity

90

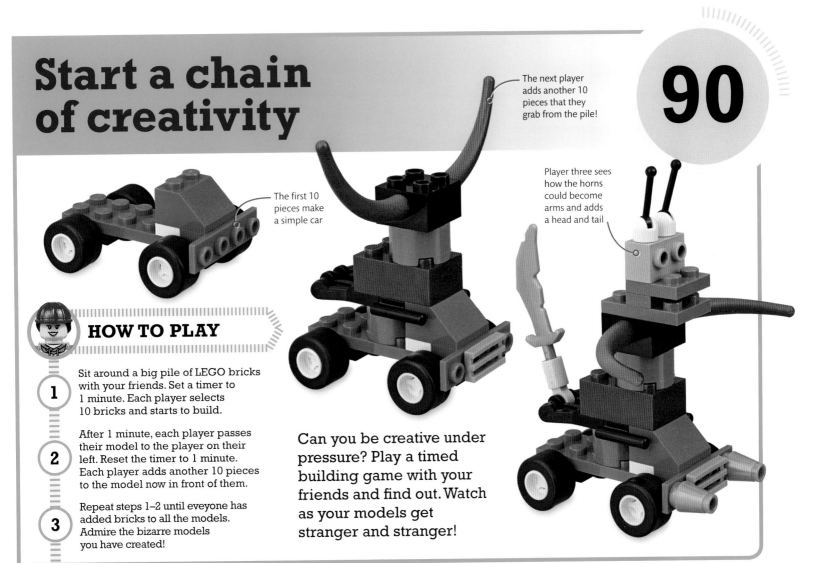

The first 10 pieces make a simple car

The next player adds another 10 pieces that they grab from the pile!

Player three sees how the horns could become arms and adds a head and tail

HOW TO PLAY

1. Sit around a big pile of LEGO bricks with your friends. Set a timer to 1 minute. Each player selects 10 bricks and starts to build.

2. After 1 minute, each player passes their model to the player on their left. Reset the timer to 1 minute. Each player adds another 10 pieces to the model now in front of them.

3. Repeat steps 1–2 until eveyone has added bricks to all the models. Admire the bizarre models you have created!

Can you be creative under pressure? Play a timed building game with your friends and find out. Watch as your models get stranger and stranger!

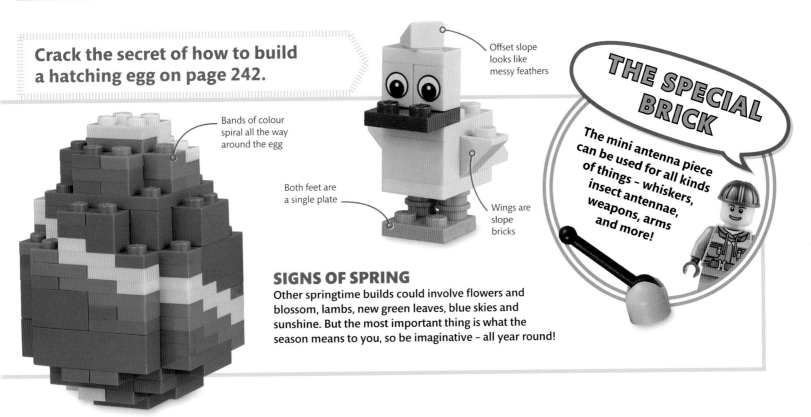

Crack the secret of how to build a hatching egg on page 242.

Bands of colour spiral all the way around the egg

Both feet are a single plate

Offset slope looks like messy feathers

Wings are slope bricks

THE SPECIAL BRICK

The mini antenna piece can be used for all kinds of things – whiskers, insect antennae, weapons, arms and more!

SIGNS OF SPRING

Other springtime builds could involve flowers and blossom, lambs, new green leaves, blue skies and sunshine. But the most important thing is what the season means to you, so be imaginative – all year round!

91 Put on a LEGO magic show

Roll up! Roll up! See a minifigure disappear before your very eyes! Gasp as rabbits are pulled from a hat! Question everything you thought possible as a pizza is shrunk to the size of a coin! Ladies and gentlemen, boys and girls, see all this and more with your very own LEGO magic models!

Doors have grey plates with side rails at the tops and bottoms, which allow the doors to slide open and shut

Dazzling stars distract the eye

THE SPECIAL BRICK

Plates with side rails are perfect for making sliding doors. The rails slide along bricks with a groove.

MINIFIGURE MAGIC

Make a minifigure disappear! You'll need to build a magician's cabinet with closing doors and a revolving wall. The minifigure stands on a platform attached to the revolving wall. When the wall is turned, an identical platform is revealed – but there is no minifigure! A successful magic trick is all about distracting the eye, so make sure your cabinet is as colourful and creative as possible, and remember to wave your magic wand with one hand as you turn the revolving wall with the other!

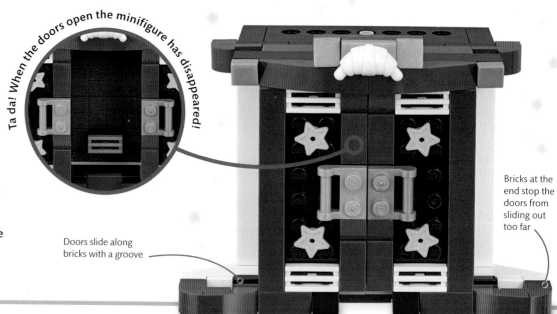

Ta da! When the doors open the minifigure has disappeared!

Doors slide along bricks with a groove

Bricks at the end stop the doors from sliding out too far

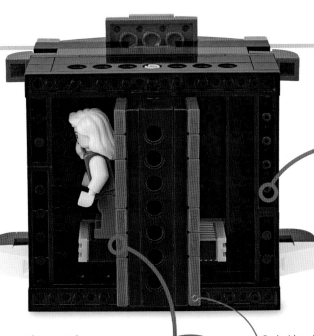

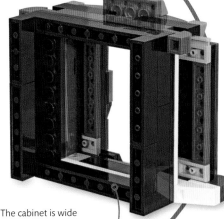

The revolving wall turns on LEGO Technic pins at the top and bottom

The cabinet is wide and deep enough for the revolving wall to turn without hitting the doors

The minifigure stands on a brick platform – her legs attach to hidden studs on the wall, which stop her from falling off as she is turned!

Both sides of the wall are decorated with the same red tile pattern

You could also use two different minifigures to perform a minifigure changing trick!

Angled ears are created with click hinges

Cute rabbit nose is a tooth plate

Curved pieces give the hat its rounded shape

The brim is built in four sections, which attach to bricks with side studs

MAGICIAN'S BUNNY

Every good magician has a rabbit in a hat! You could turn these great props into tricks by building your hat with a hidden compartment, or by making the rabbit with lots of hinge pieces, so that it folds down inside the hat and seems impossibly large when it is lifted out!

Begin the hat by building a box

WAND WIZARDRY

Wave your magic wand to distract attention as you make this pizza build disappear (slip it quickly into your hand or up your sleeve!). Then find the tiny pizza tile behind an audience member's ear. The trick is to have the pizza tile hidden between two of your fingers until you slide it up to your forefinger and thumb. What else could you shrink?

Thread LEGO Technic axles through the wand to stop it from coming apart

2x2 brick with hole

A white round plate with curved underside completes the end

Four curved plates make up the pizza base

92 Give yourself a medal

Do you know someone who deserves a medal? Maybe it's you! Make first, second and third place medals and award them for the games in this book.

Use two layers of round plates to create the numbers

You could thread a ribbon through this curved plate with hole

93

RAMP IT UP

One way to build a racing ramp is to link together LEGO base plates and prop them up with a shallow stack of books. If the studs slow things down too much, turn the base plates upside down. Don't make the ramp too steep, or the cars will simply fall off it.

Small front wheels for extra speed

Here is a puzzle to build, solve – and then set for your friends! A farmer needs to get a fox, chickens and some grain across a river – but he only has room in his boat for himself and one of those three things! He will have to make several trips, but he knows that if he leaves the chickens behind with the grain, they will eat it – and if he leaves the fox with the chickens, it will eat them! In what order will he get everything across?

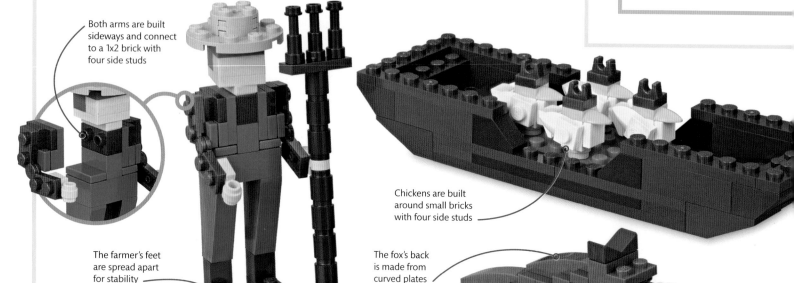

Both arms are built sideways and connect to a 1x2 brick with four side studs

The farmer's feet are spread apart for stability

Chickens are built around small bricks with four side studs

The fox's back is made from curved plates

Solve the farmer's puzzle

You can find the solution on page 253 ▶

Find your fastest car

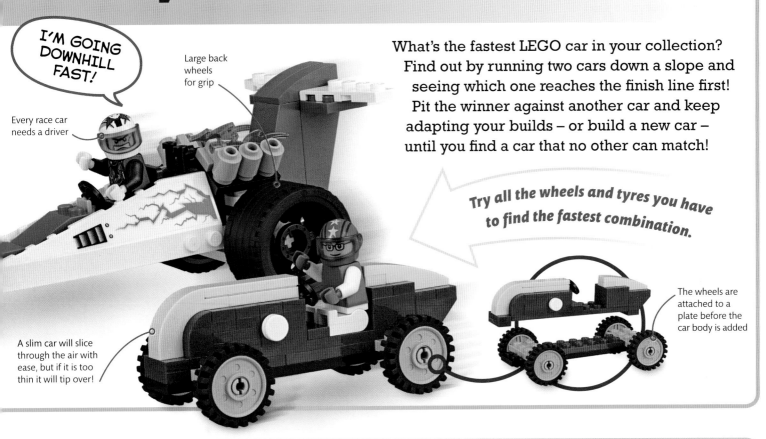

"I'M GOING DOWNHILL FAST!"

Large back wheels for grip

Every race car needs a driver

A slim car will slice through the air with ease, but if it is too thin it will tip over!

What's the fastest LEGO car in your collection? Find out by running two cars down a slope and seeing which one reaches the finish line first! Pit the winner against another car and keep adapting your builds – or build a new car – until you find a car that no other can match!

Try all the wheels and tyres you have to find the fastest combination.

The wheels are attached to a plate before the car body is added

The grain is stacks of small round bricks

The minifigures add equal weight at both ends

Hinge cylinder pieces hold the two sides at the same angle

The seesaw balances on a LEGO Technic pin with ball connector

The base is a large radar dish

These two minifigures rock back and forth on one tiny ball, but they don't tip over! Can you add more or different pieces and still make the seesaw swing?

94

Make a seesaw for minifigures

95

96 Create a friendly gnome

THERE'S GNOME PLACE LIKE HOME!

Hat is made from rocket and nose cone pieces

Spectacles are transparent round tiles

Toadstool cap is a construction worker's helmet

Hoe for cutting weeds

Lance makes a perfect fishing rod

Feel like giving a gnome a home? This gnome will look great watching over your pot plants or window boxes. Gnomes are friendly, but they can get up to mischief, so don't leave them outside or you might find they wander off!

Play football with straws

97

Challenge your friends with this scaled-down football game. Two players each have a straw, which they use to try to get the ball into their opponent's LEGO goal – just by blowing!

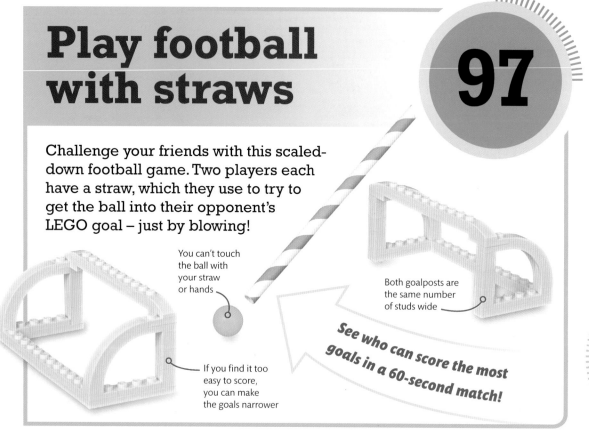

You can't touch the ball with your straw or hands

Both goalposts are the same number of studs wide

If you find it too easy to score, you can make the goals narrower

See who can score the most goals in a 60-second match!

MAKE IT SNAPPY
The build is really one big hinge, linked by LEGO Technic pins at the back of the head. The two halves of the mouth are built separately, and then connected by the pins. Add a long brick coming out of the back of the top half – when you push down on it, the shark's jaws will open wide!

98

KNOW YOUR GNOMES

Most gnomes are short and plump, with pointy hats, beards and brightly coloured outfits. They like to help out in the garden, so they often carry shovels or push wheelbarrows. If there is water nearby, they also enjoy a spot of fishing. What will your gnome be doing?

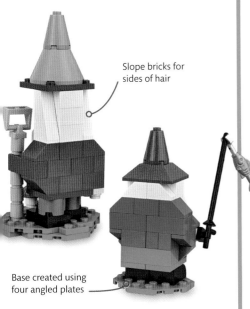

Slope bricks for sides of hair

Base created using four angled plates

Why not make different racks for different kinds of video games?

The cases rest on smooth tiles

Put your video game collection in order with a LEGO rack for your game cases. Place what you're playing at the front, so you can see its stylish cover art.

This rack has room for three video game cases

Add a decoration – this musical note shows that this rack is for dance and karaoke-style games

99 Organise your games

Press here to open

LEGO Technic pins connect the two halves of the mouth

Curved pieces add a smooth finish above and below the teeth

The teeth sections fit sideways onto angle plates at the front and sides of the mouth

Don't be scared by this great white shark – all it eats is paper clips! Press the lever at the back and its mouth opens wide. Reach inside and claim the clips you need before its shiny white jaws snap shut again!

Build a shark with bite

THE SPECIAL BRICK

1x1 tooth plates aren't just for making teeth! They can also look like ice, claws, noses, beaks and much more!

100 Give a LEGO greetings card

Show someone how much you care with a greetings card to mark a special occasion – or just to say hello! These cards aren't for sending in the post, so you get to give them in person. You could also leave one on display, so the lucky person you made it for gets a surprise!

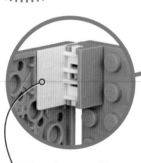

Both cards open on hinge bricks at the top, middle and bottom

Bright, colourful decorations will make your card stand out

You will need two large plates the same size to make your card.

A message is spelt out with LEGO plates inside

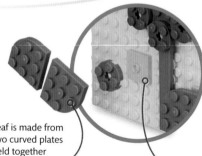

Leaf is made from two curved plates held together by a round plate

The round plate attaches to a jumper plate, connecting the leaf to the card

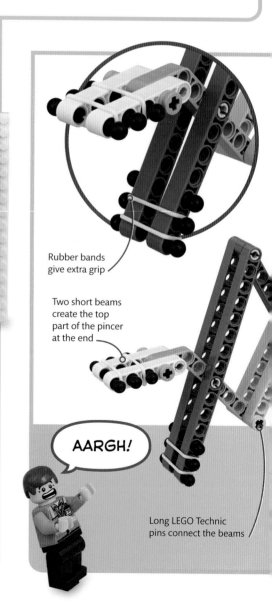

Rubber bands give extra grip

Two short beams create the top part of the pincer at the end

AARGH!

Long LEGO Technic pins connect the beams

BUILDER'S TIP

You could also build a card from the bottom up using bricks instead of plates, with hinge plates to connect the two sides.

A CARD FOR ANY OCCASION

As well as birthday cards and season's greetings, you could also make get well messages, thank you cards and cards that congratulate people on passing school tests or getting new jobs. Make the picture on the front reflect the kind of card that you are making, or add the favourite things of the person that you are making it for.

101 Put your memory to the test

Use pieces that are easy to name, such as a skateboard or snake

Take on your friends with this tricky memory challenge! Spread 20 or 30 pieces out on a table and ask all the players to study them for one minute, then cover them up. Next, everyone has two minutes to write down as many pieces as they can remember. Whoever lists the most correct pieces is the winner!

Here is a great way to keep your room tidy without having to break a sweat! Grasping the end of this extending arm makes it reach out for almost 76cm (30 inches), grabbing onto whatever it finds in its path. Nothing can escape its clutches!

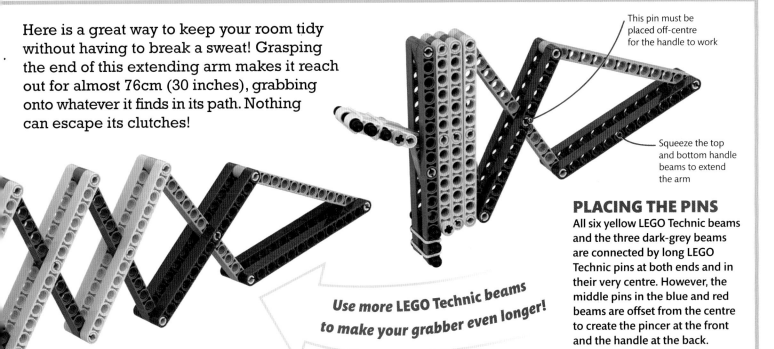

This pin must be placed off-centre for the handle to work

Squeeze the top and bottom handle beams to extend the arm

Use more LEGO Technic beams to make your grabber even longer!

PLACING THE PINS

All six yellow LEGO Technic beams and the three dark-grey beams are connected by long LEGO Technic pins at both ends and in their very centre. However, the middle pins in the blue and red beams are offset from the centre to create the pincer at the front and the handle at the back.

Make a long-armed grabber

102

103 Keep yourself cool

Smooth tile decorations stop sections from getting stuck to each other when the fan is folded in

Tile is on top section only

THIS TRULY IS MY BIGGEST FAN.

Wall panel pieces below each hinge stop the sections from opening out too far

Hinge plates link each section

Each section is a long angled plate

Hand fans have been used throughout history to keep people cool and help them look cool, too! What colours and pieces will you use to decorate your folding LEGO fan?

104 Put together some percussion

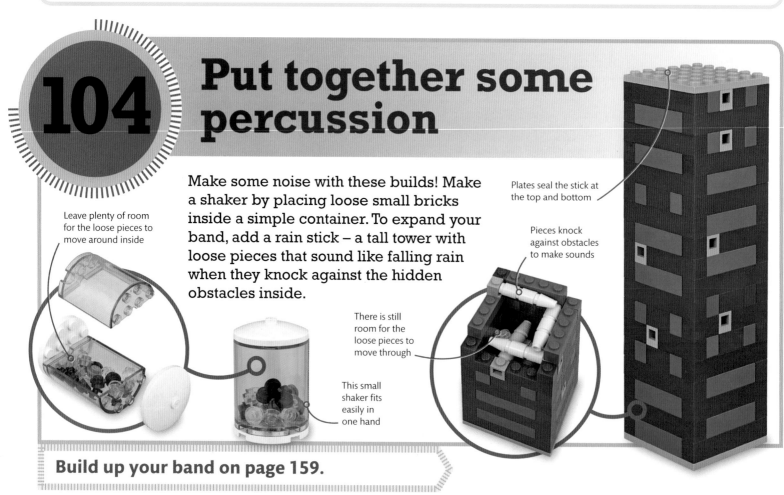

Make some noise with these builds! Make a shaker by placing loose small bricks inside a simple container. To expand your band, add a rain stick – a tall tower with loose pieces that sound like falling rain when they knock against the hidden obstacles inside.

Leave plenty of room for the loose pieces to move around inside

There is still room for the loose pieces to move through

This small shaker fits easily in one hand

Plates seal the stick at the top and bottom

Pieces knock against obstacles to make sounds

Build up your band on page 159.

Build a paper aeroplane launcher

105

Give your paper aeroplanes an extra boost with a smooth runway and a flick-firing launch mechanism made from LEGO Technic pieces. Use a small piece of paper to make an aeroplane and then take turns with a friend using the launcher and see who can make their plane fly the furthest.

Watch your paper aeroplane soar through the sky!

Two grille slopes support the plane before launch

Flick here to send your plane up, up and away!

When released, the lever pushes the aeroplane up from the bottom

Long LEGO Technic pin limits the movement of the beam

The plane sits loosely within this channel

Tyres attach to long LEGO Technic pin

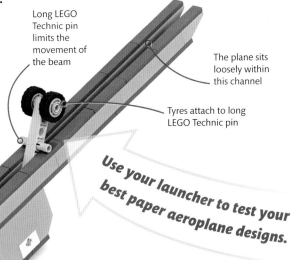

The lever is a LEGO Technic beam that fits onto an axle

Use your launcher to test your best paper aeroplane designs.

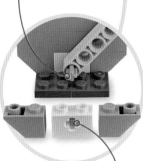

The axle slots into a brick with a cross hole, which is built into the stand

LIFT-OFF LEVER
The firing mechanism is a lever that pivots on a LEGO Technic axle in the base of the launcher. The lever's length adds to its power, while the tyres make it easier to flick and give it extra momentum when it is in motion.

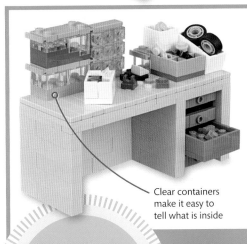

Sorting your bricks by size and type can make building even more fun because you can find the parts more quickly and easily. Collect small plastic tubs to store all your different parts. Try organising parts by shape first of all. Sorting by colour can make finding things harder – imagine trying to find a particular yellow piece in a box full of yellow pieces!

Clear containers make it easy to tell what is inside

106 # Sort your LEGO bricks

Brick-drop challenge

Test your nerves in this exciting two-player game! Inside the brick-drop tower are lots of loose LEGO pieces, supported by sticks made from LEGO Technic axles. Players take turns removing the sticks – and then watch as the loose pieces take a tumble!

LEGO Technic axles overlap to create a lattice to hold the pieces

HOW TO PLAY

1 Place all the sticks in the tower, then pour a handful of small pieces into the top.

2 Each player sits in front of one of the two trays. Take turns removing a stick from the tower – gently!

3 As sticks are removed, the bricks will start to fall and land in the trays. Peek through the sides of the tower to guess which way you think the pieces will fall.

4 When all the sticks have been removed, the winner is the player with the fewest pieces in their tray.

Transparent rock bricks let players see inside the tower

Layers of bricks with holes allow sticks to cross through the model

Pieces on the end of the sticks stop them from sliding through the model

Lid rests on a layer of smooth tiles

Ornate pillars are decorative – but not essential!

Slope bricks help hold the tower clear of the base

107

Tiles stop the tray from sliding on the base

Tray is a square wall element

Add the bricks with holes at different levels on alternate sides.

FROM TOP TO BOTTOM
The brick-drop tower is hollow and open at both ends so that the loose pieces can be added, and can then fall through to the trays below. The trays slot neatly into place between decorative tiles on the base, but do not attach to anything. They are easy to remove so that you can pour the loose pieces back into the top and play again!

108 Build a pair of bookend buddies

Ears are grille slopes

Layers of curved plates surround the eyes

The tail is made from a mixture of angled plates

BEING A BOOKEND IS A REAL HOOT!

The owl's feathery front is created with croissant pieces

This friendly fox and wise old owl are great pals. They never let anything come between them – unless it's a good book! They spend their days back to back, guarding all the knowledge and excitement that is found on a bookshelf, and making any room much more colourful!

The backs of the bookends are completely flat

Make sure your bookend can support one or two books before adding more

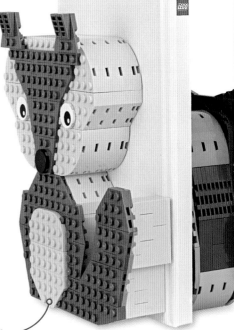

Key details are created with a top layer of plates

BALANCING THE BOOKS

Both animals are built sideways from a base of thin plates using curved and angled bricks to make a simple outline. Make sure the bookends are deep enough not to tip over. Adding bricks all through the insides, rather than having hollow space, also gives them the solid weight they need to support real books.

BUILDER'S TIP

Construct the main part of the tower away from the base, then attach it to the red legs. This will be more stable than building up from the legs.

Spot the difference

Challenge your friends and family with a pair of near-identical LEGO scenes and see if they can spot the differences against the clock! Ten things have changed in each of these scenes. Can you identify them all in three minutes? Try to build your own pair of scenes too. Remember to include lots of small details!

1

Keep key pieces, like this blue base plate, the same in both builds

LEGO Technic connectors create a curvy tree trunk

1

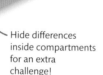

Build in lots of opportunities to add detail, like this brick with clip

Hide differences inside compartments for an extra challenge!

2

2

109

WHAT TO SPOT

A good spot-the-difference game will have lots of detail, with things added, things taken away, things that have changed colour, and items that have been swapped for other things. Don't forget to let people know how many changes they are looking for!

Find the full list of differences for each model on page 253 ▶

110 Take aim in tin can alley

Bring all the fun of the fairground into your own home with this classic tin can target game. Take turns with your friends seeing how many cans you can knock down, or try to hit them all in 30 seconds.

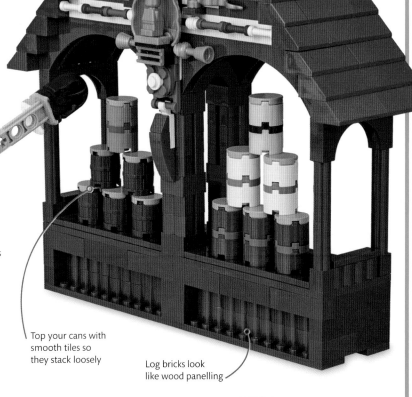

The launcher can swivel from side to side on this turntable

Look through this LEGO® BIONICLE® sight to take aim

Turn the cogs to tilt the launcher up and down

Use this handle to aim the launcher left and right

Top your cans with smooth tiles so they stack loosely

Log bricks look like wood panelling

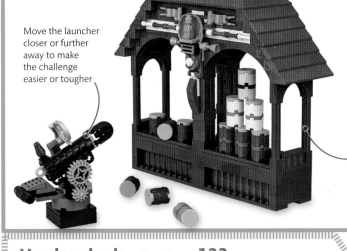

Move the launcher closer or further away to make the challenge easier or tougher

FAIREST OF THEM ALL
Fancy stalls in carnival colours add to the excitement of funfair games. Make your tin can alley stall as appealing as the real thing by adding decoration and detail all over.

Tall round bricks look like wooden poles

THE SPECIAL BRICK

This chunky housing has a spring-release mechanism that fires a missile when the lever at the back is pulled.

Hook a duck on page 133.

111 Decorate your furniture

Building around table legs is a fun way to liven up parts of furniture that often go unnoticed. Surprise visitors by decorating the legs on your dining table, desk or even bed! Add minifigures to a simple square shape or try building different patterns.

Most table legs are not very exciting!

Stack alternating bricks from both connecting walls to create strong corners

AN IDEA WITH LEGS

Make sure your decoration fits the table leg perfectly by building on site. Begin by creating a frame of thin plates around the leg and then start stacking. If you prefer, try leaving a gap in your build so that it can slot on and off the table leg without you having to take apart your model.

A BIG STEP FOR A MINIFIGURE!

Build around your table leg, but not underneath it.

Single-colour stairs allow colourful minifigures to stand out

Can you collect more carrots than your rival rabbit? Find out with this bunny-based board game. Hop from square to square in search of a sprouting snack, but watch out for the prickly thorns! A carrot spinner decides which way your bunny bounces, but you decide how far it can move! This board is big enough for two players but you could build a larger one if you have more players.

112

113 Take on the Alphabet Building Challenge

Slope bricks create a curved handle shape

Comb, cat, crayon or car could all be good "C" builds

Comb teeth are thin bar pieces

The Alphabet Building Challenge is as easy as A, B, C! Give your friend a letter from the alphabet and 30 seconds to pick an object to build that begins with that letter. Let them choose a letter for you, decide on an object, and race to create your chosen builds.

HOW TO PLAY

1 Each player places their rabbit on the board, on a square of their choice.

2 Take turns spinning the carrot. See which way it points: up, down, left or right.

3 Move any number of squares you wish in that direction. If you land on a square with a carrot top – collect the piece!

4 You cannot land on or pass over squares with thorns, so you must wait for your next turn to go around them.

5 When all the carrot tops have been picked, the winner is the player who has collected the most!

RULES OF THE FIELD

Place an odd number of carrots and a few obstacles on your board before you play. Space them out and change their position in between games. Make sure that both players are sitting on the same side of the board as the carrot spinner, so that you both agree which way is up!

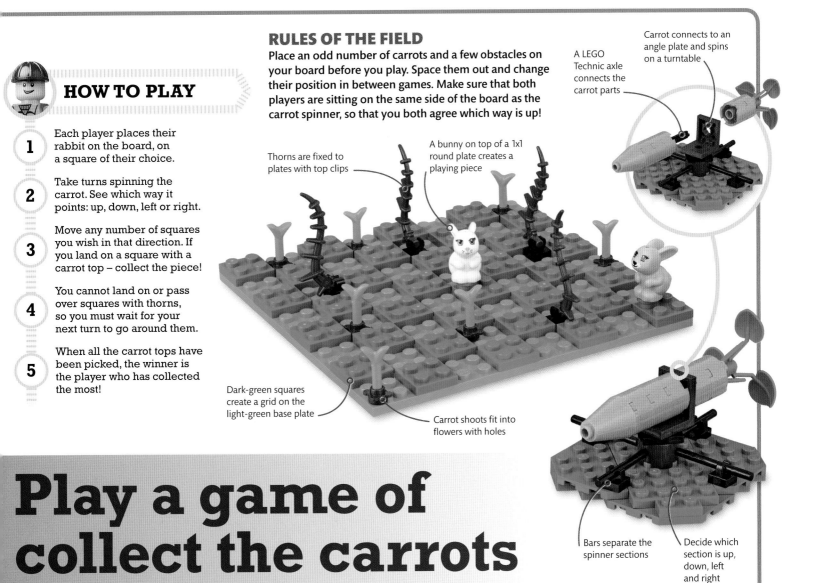

Thorns are fixed to plates with top clips

A bunny on top of a 1x1 round plate creates a playing piece

A LEGO Technic axle connects the carrot parts

Carrot connects to an angle plate and spins on a turntable

Dark-green squares create a grid on the light-green base plate

Carrot shoots fit into flowers with holes

Bars separate the spinner sections

Decide which section is up, down, left and right

Play a game of collect the carrots

114 Hunt for the hidden pirate

Turn a pirate into treasure by hiding him all around the house! Show the model to your friends, then break the model down into several parts, and ask someone who is not playing to put each part in a different place. Set a timer, and see how quickly it takes you and your friends to find them.

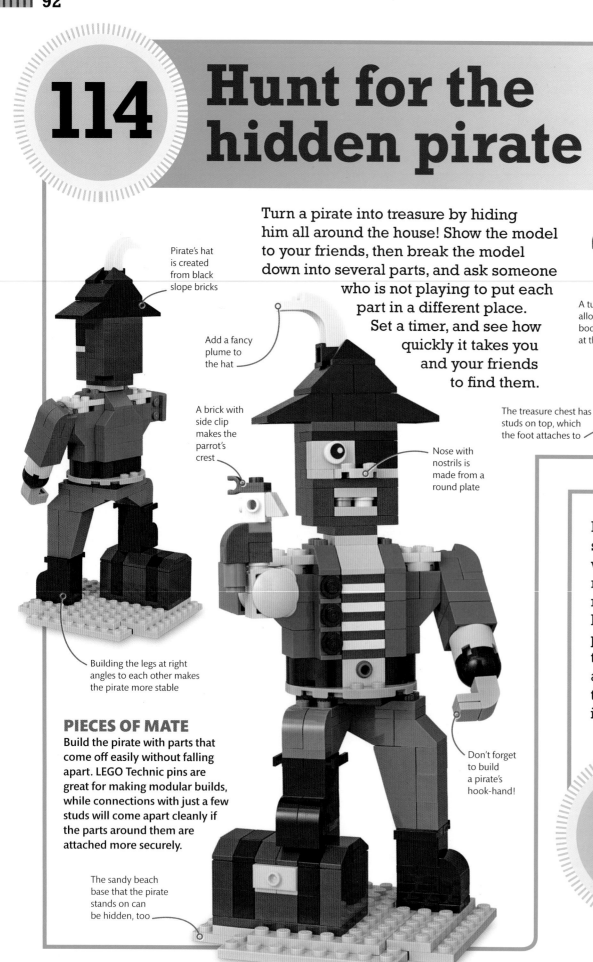

The pirate breaks down into six parts to be hidden

A turntable allows the body to twist at the waist

The treasure chest has studs on top, which the foot attaches to

Pirate's hat is created from black slope bricks

Add a fancy plume to the hat

A brick with side clip makes the parrot's crest

Nose with nostrils is made from a round plate

Building the legs at right angles to each other makes the pirate more stable

Don't forget to build a pirate's hook-hand!

The sandy beach base that the pirate stands on can be hidden, too

PIECES OF MATE
Build the pirate with parts that come off easily without falling apart. LEGO Technic pins are great for making modular builds, while connections with just a few studs will come apart cleanly if the parts around them are attached more securely.

Play back your building session as it happened with a cool time-lapse movie! Take photos at regular intervals as you build, and record the process from beginning to end. Play the pictures as a movie or slideshow to see your model made in a matter of seconds!

115

Take the 20-to-1 challenge

116

Take 10 pairs of matching bricks and see what you can build using all of them. Then take one brick away and build something completely different with the 19 pieces you have left. Keep rebuilding with one brick fewer every time. How close can you get to making 20 different things?

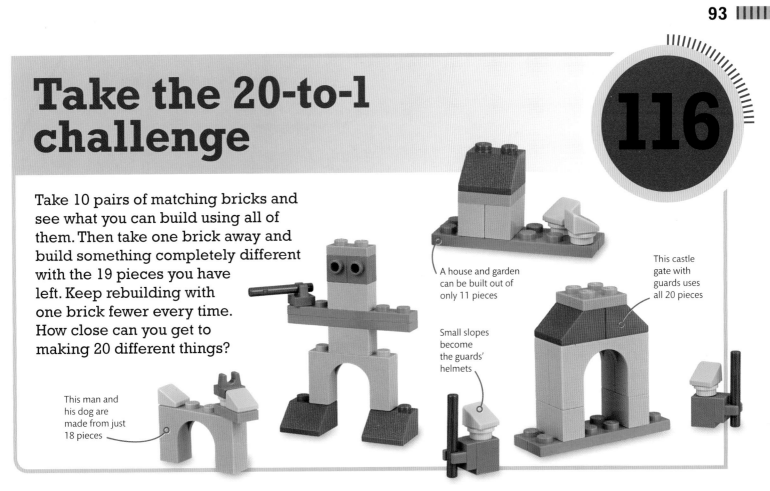

A house and garden can be built out of only 11 pieces

This castle gate with guards uses all 20 pieces

Small slopes become the guards' helmets

This man and his dog are made from just 18 pieces

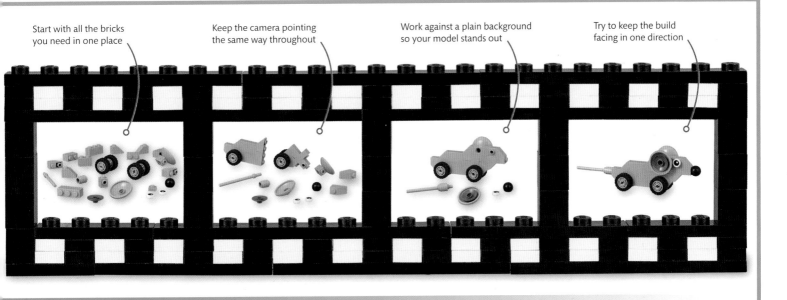

Start with all the bricks you need in one place

Keep the camera pointing the same way throughout

Work against a plain background so your model stands out

Try to keep the build facing in one direction

Make a time-lapse video of your building session

Get tips on taking great LEGO photos on page 42.

117 Keep building on the go

Make your journeys go faster by taking a LEGO travel pack with you. All you need is a box with a secure lid, a choice selection of bricks and some homemade challenge cards to choose from. To make it harder, build against the clock!

A handful of bricks can connect in hundreds of different ways

Use your bricks to recreate the models on your cards.

Keep your builds relatively small and simple

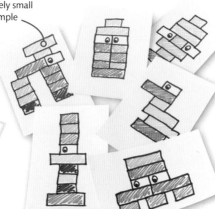

Take two of each brick you need, so you can play with a friend

If you want to show off your photos in style, why not make a LEGO picture stand? This one has a simple clip that snaps shut to hold a photograph without damaging it.

The entire stand is built sideways

Leave this space for the hinge

A broad base keeps it stable

The clip opens at the hinge – the rubber band closes it

Make a snappy picture stand

118

The bumpers are secured by LEGO Technic half pins.

Flick the flipper, tilt the table and try to get the ball into the centre slots in this action-packed arcade game! Give yourself an extra challenge by seeing how many times you can hit the target in two minutes, or try to land the ball in all four slots in turn.

119

Play a little pinball

Curved channel for the ball is formed from large and small half arch bricks

Flick the flipper downwards to launch the ball

Score points by getting the ball into the yellow slots.

The flipper is a LEGO Technic beam that pivots on a central LEGO Technic pin

A GAME OF TWO LAYERS

The pinball table is built sideways with just two layers of bricks, each one-stud deep. The bottom layer is mostly white and flat, but with some coloured bricks extending upwards to form part of the top layer. All the curves and slopes are on the top layer only, except for the slopes on the outside edges.

Make a mealtime train

All aboard! This train is bound for all destinations around the dinner table, calling at cutlery, condiments, napkins and serving spoons! It makes a great decoration when set up on a track around the middle of a table, and you could even add an electric motor!

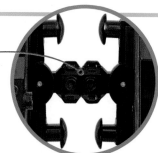

Train buffers connect with magnetic couplings

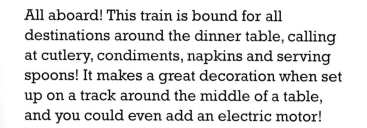

Numbers are built into the sides of the carriages using small black bricks and plates

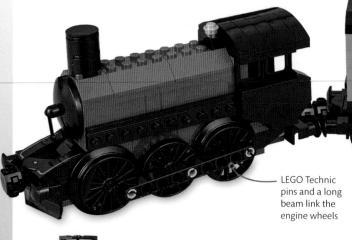

LEGO Technic pins and a long beam link the engine wheels

Carriage wheels turn on bogie plates

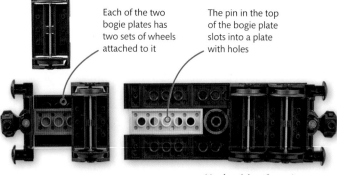

Each of the two bogie plates has two sets of wheels attached to it

The pin in the top of the bogie plate slots into a plate with holes

Underside of carriage

FULL STEAM AHEAD

Even if you don't have train wheels and tracks, you can still build a LEGO train! Large automobile wheels without their tyres and even LEGO Technic gears can make train wheels that run without a track, while smooth tiles or plates with rails can be used to construct straight lengths of track.

THE SPECIAL BRICK

Bogie plates are 4x6 pieces with a pin on top that let train wheels turn with bends in the track.

120

HOW TO PLAY

1 The first player places one piece at the flat end of the board, slightly overhanging the edge, and flicks it once along the board.

2 The same player repeats this with four more pieces, leaving each piece where it lands.

3 The player scores one point for each piece that lands on a different colour and is not on a white line.

4 The pieces are collected up, and the next player begins their turn following the steps above. The winner is the player with the highest score after three turns each.

121

Both carriages can hold items to be passed around the table

A red light indicates which end is the back of the carriage

122 Pick out a pattern

Look around, you'll see patterns everywhere – on walls, floors, clothes and cushions! Look at how they repeat colours and shapes, then invent a new pattern using the techniques you have seen.

This tartan pattern looks the same whichever way you turn it

This Aztec pattern uses claw pieces to make curves

This game is easy to learn, but harder than it looks to master! Players slide their playing pieces along the board, trying to get them all into different coloured sections. Landing on a colour scores a point – but landing on a white line scores nothing at all!

Use curved pieces to create the end barrier

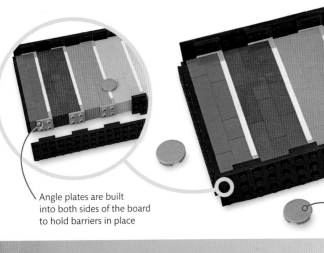

Barriers stop the playing pieces from coming off the board

Angle plates are built into both sides of the board to hold barriers in place

Playing pieces are round tiles

BUILDING THE BOARD
The shuffleboard is built as a high brick wall and laid on its side for playing the game. Building a smaller board or dividing it into fewer sections makes the game easier to play, but not so exciting to watch!

Build a colourful shuffleboard game

123 Perform a puzzle box magic trick

WHAT'S IN THE BOX?

The secret is two LEGO Technic axles on the small box, which slot into bricks with holes in the bigger box when the puzzle is tilted a certain way. This makes the two boxes lock together – until they are tilted back the other way!

The handle is made from corner panel pieces

Each axle fits inside two layers of bricks with holes

The orange squares show which end of each box is the locking part

A third layer of bricks stops the axles from sliding in the wrong direction

Line up the orange corners when putting the small box back inside

When the boxes are tilted downwards, the axles slide into these bricks with holes, locking the boxes together

The axles slide in and out as the boxes are tilted

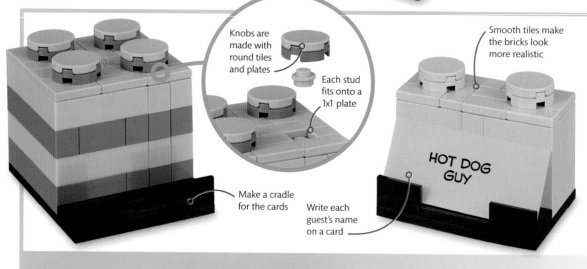

Knobs are made with round tiles and plates

Each stud fits onto a 1x1 plate

Make a cradle for the cards

Write each guest's name on a card

Smooth tiles make the bricks look more realistic

HOT DOG GUY

There is no need to guess who is coming to dinner when you use these stylish place card holders! Each one is shaped like a giant LEGO brick, with a stand at the front for a name.

Set a dinner table in style

124

Amaze your friends and family with this mystifying puzzle box! Hand it over with the orange corners tilting downwards and no one will be able to lift the smaller box out of the big one. Take it back with the orange corners upwards and the magic boxes will slide apart with ease! You could even set a timer and see who can solve it in the shortest amount of time.

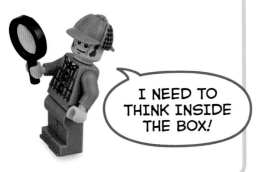

I NEED TO THINK INSIDE THE BOX!

Make a duck pond

125

Create a water feature for your home without getting wet! It is easy to build a pond or puddle shape. Then all you need to do is add animals and plants to make a cute scene.

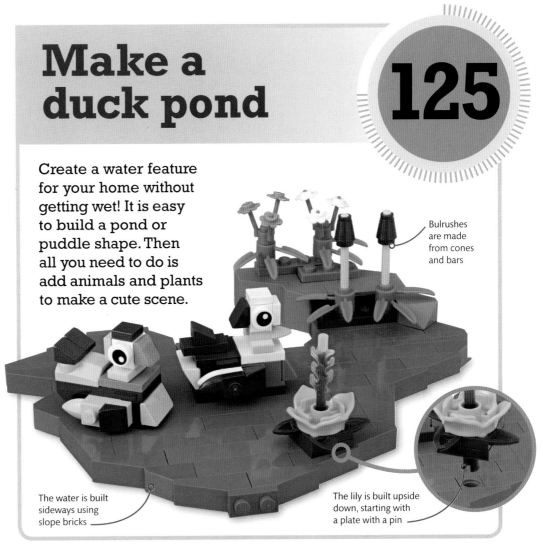

Bulrushes are made from cones and bars

The water is built sideways using slope bricks

The lily is built upside down, starting with a plate with a pin

Build a brickie

126

It takes a second to take a selfie, but how quickly can you build a brickie? Challenge your friends to make LEGO self-portraits in 10 minutes and then compare your funny faces!

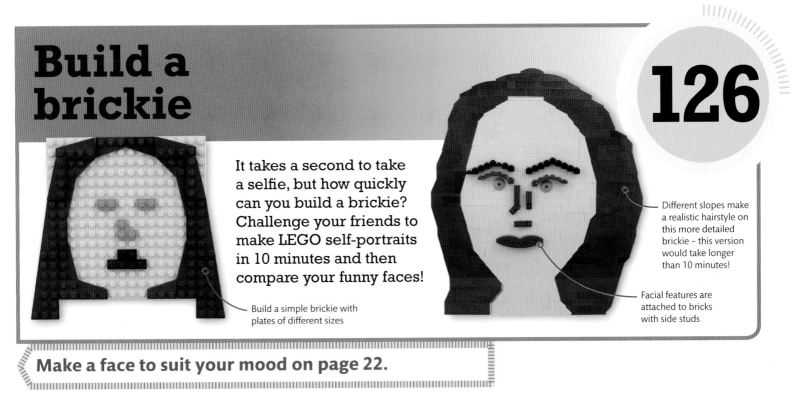

Different slopes make a realistic hairstyle on this more detailed brickie – this version would take longer than 10 minutes!

Build a simple brickie with plates of different sizes

Facial features are attached to bricks with side studs

Make a face to suit your mood on page 22.

Size up a scale challenge

127

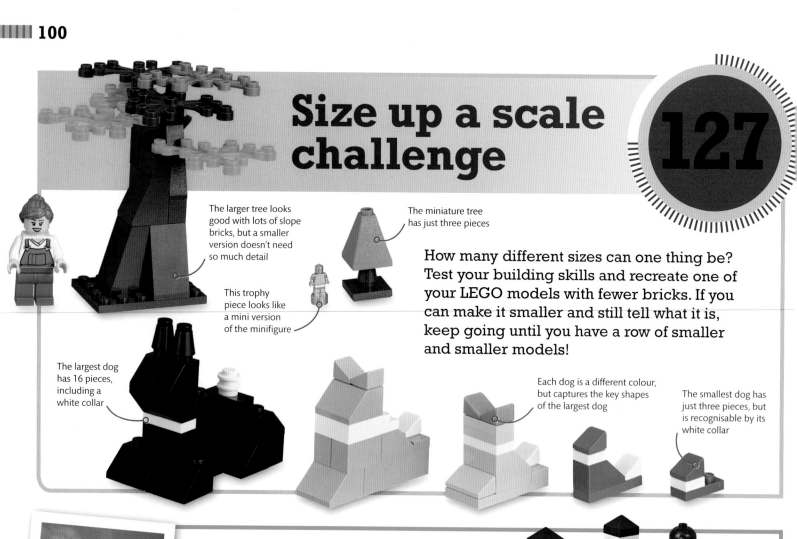

The larger tree looks good with lots of slope bricks, but a smaller version doesn't need so much detail

The miniature tree has just three pieces

This trophy piece looks like a mini version of the minifigure

How many different sizes can one thing be? Test your building skills and recreate one of your LEGO models with fewer bricks. If you can make it smaller and still tell what it is, keep going until you have a row of smaller and smaller models!

The largest dog has 16 pieces, including a white collar

Each dog is a different colour, but captures the key shapes of the largest dog

The smallest dog has just three pieces, but is recognisable by its white collar

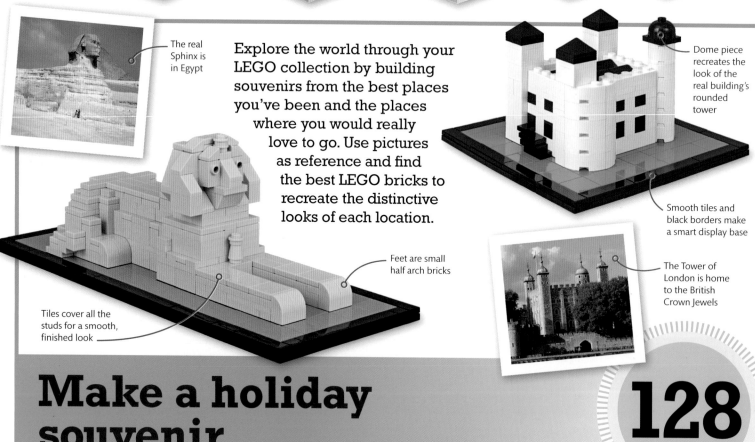

The real Sphinx is in Egypt

Explore the world through your LEGO collection by building souvenirs from the best places you've been and the places where you would really love to go. Use pictures as reference and find the best LEGO bricks to recreate the distinctive looks of each location.

Dome piece recreates the look of the real building's rounded tower

Smooth tiles and black borders make a smart display base

Feet are small half arch bricks

The Tower of London is home to the British Crown Jewels

Tiles cover all the studs for a smooth, finished look

Make a holiday souvenir

128

129 Fool the eye with forced perspective

Far-off ocean liner is just two small pieces

Distant mountain range made from dark-grey bricks

Houses are smaller than mountains, but look bigger because they are closer

Make your builds look much bigger than they really are – by making some of the parts smaller! Forced perspective is a way to create a sense of depth by putting larger things in the foreground, and smaller things further away. The eye treats all the objects as if they are the same scale, so it assumes that the small things must be very far away!

The minifigure is actually only one brick higher than the scene!

This minifigure seems to be looking out on the scene from high up

PHOTO FINISH

Forced perspective scenes only work when seen from the right direction, which means they can look especially good when photographed with care. Take photos of your forced perspective builds from their best angles – and you could turn them into a gallery of your greatest optical illusions!

BUILDER'S TIP

Place minifigures in the foreground of your forced perspective scenes for an instant sense of scale.

Use transparent parts to create a different kind of illusion!

The near half of the tennis court is actually two-thirds of the build

The net is a small fence piece just five studs from the far end

The other player is a tiny trophy accessory

This minifigure is leaping for the ball

A small round plate is the tennis ball in mid-air

The player on the far side of the net looks very far away

The build is much wider at this end than the other end

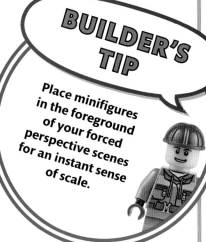

Find out how to build other optical illusions on pages 34–35.

130 Make some numbers

From lucky numbers to birthdays, some numbers are always worth remembering. Rather than simply writing them down, though, you could build them instead! You can display them to mark significant dates, use them to remember important numbers, or mix them up to make maths puzzles!

These numbers run through a rainbow of colours

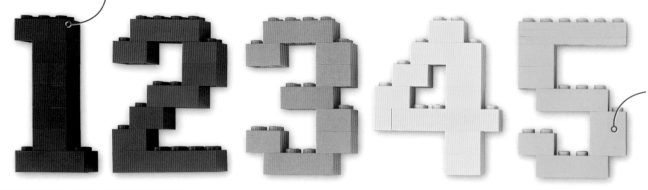

Brick-built numbers can lay flat or stand up on a base plate

BUILDER'S TIP

If you are inventing a book cover from scratch, sketch your idea out on paper before you start to build.

131 Build a book cover

You could make up your own book – this one is about a New York taxi driver!

A good book paints a picture in your mind, so why not build those pictures out of LEGO bricks! Take your favourite book and think about what you would put on its cover – it should give people an idea of what the story is about. Build it in 3-D for a challenge, or make your cover flat using a base plate.

The 3-D effect is achieved by attaching pieces to bricks that are sticking out of the background

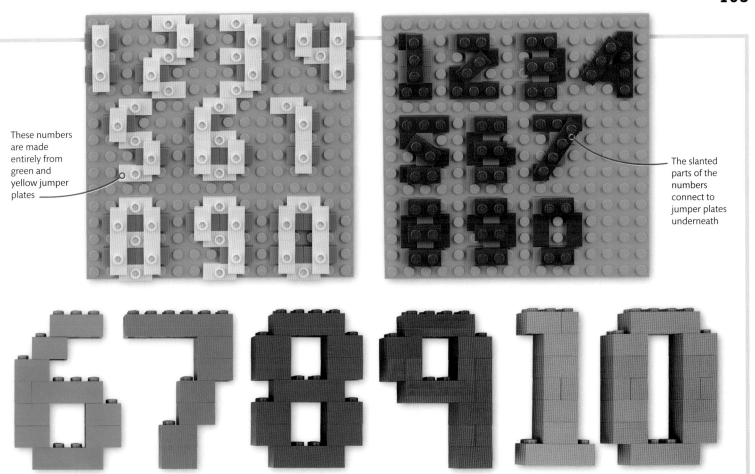

These numbers are made entirely from green and yellow jumper plates

The slanted parts of the numbers connect to jumper plates underneath

Hold an award ceremony

If you have already played some of the games in this book, then you or somebody you know probably deserves a winner's award! This cup is a classic trophy shape and should be given with a lot of ceremony. You could also give it to someone to say thank you for being the best at what they do.

Make the cup with cut-off corners for a rounded shape

Add two strong handles for holding the cup in the air

The lid is a dome brick surrounded by slopes

A sturdy base will stop your cup from tipping over

I'VE WON THE COFFEE CUP!

132

133 Make a working sundial

Tell the time with a LEGO sundial. It looks like a normal clock but with a pointer at 12 o'clock. Place in the sunshine at the start of an hour, and line up the shadow to the right time. Come back throughout the day for regular time checks!

The shadow will be here when it is 11 o'clock

This marker will be in the shade at 3 o'clock

This long shadow shows that it is just after 5 o'clock

IT'S PAST 5 O'CLOCK – TIME FOR A SNACK!

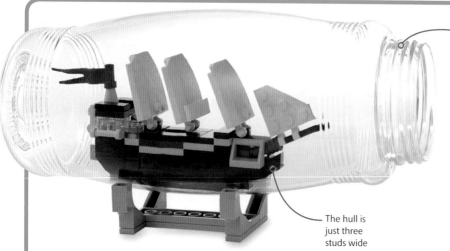

Look for a bottle with a neck big enough for the hull, but too small for it to fit with raised sails

The hull is just three studs wide

These sails fold forward

SETTING SAIL

To fit the ship inside the bottle, build it with sails fixed to clips so they can fold forward or to the side. With the sails folded down, the ship should fit through the neck of the bottle. Once it is inside, use a stick to gently nudge the sails into an upright position.

Fold this sail to the side first

Bars on the sails attach to clips on the deck

Stand is made from upside-down half arch bricks

How does this LEGO ship fit inside the bottle? It looks impossible, but the secret is in the sails! Sailors have been making ships in bottles for hundreds of years. No self-respecting pirate would be without one!

134 Build a ship in a bottle

135 Put the head on the minifigure

Give a classic party game a LEGO twist by trying to pin the head on a minifigure! Players take turns wearing a blindfold and try to place the head. It is sure to make you laugh your head off!

THE SPECIAL BRICK

Use angled plates to create interesting shapes. Two 2x4 angled plates form each of the minifigure's arms.

LEGO Technic half pins poke through for the eyes to attach to on the other side

Sideways headlight brick allows you to attach the head to the board

The body includes a long neck stud, just like a real minifigure

Pick minifigures with distinctive parts

Plates creating the minifigure shape and white background attach to two base plates underneath

A STUDY IN STUDS
The body is built with studs facing out so that the head can be attached anywhere. The background can be as big as you like, but the larger you make it, the more likely it is that blindfolded players will attach the head in completely the wrong place!

136 Guess the minifigure

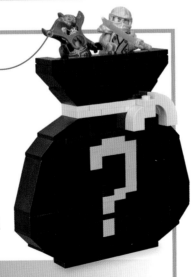

Can you identify minifigures just by how they feel? Place 10 minifigures inside a fabric bag and give your friends one minute each to feel the minifigures through the bag. The winner is the player who guesses the most minifigures correctly!

Keep your kitchen tidy

Build taller compartments for your longest utensils

ONE TABLESPOON OF FLOUR... THAT'S GOING TO BE HEAVY!

The base is made from two plates

Add tiles on top for a smooth finish

PERFECTING THE RECIPE

Design your utensil holder in colours to match the kitchen it will go in. Before you start to build, ask permission to borrow some safe utensils so you can see how big and tall it needs to be. If all the utensils are roughly the same size, make it with just one large compartment.

137

Make room for big utensils in even the smallest kitchen with this useful storage solution. It has four sections at different heights to hold longer and shorter items, and small holes at the bottom to stop crumbs from gathering inside. Any budding chef would be glad to get it as a gift!

The shape of this window is made by half arch bricks on both sides of the transparent bricks

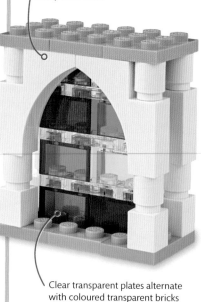

Clear transparent plates alternate with coloured transparent bricks

Add colourful light effects to your LEGO buildings by giving them stained-glass windows! There are lots of ways to do this using different transparent bricks and interesting lattice pieces. The best effects mix several colours at once. Hold your finished windows up to the light to see them really glow!

138

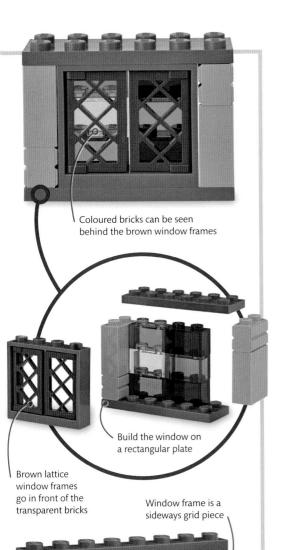

Coloured bricks can be seen behind the brown window frames

Build the window on a rectangular plate

Brown lattice window frames go in front of the transparent bricks

Window frame is a sideways grid piece

Sort at speed!

139

For this game, every player has a cup full of random bricks. Decide how to sort the bricks – by colour, size or brick type. The first player to sort all of their bricks is the winner! To make the game fair, swap your cups of random bricks after every go. Why not time yourselves and start a sorting leader board?

Put your mixed bricks into three cups for sorting

These bricks have been sorted by brick type

Build a filtering device for finding your smallest LEGO pieces on page 50.

Transparent plates plug into the underside of the grid to form a pattern

The grid fits onto bricks with side studs so that it can be built into a bigger wall

LET THERE BE LIGHT

If you make a building with a stained-glass window, leave the back wall open so light can shine through it from behind. Or build a LEGO light brick into the structure to give a warm glow that will bring the whole building to life.

Make a beautiful stained-glass window

140 Build your own zoo

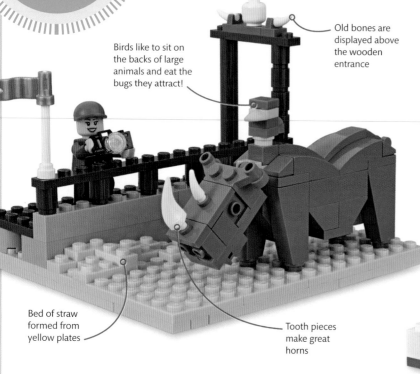

Birds like to sit on the backs of large animals and eat the bugs they attract!

Old bones are displayed above the wooden entrance

Bed of straw formed from yellow plates

Tooth pieces make great horns

WATCH THE WILDLIFE

Think about how big the animals should be alongside minifigures. Make use of unusually shaped pieces and sideways building to create realistic, characterful creatures. Add hinge pieces to create movement and natural-looking angles, such as the tilted head of the rhino.

Only the zookeeper is allowed on this side of the barrier!

The penguin's eyes are side studs

A penguin's head with no body looks like it is underwater!

Find out more online or in books about how animals like to live, then decide what to include in each enclosure.

Go wild with models of all your favourite animals in your very own LEGO zoo. Think about the conditions they like to live in and build an enclosure for each animal. Why not ask your friends to build their own favourites and then bring them all together in one big wildlife park!

Gorilla's ears are bricks with side studs

Shoulders are half arch pieces

EEK!

Brown round plates make droppings!

Find a penguin parade on page 246.

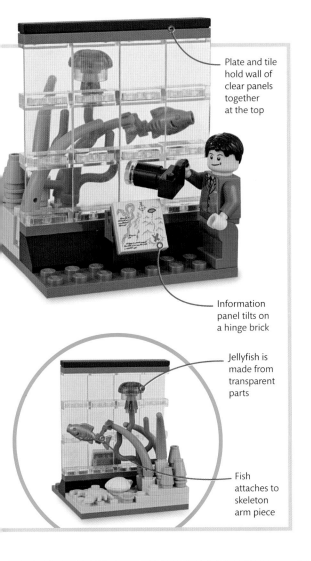

Plate and tile hold wall of clear panels together at the top

Information panel tilts on a hinge brick

Jellyfish is made from transparent parts

Fish attaches to skeleton arm piece

Play the ball-in-the-hole game

142

Get all five balls into their colour-coded holes – just by tilting the box. For an even tougher challenge, try doing it against the clock!

Circular elements from LEGO NINJAGO sets

Balls run smoothly on tiles

Build the sides high enough to stop the balls from rolling out.

Begin with a square base plate

Use your transparent pieces in a different way to make neon signs. Build a picture using transparent pieces and black pieces only. Position your finished sign in front of a torch to see it shine!

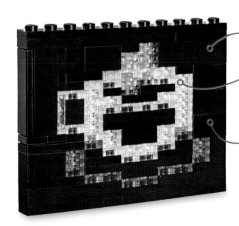

Picture is one-stud deep

Transparent plates form the shape of a coffee cup and saucer

Black bricks will really make the colours stand out

Ice-cream scoops are transparent radar dishes

Ice-cream cone is made from transparent round bricks

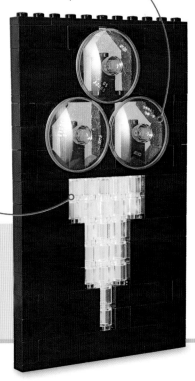

141

Make a sign that shines

143 Make a picture-perfect easel

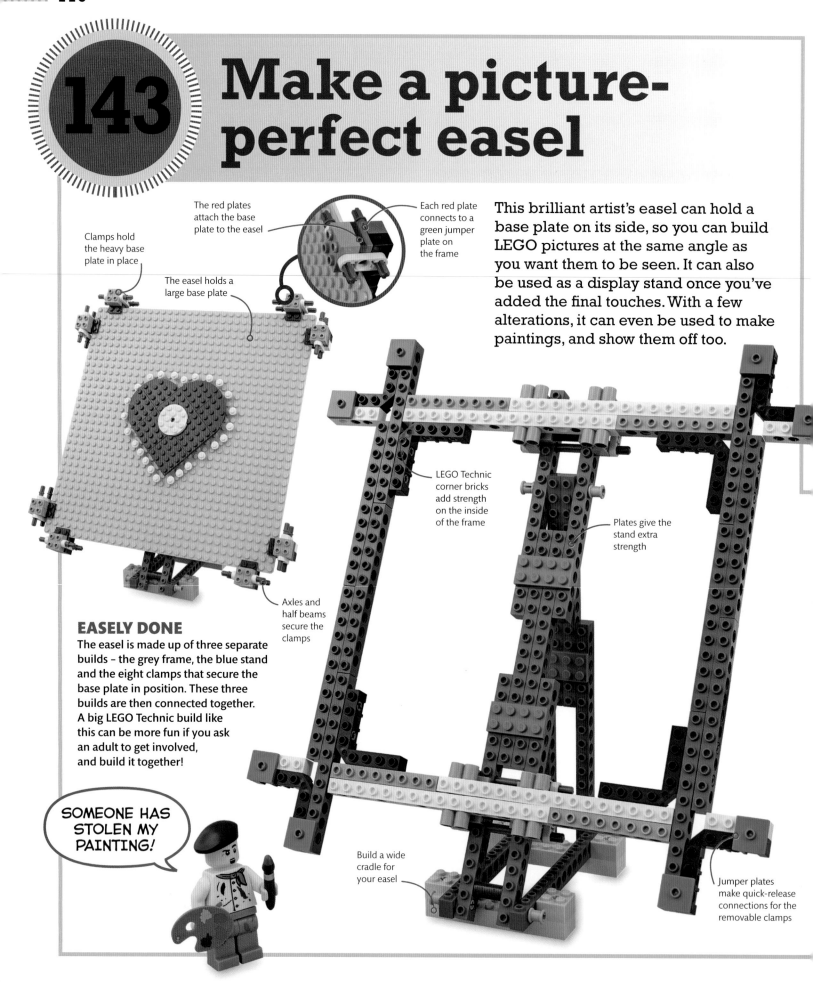

The red plates attach the base plate to the easel

Each red plate connects to a green jumper plate on the frame

Clamps hold the heavy base plate in place

The easel holds a large base plate

This brilliant artist's easel can hold a base plate on its side, so you can build LEGO pictures at the same angle as you want them to be seen. It can also be used as a display stand once you've added the final touches. With a few alterations, it can even be used to make paintings, and show them off too.

LEGO Technic corner bricks add strength on the inside of the frame

Plates give the stand extra strength

Axles and half beams secure the clamps

EASELY DONE
The easel is made up of three separate builds – the grey frame, the blue stand and the eight clamps that secure the base plate in position. These three builds are then connected together. A big LEGO Technic build like this can be more fun if you ask an adult to get involved, and build it together!

SOMEONE HAS STOLEN MY PAINTING!

Build a wide cradle for your easel

Jumper plates make quick-release connections for the removable clamps

Build a coaster puzzle

144

This puzzle doesn't take too long to solve, and when it is done, it becomes a cool-looking drinks coaster! Set a timer to see how quickly you can solve it, then match up the pieces so that no two tiles of the same colour touch. Reward yourself with a cold drink and a stylish pattern to rest it on!

Use corner plates to make the edge pieces

The base has a raised lip to hold the puzzle pieces in place

Build the puzzle pieces as shown here, making sure no two tiles of the same colour touch

64 square tiles are used to make the chequered pattern

Build a different pattern puzzle on page 234.

The frame rests against these smooth tiles when it is fixed in place

You can adjust the angle of the stand by moving where these top pins connect.

THE SPECIAL BRICK

Crossblocks are very useful LEGO Technic connectors that link elements in two different directions.

Connect the frame to the stand by slotting axles through these crossblocks

Lock the axles in place with small half beams

MAKING A STAND
The stand that supports the easel frame is built as a large triangle, held together with LEGO Technic pins. The frame is securely attached to the stand, and the whole thing stands on a wide base to keep it from tipping over.

The stand is made from long LEGO Technic bricks

Connect the sides of the triangle using long pins with bush ends (grey round pieces) to secure them

Make a micro-scale set

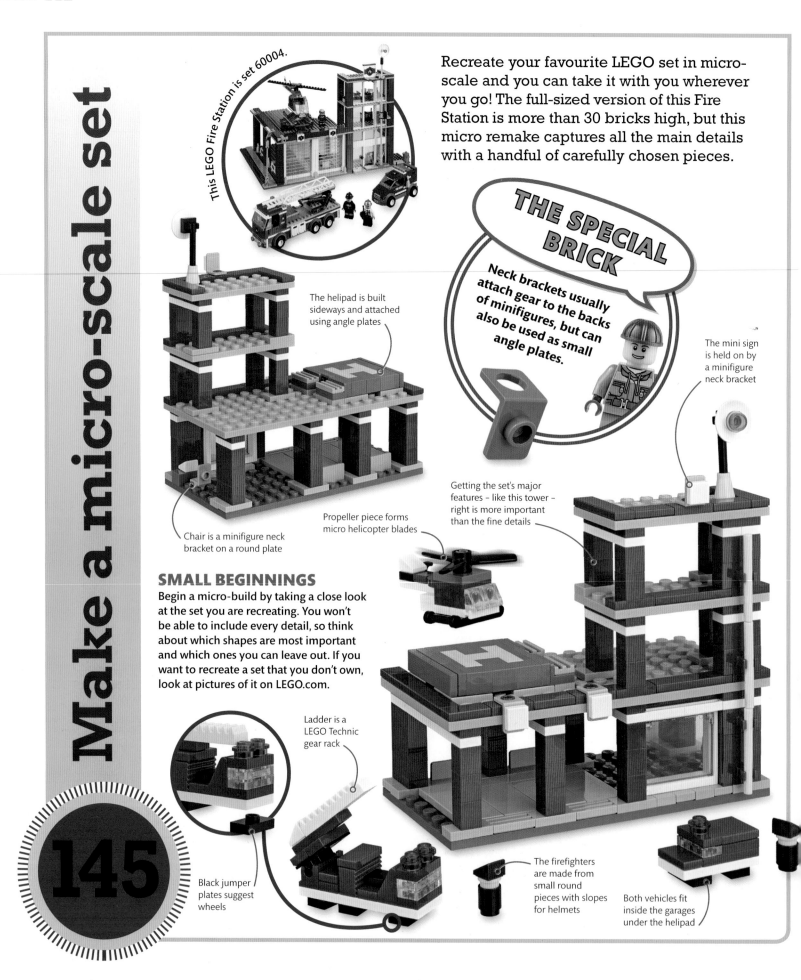

This LEGO Fire Station is set 60004.

Recreate your favourite LEGO set in micro-scale and you can take it with you wherever you go! The full-sized version of this Fire Station is more than 30 bricks high, but this micro remake captures all the main details with a handful of carefully chosen pieces.

The helipad is built sideways and attached using angle plates

THE SPECIAL BRICK

Neck brackets usually attach gear to the backs of minifigures, but can also be used as small angle plates.

The mini sign is held on by a minifigure neck bracket

Chair is a minifigure neck bracket on a round plate

Propeller piece forms micro helicopter blades

Getting the set's major features – like this tower – right is more important than the fine details

SMALL BEGINNINGS

Begin a micro-build by taking a close look at the set you are recreating. You won't be able to include every detail, so think about which shapes are most important and which ones you can leave out. If you want to recreate a set that you don't own, look at pictures of it on LEGO.com.

Ladder is a LEGO Technic gear rack

Black jumper plates suggest wheels

The firefighters are made from small round pieces with slopes for helmets

Both vehicles fit inside the garages under the helipad

145

Play a game of peg solitaire

146

Plunge into a game of strategy and skill with this classic one-player puzzle. Whether you build a round board or a square one, there is no way to cut corners – you need to make the right moves right from the start!

32 small round bricks for playing pieces

The base is made from four curved bricks

Alternating plates form a cross-shaped grid

The pegs are spaced out so that they are easy to grasp

Use these spaces to store pegs removed from the board

HOW TO PLAY

1 Start with 32 pegs – one on every square except the centre one. Move one peg at a time by jumping it over another peg into a vacant square (your first move will be into the centre square).

2 Pegs can jump in any direction except diagonally, and you can only jump over one peg at a time. Every time a peg moves, the peg that it jumps over is removed from the board.

3 The object of the game is to move the pegs in a sequence that leaves no peg stranded in a position where it cannot jump over another. You win the game when there is just one peg left on the board. Once you've solved it, try playing against the clock for an even tougher challenge!

Smooth tiles look like a wall of multicoloured LEGO bricks

Chain connects to built-in plates with bars

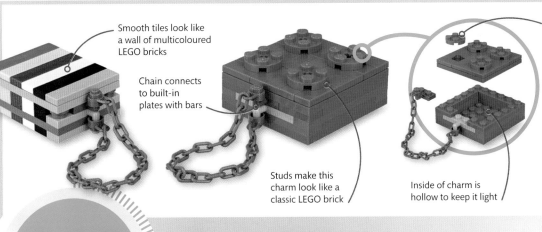

Studs make this charm look like a classic LEGO brick

Inside of charm is hollow to keep it light

Each 2x2 round plate attaches to a 1x1 plate surrounded by smooth tiles

Use a LEGO chain piece to add a unique charm to your favourite bag or backpack. These charms look like giant LEGO bricks, but you can make yours look like anything!

147 # Build a charm for your bag

148 See things in black and white

These builds look like they have been photographed in black and white, but in fact they are built entirely out of black, white, and grey pieces! You can create striking models by using lots of shapes and textures in this way. Who needs colours, anyway?

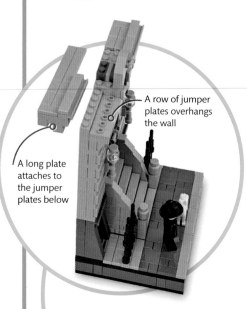

A row of jumper plates overhangs the wall

A long plate attaches to the jumper plates below

Toadstools come in all shapes and sizes

The grass is made from fang pieces and cone bricks

The snail is leaving a shiny white trail!

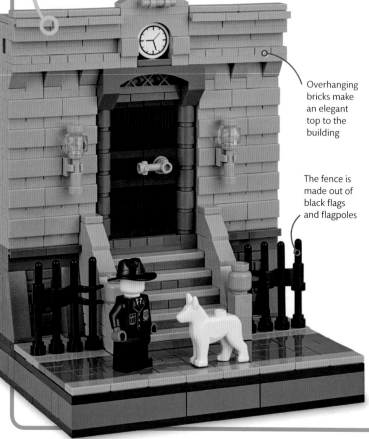

Overhanging bricks make an elegant top to the building

The fence is made out of black flags and flagpoles

Everyone loves to unwrap a LEGO present, and in LEGO pass the parcel, there are bricks between every layer of paper! Play music as the parcel is handed around the group, and when the music stops, the person holding the package removes a layer of gift wrap and uncovers a handful of bricks. Once all the layers are unwrapped, players build models from their handful (or handfuls, if they're lucky!) of bricks.

Play pass the parcel

150 Crack the vanishing egg trick

How many eggs can you see in the grass below? How about in the model at the bottom of the page? They are both the same model, but in the second picture, one of the eggs has disappeared! It hasn't been rebuilt brick by brick – it is just the result of an eggs-tremely quick and clever change!

Crest is a curved slope

The model breaks into three sections

Just a few studs connect the top and bottom pieces so the top sections can be swapped easily

The white pieces must be positioned very carefully for the trick to work

Perform the trick the other way around to make the chicken lay an egg!

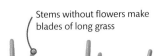

MIXING EGGS

The trick works because one of the nine eggs in the top picture is entirely within the upper part of the build. Perform the trick by quickly swapping the two top sections. This will make the small egg line up with one of the others to become a single, slightly larger egg.

The chicken seems to have moved by itself!

Stems without flowers make blades of long grass

Chunky wing is a sideways corner slope

The person stopping the music should ensure it stops on each person once

A player may have more than once chance to unwrap a layer

149

See what's inside a hatching egg on page 242.

151 Play snakes and ladders

HOW TO PLAY

1 All players start with a counter in the bottom-left square of the board. Roll a die before the game begins. The player who rolls the highest number goes first.

2 Roll the die and move your counter forward by the number of squares shown. At the end of each row, travel along the next row in the opposite direction.

3 If your move ends on a snake's head or the bottom of a ladder, travel to the square at the other end of that snake or ladder. If you land on a square that is obscured by **another** part of a snake or ladder, move forward one square.

4 The winner is the first player to reach the yellow square in the top-right corner of the board.

BUILDING THE BOARD

Your board can be as big as you like. This one has nine rows of nine squares, built on a number of larger base plates. Make sure it is clear where the snakes and ladders begin and end, and that the snakes' heads are all higher up than their tails!

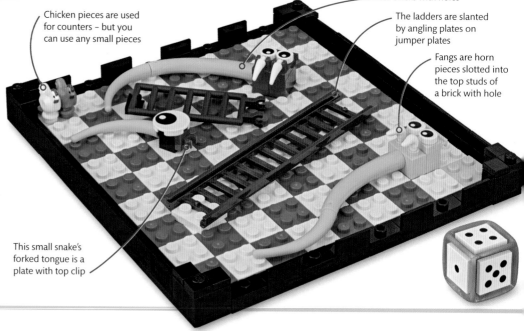

Chicken pieces are used for counters – but you can use any small pieces

The snakes' bodies slot into bricks with holes

The ladders are slanted by angling plates on jumper plates

Fangs are horn pieces slotted into the top studs of a brick with hole

This small snake's forked tongue is a plate with top clip

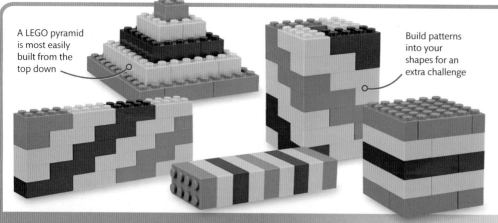

A LEGO pyramid is most easily built from the top down

Build patterns into your shapes for an extra challenge

How many different shapes can you make in ten minutes? Try to make a square, a long rectangle, a tall rectangle, a cube, a cone, a pyramid and even a sphere out of a selection of simple bricks.

Make shapes against the clock 152

THE SPECIAL BRICK

The snake's tail pieces come in middle and end sections that can also be used to make tentacles, horns and plants.

Make your own LEGO version of this brilliant board game and you can decide how many snakes and ladders there are, where they go, and what they look like! You could build a friendly board that is nearly all ladders, or you could swap all the snakes for water slides.

Give make-up a makeover

154

Make tall compartments for long brushes

Design your make-up organiser to perfectly fit its contents.

If you don't have enough matching clear pieces, make a colourful patchwork design instead!

Blue pieces make it easy to see how the sections divide

Give a dressing table a touch of sparkle with this make-up organiser. Made mostly from clear pieces, it looks like shimmering crystal and has different-sized sections for mascara, lipsticks and more.

153

Get results with a LEGO graph

Display the results of a survey or contest by making a LEGO bar chart. Whether it is for a school project or a game at home, LEGO bricks are a great way to count votes and scores in a visual way.

Ask your friends to choose their favourite minifigure, then display the results

Each minifigure stands in front of its number of votes

Recreate a creepy-crawly

155

Curly antennae are black plant pieces

Try not to give yourself a fright when you build these giant bugs! Insects have lots of strange, scuttling parts, and you can learn a lot about them by making LEGO models. Copy pictures from books or online, or get up close to the real thing – if you dare!

Claws fit into robot arm pieces

The back legs can move on hinge plates

Realistic-looking shells are made from curved slope bricks

I SAID I WANTED A BIG *HUG!*

Fill your home with funny bugs on page 226.

156

Bake a batch of LEGO cakes

This brownie is a box piece with a plate on top

Have your cake, but don't eat it, with these great LEGO bakes! Perfect for a dolls' tea party or teddy bears' picnic, these cakes and biscuits also make great decorations for a real party – before the genuine treats come out!

TIME FOR A COFFEE BREAK!

Three round plates make a chocolate biscuit

Use quarter domes for this pretty petit four

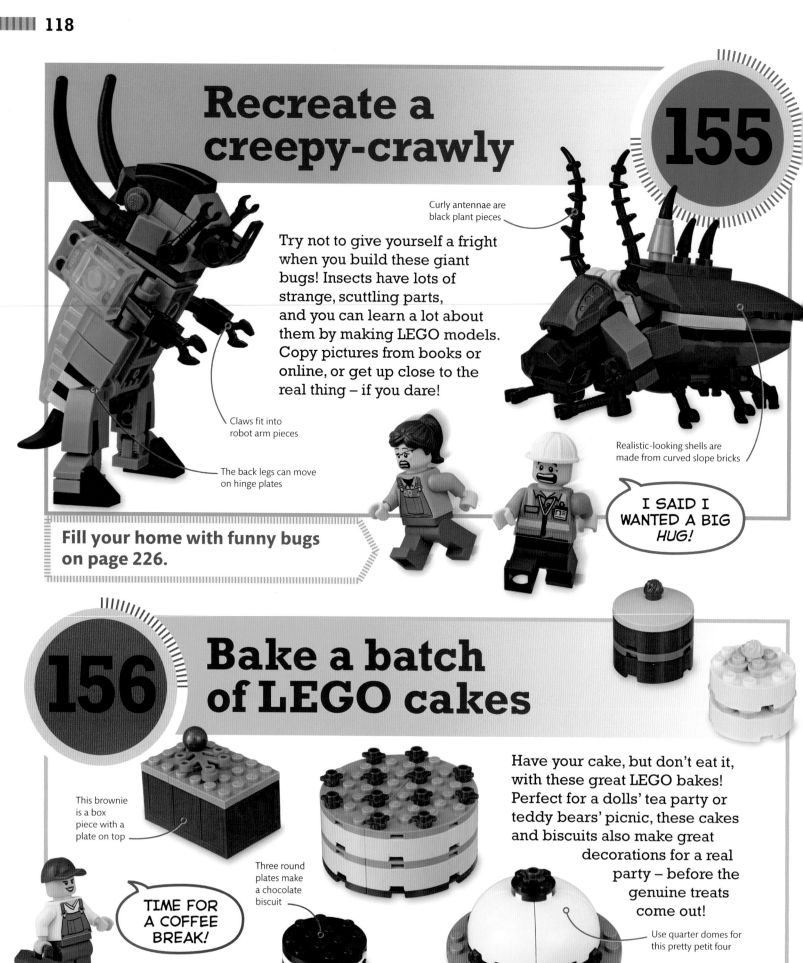

157 Make a magical island

Make a fantasy world where nothing stays the same for long! A modular micro-landscape can be easily expanded and rearranged in seconds. Each section is built on bricks with holes, so you can slot them together and pull them apart.

This fantasy land has a dragon in the mountains!

The clouds are ice-cream parts fitted sideways

Spire is a unicorn horn on top of a cone brick

Connect the sections in any shape you like

Make each section the same size so you can swap their places.

Plates with top clips grip the sails of this tiny ship

LEGO Technic pins connect sections

158 Put your best builds on display

Treat your top models like pieces of sculpture by showing them off on stylish display stands. It's amazing how much difference a raised plinth or platform can make, and even a simple build will look like a work of art if you make it part of your gallery.

WE'RE HONOURED TO BE CHOSEN!

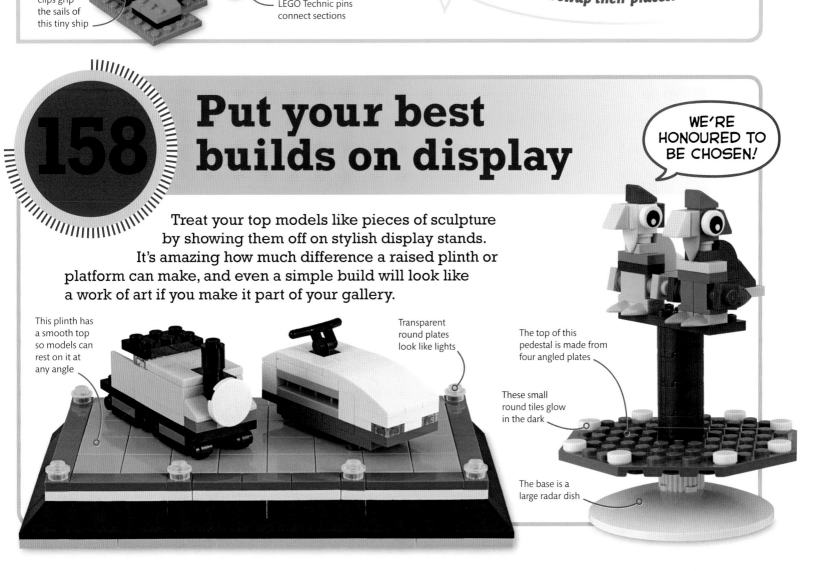

This plinth has a smooth top so models can rest on it at any angle

Transparent round plates look like lights

The top of this pedestal is made from four angled plates

These small round tiles glow in the dark

The base is a large radar dish

159 Make any shape

Everyone knows how to build a LEGO square, but how about a triangle, a hexagon or a 12-sided dodecagon? With a little bit of imagination and experimentation, there isn't a single shape that can't be built in one way or another!

How many different shapes can you make using hinge plates?

The inner ring of hinge plates stops the shape from distorting

The 12 sides of this dodecagon are so short that it looks like a circle

This hexagon is made from six triangles – three green ones at the front and three yellow ones at the back

When chess doesn't offer a big enough challenge, why not try your hand at super chess? Even the world's greatest minds have never played chess on a board like this, so with practice you might just become the world's first super chess grandmaster! To play regular chess instead, simply build an 8x8 square board.

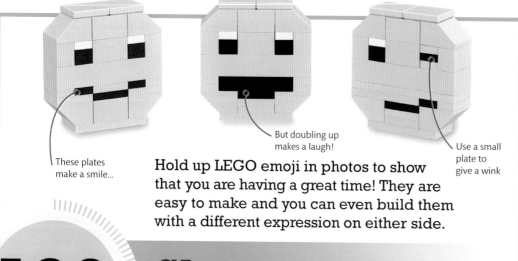

These plates make a smile...

But doubling up makes a laugh!

Use a small plate to give a wink

Hold up LEGO emoji in photos to show that you are having a great time! They are easy to make and you can even build them with a different expression on either side.

160 Show some LEGO emoji

161

SHAPING UP

Once you have built a multi-sided shape using plates, you can use it as a stable base for a much bigger build. By adding walls to the six sides of a hexagon, you can create a fairytale tower or a realistic space station. Adding another hexagon on the top will hold the angled walls in place.

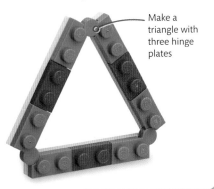

Make a triangle with three hinge plates

Pick-a-brick challenge

162

This tree is almost entirely made from green slope bricks

How many ways can you use one kind of piece? Choose a piece that you have plenty of, such as a slope brick, and set yourself a 10-minute challenge to use it in three builds.

This witch has green slopes from head to toe!

Use special bricks to finish off your builds

Caterpillar legs are slopes on their side

The broom is also made using slopes

HOW TO PLAY

1 The game is played like regular chess, but with each side split into two halves.

2 Set up one half with the King, one Bishop, one Knight, one Rook and four Pawns, placing them in any order within the black-and-grey section.

3 Set up the other half in the same way but with the Queen instead of a King.

4 To begin, white plays first, with a move into the black-and-white section.

Have fun coming up with new tactics to beat your opponent!

Knights have sloped tops

Rooks have flat tops

Kings have swirly tops

Bishops have rounded tops

Queens have tall round tops

Pawns are 1x1 round bricks

Pawns can only move forward, so keep track of the direction they are moving in

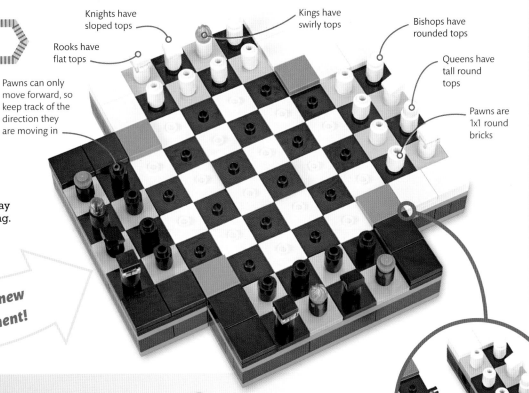

The board is built as separate modules that can be pulled apart

The modules are attached using bricks with holes and LEGO Technic pins

Play a game of super chess

163 Build a mighty mech

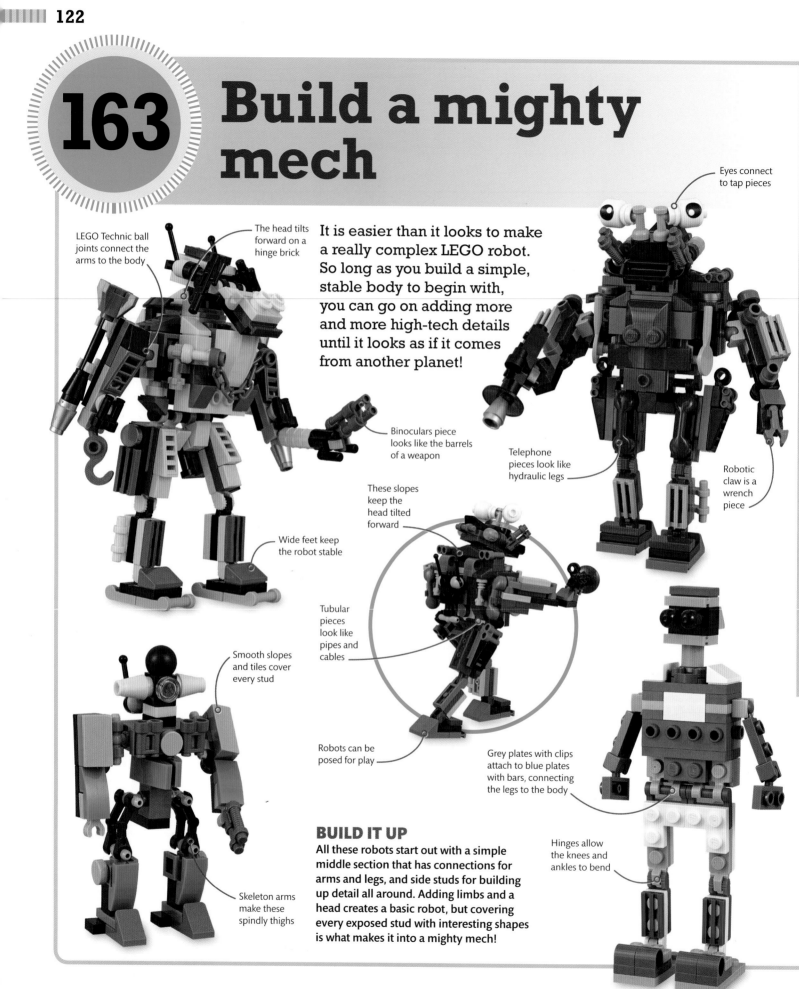

It is easier than it looks to make a really complex LEGO robot. So long as you build a simple, stable body to begin with, you can go on adding more and more high-tech details until it looks as if it comes from another planet!

LEGO Technic ball joints connect the arms to the body

The head tilts forward on a hinge brick

Binoculars piece looks like the barrels of a weapon

Wide feet keep the robot stable

Eyes connect to tap pieces

Telephone pieces look like hydraulic legs

Robotic claw is a wrench piece

These slopes keep the head tilted forward

Tubular pieces look like pipes and cables

Robots can be posed for play

Smooth slopes and tiles cover every stud

Skeleton arms make these spindly thighs

Grey plates with clips attach to blue plates with bars, connecting the legs to the body

Hinges allow the knees and ankles to bend

BUILD IT UP

All these robots start out with a simple middle section that has connections for arms and legs, and side studs for building up detail all around. Adding limbs and a head creates a basic robot, but covering every exposed stud with interesting shapes is what makes it into a mighty mech!

Give a 3-D greetings card

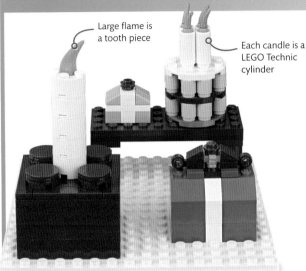

Large flame is a tooth piece

Each candle is a LEGO Technic cylinder

Green cherry pieces look like fruit in a bowl

Remove a minifigure's legs to make it look like he is tucked up in bed

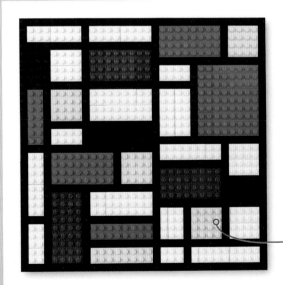

Smooth tiles used to create a rug

A brightly coloured floor makes the contents of the room stand out

When someone you know is celebrating – or sick – make them feel really special by building them a LEGO scene as a greetings card. You could give them the scene to keep, or you could photograph it and turn it into a card so that you can add a written message.

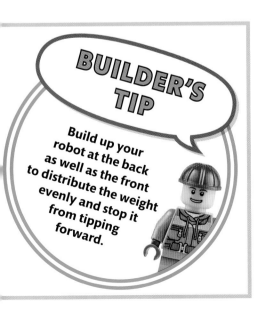

BUILDER'S TIP

Build up your robot at the back as well as the front to distribute the weight evenly and stop it from tipping forward.

Show off your modern art skills by making abstract images out of LEGO bricks. In the 20th century, abstract artists such as Piet Mondrian were fascinated by straight lines and bold colours. Mondrian would have loved being able to work with LEGO bricks!

Just a few bold colours make up this striking design

Make a piece of modern art

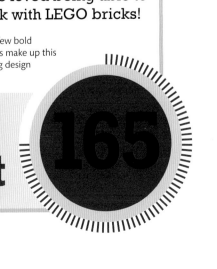

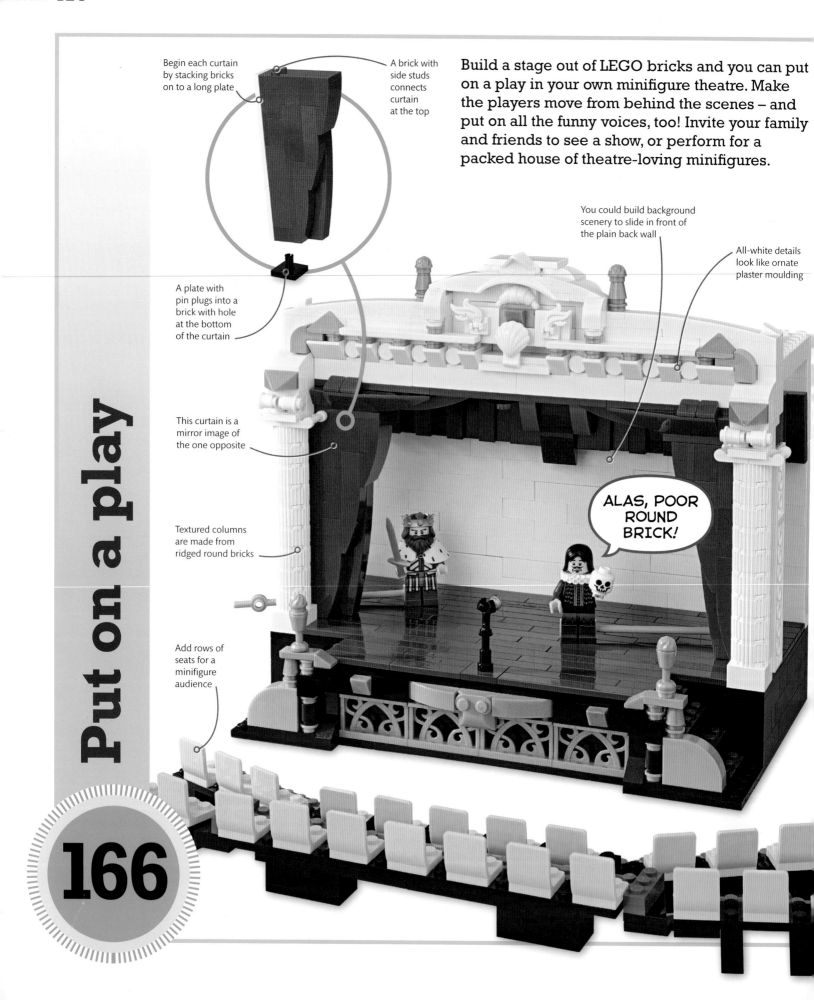

Begin each curtain by stacking bricks on to a long plate

A brick with side studs connects curtain at the top

Build a stage out of LEGO bricks and you can put on a play in your own minifigure theatre. Make the players move from behind the scenes – and put on all the funny voices, too! Invite your family and friends to see a show, or perform for a packed house of theatre-loving minifigures.

You could build background scenery to slide in front of the plain back wall

All-white details look like ornate plaster moulding

A plate with pin plugs into a brick with hole at the bottom of the curtain

This curtain is a mirror image of the one opposite

Put on a play

Textured columns are made from ridged round bricks

ALAS, POOR ROUND BRICK!

Add rows of seats for a minifigure audience

166

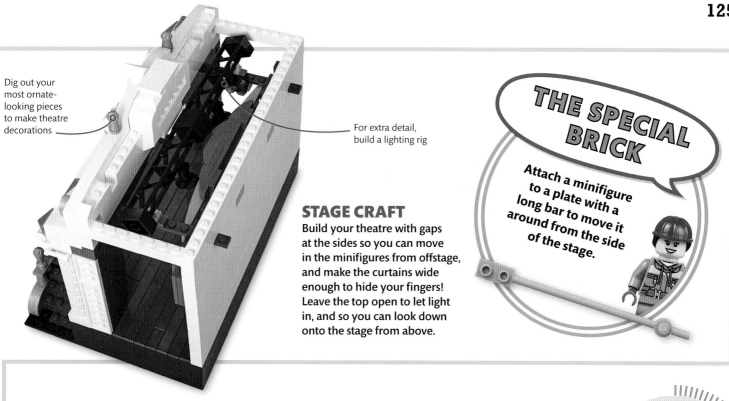

Dig out your most ornate-looking pieces to make theatre decorations

For extra detail, build a lighting rig

STAGE CRAFT

Build your theatre with gaps at the sides so you can move in the minifigures from offstage, and make the curtains wide enough to hide your fingers! Leave the top open to let light in, and so you can look down onto the stage from above.

THE SPECIAL BRICK

Attach a minifigure to a plate with a long bar to move it around from the side of the stage.

Bring back the dinosaurs

167

Dinosaurs haven't lived on Earth for millions of years. Can you bring them back in five minutes? Set a timer and build a micro-dinosaur using the smallest pieces you have.

A small plate is the starting point for the Ankylosaurus

Huge teeth are actually two small round plates!

WE JUST WANT TO BE FRIENDS...

Tiny T. rex arms are made from a plate with a side clip

Brachiosaurus eyes are a single black plate

Use slope bricks for feet

RUN, HOT DOG MAN, RUN!

Head can be posed with a click hinge

This spiky Ankylosaurus has tooth plates along its sides

168 Make a cityscape for your room

Give your room some big-city style with a scene packed full of skyscrapers! For a really cool picture, build up a few layers of plates for a sense of depth, using light colours at the back and darker ones at the front.

Cable pieces are held in place by plates with clips on top

This scene shows the Seattle skyline

A row of blue plates links two large base plates

If you build a real city, show which one it is by including some landmarks like Big Ben

This piece looks like a ferris wheel – perfect for the London Eye

Each petal clips onto a round plate with a ring of bars

The stem top is a tail tip piece

Bring a smile to someone's face with the gift of flowers. Unlike real flowers, these brightly coloured blooms will last a lifetime, and are perfect for any room – even one that doesn't get much sunlight!

Curved slopes make great petals

The stems are stacked small round bricks

A plate holds the base together

Build the vase from curved bricks and plates, or use a real plastic jar.

Give a beautiful bunch of flowers 169

THE SPECIAL BRICK

Just like smooth tiles, curved slopes give builds a realistic look, because of their stud-free surfaces.

Unusual plates make details for the tops of buildings

Mirror image looks like a reflection in water

BY THE BOOK

Build your book flat, starting with a base of plates for the back cover before adding white or tan bricks for the pages. The bricks for the pages should be placed one stud away from the base's edge on three sides. Place them right up to the edge on one of the longer sides. This side will become the book's spine.

A wall of textured bricks creates the look of pages

Smooth tiles hide the studs on the front and back covers

SHH! I'M READING!

There are lots of things you can do with a LEGO book! Make it solid and you can use it as a bookend. Make it hollow and you can use it as a secret hiding place. Make it as realistic-looking as possible and you can use it to play a prank on someone!

Use smooth tiles to make your own design on the front cover.

Bricks with side studs connect the spine to the book

Place plates under four of the curved slopes to make them stick out from the spine

Curved slopes mounted on a long plate form the book's spine

171 Review your favourite set

Tell everyone how much you love your favourite LEGO set by making a video of yourself talking about it. Show off all of its features and say what you like best about it. Ask an adult to put your video online and you might become an Internet sensation!

Build a clapperboard out of LEGO bricks to make your videos extra special!

These stripes are white tiles

A hinge plate holds the two parts of the clapperboard together

SPOTTED PATTERNS
Keep an eye out for interesting tiled and paved patterns when you are out and about and see if you can recreate them using LEGO tiles. You could even start a collection of pattern ideas by taking photos of the best ones you see.

The top layer of tiles connects to small round plates

This cobblestone pattern looks complex, but it is mostly built on one layer

Built-in jumper plates allow you to add extra details, like furniture

Offset rows of grey tiles look like paving slabs

Each white tile attaches to a jumper plate

You can make a LEGO building look even more realistic when you hide its studded floor with tiles. Using all one kind will do the trick, but mixing different shapes and colours will create a really classy finish.

A top layer of tiles hides the gaps around the edge of this pattern

Each black tile attaches to a small round plate

172 Use tiles to make a fancy floor

173 Impress with a paperweight

Use lots of small pieces – they will weigh more than a few large pieces.

Transparent bricks over coloured bricks make interesting effects

Panda's eyes are black small round plates

Build the panda on its back, starting with this long plate

These bamboo shoots are stacked flower stems

A paperweight needs to have a stable base

A paperweight makes a great gift for someone with a desk to keep tidy. Not only will it decorate their office, but it will also make them think of you every time they look at it.

Play a game of pick-up sticks

174

Start by gathering lots of long, thin pieces into a pile. Set your timer to 60 seconds. Players take turns removing one piece at a time – without making any of the other pieces move! If you succeed, you keep the piece, and if not, it goes on a discard pile. The winner is the player with the most pieces when the time runs out!

THIS IS A STICKY SITUATION!

You could make up scores for different pieces or colours

Antenna pieces are ideal, but you could also use long swords, LEGO Technic axles or a mixture of pieces

175 Make a table centrepiece

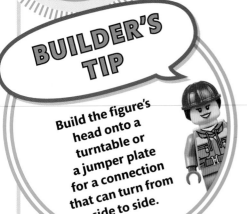

BUILDER'S TIP

Build the figure's head onto a turntable or a jumper plate for a connection that can turn from side to side.

Mark a special occasion with a thoughtful themed build. This bride and groom would look great on the top table at a wedding! Build them to look just like the happy couple.

Hat brim is made from two angled plates

Tiara is four silver tiles

Tall slope bricks shape the dress

Slopes look like shiny shoes

Each wing connects to a brick with a side stud

Dragonfly wings are a new way to use these transparent ring plates

Round bricks create this beast's long nose

Small slopes run all down the back

The back of the beast is made from a single staircase element

There is more than one way to use every LEGO piece! Find the most unusual part you can and turn it into something totally new. Give yourself five minutes, and see what you come up with!

176 Use special pieces in new ways

177

Race for the rocket

If all your board games seem a little flat, why not build one that reaches for the moon? In this space-themed game, you race to be the first to get to the rocket. It works like a normal board game, but also makes a cool decoration when it is not being played!

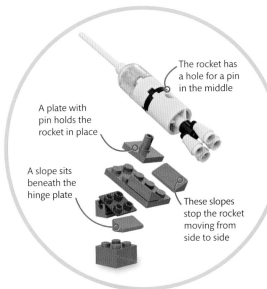

A plate with pin holds the rocket in place

The rocket has a hole for a pin in the middle

A slope sits beneath the hinge plate

These slopes stop the rocket moving from side to side

Bricks with grooves add detail to the top of the tower

The red squares can be smooth tiles because no player can stop on these

Each grey square is a jumper plate for the minifigure to attach to

Space-themed plates attach to bricks with side studs

HOW TO PLAY

1 Two players take turns rolling a die and move the number of spaces shown.

2 Land on a red square, and you must move back two spaces. Land on the other player, and they must move back one space. (If they then land on a red square, they must move back another two spaces!)

3 The winner is the first player to reach the rocket by landing on the top, white square, from where they may launch the rocket!

STEPPING UP

The tower is built on a square plate and is solid all the way up. The first three flights of stairs are all the same size, then the next two are one step shorter. The sixth and final flight is one step shorter again.

To make a micro-scale space base, turn to page 48.

178 Get some target practice

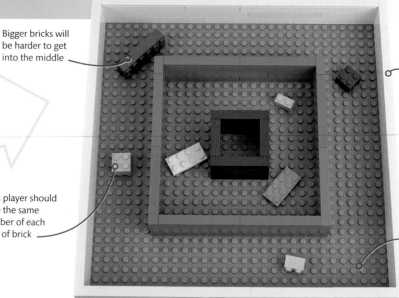

Bigger bricks will be harder to get into the middle

All of the walls are two bricks high

Give each player a colour and a range of big and small bricks.

Test your targeting skills by tossing bricks into this frame from five paces away. Score a point for every brick inside the blue square and five for every one inside the inner dark-red square.

Each player should have the same number of each type of brick

The game is built on a large square base plate

Create a mystery scene

179

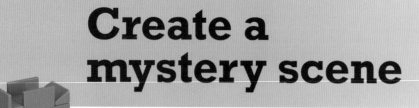

Add lots of detail to make the clues harder to spot

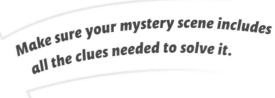

Make sure your mystery scene includes all the clues needed to solve it.

This magnifying glass is made from a loop of hinges

Build a scene where the action has already happened, and challenge your friends' detective skills! Can you work out who took the treats from this kitchen cupboard? Think about what other mysteries you could create for your friends to solve!

Paw prints reveal it was the dog who did it!

Go fishing for ducks

Play this classic fairground game and see how many rubber ducks you can catch in two minutes. Use the rod to hook the rings on the ducks' backs, and try to collect them all against the clock! Will you fit the bill or will you quack under pressure?

Experiment to find the perfect length of line

Beginners should hold the rod here

More confident players should hold it here

HOT ROD
The rod is made from several layers of long, overlapping plates to give it strength, and it has markings for where players should hold onto. The fishing line is threaded through a hook piece and then tied onto a plate with a ring at the end of the rod. Place the upright ducks on the floor or a table to begin the game – or jumble them in a bowl to make the game even harder.

Experienced players should put their hands here

This round plate has a ring on top

The eyes fit onto small radar dishes

The line is threaded through this ball

Start by building at least six ducks

Both wings attach to this 1x4 brick

A curved slope covers the top of each wing

THIS IS FOWL PLAY!

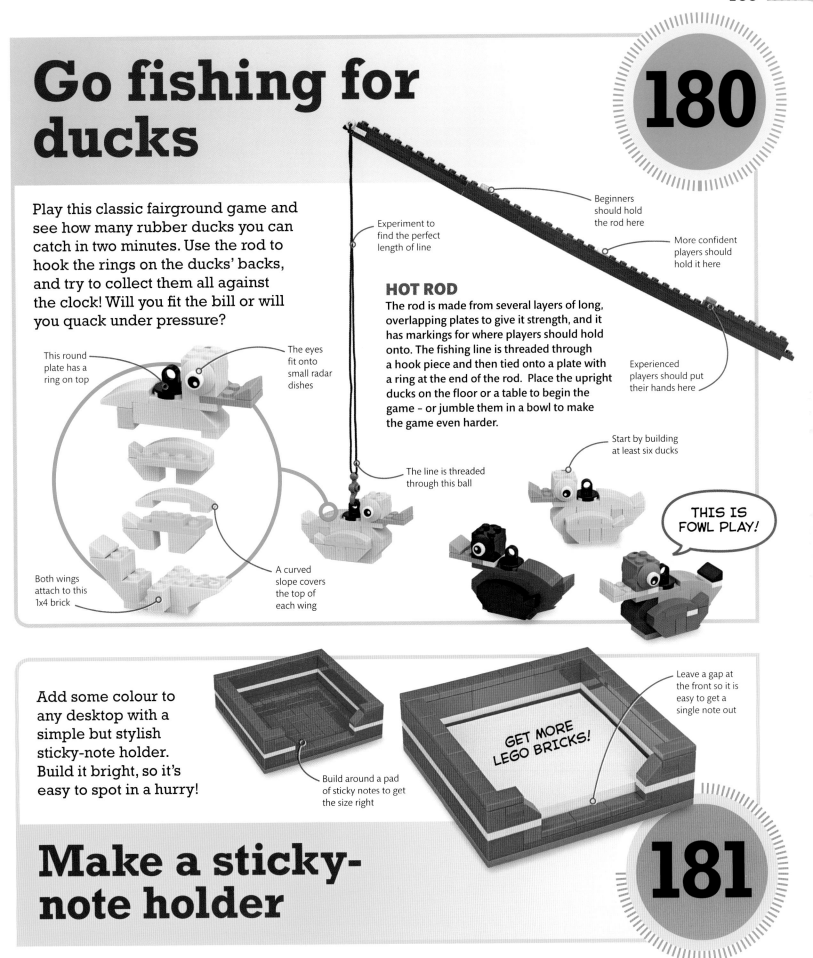

Add some colour to any desktop with a simple but stylish sticky-note holder. Build it bright, so it's easy to spot in a hurry!

Leave a gap at the front so it is easy to get a single note out

GET MORE LEGO BRICKS!

Build around a pad of sticky notes to get the size right

Make a sticky-note holder

Make a rocking pet

Real animals are always on the go, so why not try building your very own LEGO animal that can move, too? You can pick any animal you like! This colourful woodpecker rocks back and forth with a realistic pecking motion, while the happy puppy dog bounces with excitement.

Brown headlight bricks built into side of body

Legs (grey headlight bricks) attach to brown headlight bricks

BUILDING THE ROCKERS

The woodpecker has most of its weight near the top of its body, so it needs a big base to stop it from tipping over when it rocks. The base has two curved feet, built using upside-down and sideways bricks, and connected by a central plate. Because the puppy is not as tall as the woodpecker, its rocker doesn't need to be bigger than its body. It moves on two upside-down curved slopes.

Dome piece for snout

Tail is a robot arm piece

Flower stud detail behind eye

Hinged neck

Upside-down 1x4 curved slope

Use sideways building to add realistic curves to your models.

Underbelly fits onto bricks with side studs

Woodpecker stands on this 1x2 plate

2x8 plate links both rockers

Upside-down 2x4 curved slopes

Bricks with side studs connect the top of the rocker and the linking plate to the base

182

HOW TO PLAY

1 Two teams line up on opposite sides of a room, with a pile of LEGO bricks in the centre of the room.

2 Set a three-minute timer. When the timer begins, the first player in each team runs to the centre of the room, grabs a brick, and then runs back to their team, placing the brick on a table.

3 The second player in each team runs to the centre of the room, grabs a second brick, runs back to their team and builds it on top of the first brick.

4 Players take turns running back and forth, building up the size of their tower, one brick at a time. When the time runs out, the team with the tallest tower wins.

Why not build a LEGO relay racer as a trophy?

Find out how tall you are in LEGO bricks. You don't need to build a LEGO tower as tall as you are – simply make two measuring sticks that are both 10 bricks high. Lie down while a friend carefully places the sticks end to end, one after the other, starting at your feet, and working upward. Take care not to lose count!

Alternating brick colours will make it easier to count the last few at the top of your head

I'M FOUR BRICKS TALL. HOW TALL ARE YOU?

Standard minifigures are four bricks high without hair – divide your brick-height by four to get your height in minifigures!

How tall are you in LEGO bricks?

183

Feeling energetic? Run a LEGO relay race! Divide into two teams and see who can build the tallest tower as players take turns running between the bricks and their LEGO tower. Run over a short or long distance – depending on how energetic you feel!

Run a LEGO relay race

184

185 Take a look outside

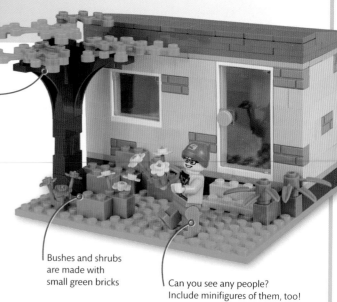

Can you see birds from your window?

The tree's branches are brown half arch bricks

Orange cone pieces become carrots

The great outdoors is full of inspiration for LEGO builds! For a random building challenge, look out of your window and build the first thing you see. It could be a bird, a garden, a plane, a shed or even a skyscraper!

All kinds of green pieces can be used in a vegetable patch

Bushes and shrubs are made with small green bricks

Can you see any people? Include minifigures of them, too!

Barbados

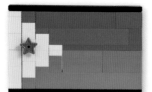

Djibouti

China

The star is attached to a brick with a side stud

United Kingdom

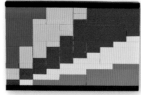

Seychelles

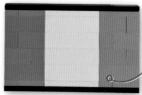

Ireland

Tricolour flags like this one are easiest to start with

Learn about different countries' flags and then recreate as many as you can using LEGO bricks. Build the flags vertically with layers of plates and bricks. Then use them in a quiz for yourself, family or friends!

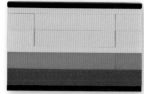

Colombia

Costa Rica

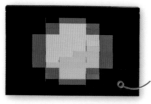

Why not make up a flag of your own?

Fly the flags of the world

186

187 Make a chest for your treasure

Keep your treasured possessions close with a trinket box you can carry around on your adventures. It looks like a pirate's treasure chest, but if you don't know any pirates, it would also make a great jewellery box for someone's dressing table.

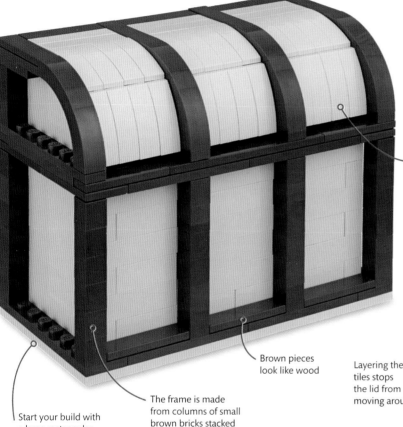

The lid has curved slopes that fit sideways on the front and curved slopes that lie flat on the top

Standard bricks are used to make the three straight edges of the lid

The lid sits on smooth tiles around the top of the box's sides

Brown pieces look like wood

Layering these tiles stops the lid from moving around

Start your build with a large rectangular base plate

The frame is made from columns of small brown bricks stacked on top of each other

PUT A LID ON IT
You could build a flat lid for your box if you prefer, and then add decorations to it. You could also add some hinges to connect the lid to your box, or a catch to keep it closed. Try adding a tray inside your box to create a separate area for your smaller special possessions.

The sides of the tray are made from panel pieces

Attach a handle to lift the tray out – this one is a round plate with a ring

The tray sits on smooth tiles built out from the box's sides

The tray's base is a single large plate

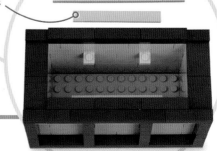

Unpick the secrets of a lock on page 174.

Take your pick with the 2x4 game

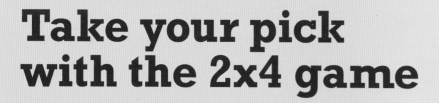

HOW TO PLAY

1 Start with 2x4 bricks on every white jumper plate. Two or more players take turns removing bricks from the board.

2 A player can remove either one or two bricks on each turn. If a player takes two bricks, the bricks must be immediately next to each other in a straight line or at right angles.

3 The winner is the player who removes the last brick.

Each brick sits on a jumper plate

You can use 2x4 bricks of any colour

Place the jumper plates in vertical and horizontal rows, with equal-sized gaps between them

Use jumper plates so it's easier to detach the 2x4 bricks

---

189 Build a stylish perfume bottle

You could put transparent coloured pieces in the bottle to look like liquid.

You don't need real perfume to make a great gift! A decorative LEGO model will last much longer and look just as good on top of a dresser.

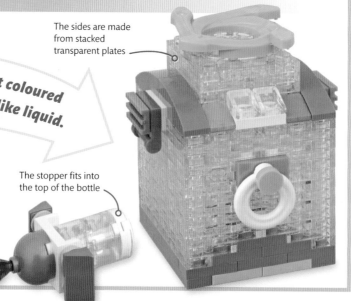

The sides are made from stacked transparent plates

The stopper fits into the top of the bottle

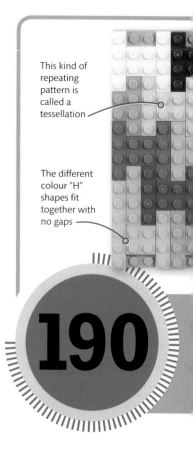

This kind of repeating pattern is called a tessellation

The different colour "H" shapes fit together with no gaps

190

188

This game uses lots of classic LEGO 2x4 bricks. To win, you will need to use strategic thinking and tactical skills to end up with the last 2x4 brick. There are only two moves to choose from, but it never plays out the same way twice!

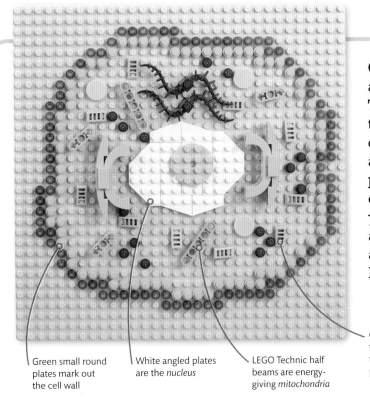

Go microscopic with a living cell model! This one shows all the parts of a plant cell and would make a brilliant science project! You could even use it to help you study by looking at a picture of a cell and seeing if you can build it from memory.

Green small round plates mark out the cell wall

White angled plates are the *nucleus*

LEGO Technic half beams are energy-giving *mitochondria*

Grille slopes are the *chloroplasts* that make a plant green

See inside a cell

191

Make a repeat pattern with plates as a decoration for your room. You can add more base plates to continue the pattern and make a bigger decoration. It can go on forever – if you have enough bricks!

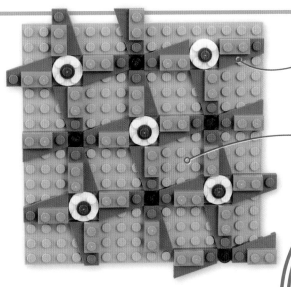

This windmill pattern is made with angled plates

The space between windmills is always the same shape, but not always the same orientation

Make a repeating pattern picture

BUILDER'S TIP

Perfect the look of your pattern pieces and work out how the loose parts will fit together before you fix them onto the base plate.

192 Make your own LEGO movie

Use lamps to light your set. Natural light is always changing, so it will make your movie look odd!

Bring your LEGO scenes to life with a stop-motion film. You will need a digital camera to take lots of pictures – and plenty of patience as you move parts of your scene a tiny amount between each shot! All the effort will be worth it when you play the pictures back and see your first blockbuster! Will it be an action movie, a tale of romance or a comedy?

You don't need to build whole buildings, just what will be seen on screen

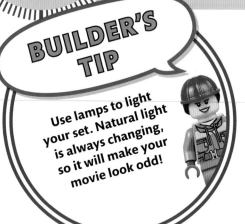

STOP MOTION!

For a stop-motion film to work, you need to keep the camera and the background in exactly the same position for every shot. For the best results, you should mount your camera on a tripod to keep it steady. Once you've taken your photos, turn them into a slideshow on your computer and see your minifigures come to life!

Make sure the base plate doesn't move between shots

Start out with a short film of a minifigure walking

Bring one leg forward and take a picture

Then bring the foot of that leg down flat and take another shot

Next, bring the other leg forward, and so on

Remember to move the arms, too, for a realistic motion

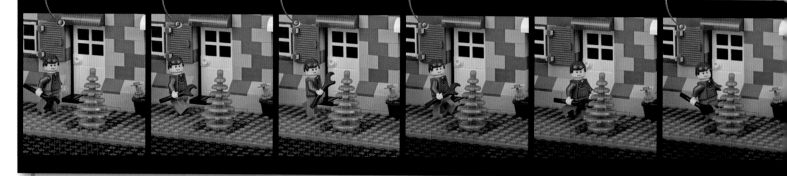

Make a time-lapse video on page 92.

193 Race to make a micro-ship

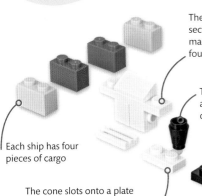
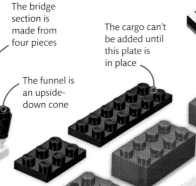

The bridge section is made from four pieces

The cargo can't be added until this plate is in place

The funnel is an upside-down cone

Choose bricks of your favourite colour for your ship

Each ship has four pieces of cargo

The cone slots onto a plate with a vertical bar – this plate needs to be added before the bridge section

Each ship has slope bricks at the front and back

Use a die or a six-sided LEGO spinner

Go full steam ahead in this fast-paced building game for two or more players! Can you set sail while your fellow sea captains are still in dock?

HOW TO PLAY

1 Each player starts with all the pieces to make a ship with cargo. Players take turns rolling a die.

2 If a player rolls a 1, 2, 3 or 4, they can add one piece to their ship (start by adding the 2x4 brick to the bottom 2x6 plate).

3 If a player rolls a 5, they must remove one piece from their ship. If a player rolls a 6, they can remove a piece from another player's ship. (If it is the player's first turn and they roll a 5 or 6, they must roll again until they get a 1, 2, 3 or 4.)

4 The winner is the first player to complete their ship with all its cargo.

194 Build a super hero

Do you sometimes wish you had a super hero ally? Well, now you can build one! Think about what tools and gadgets they would have, and design a cool costume for them. This hero is always ready to protect your favourite food from hungry family members!

Don't forget to come up with a name for your super hero!

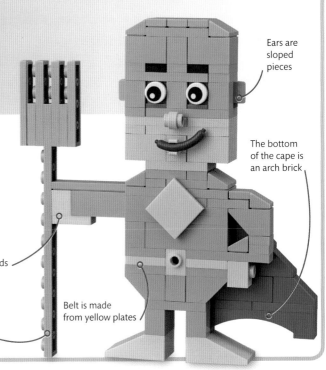

Ears are sloped pieces

The bottom of the cape is an arch brick

Both hands are bricks with side studs

Belt is made from yellow plates

Captain Cutlery always carries a fork!

195 Race across a river

Tread wisely in this two-player fast-flowing river race, where stepping stones come and go, and the tide can turn at any moment! With everything changing in midstream, you must always be thinking two steps ahead – or even two steps sideways and one step back!

If you don't have a coloured die, you could use a regular one instead.

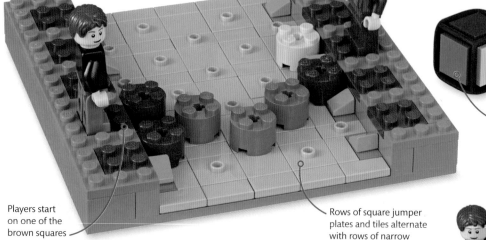

Players start on one of the brown squares

On a regular die, assign numbers to each colour (1, 2 = red; 3, 4 = blue; 5, 6 = yellow)

Each stepping stone is a round brick

Rows of square jumper plates and tiles alternate with rows of narrow jumper plates and tiles

It takes at least five stones to get across

HOW TO PLAY

1 Players start by placing their minifigure on opposite sides of the river. They then take turns rolling a die with red, blue and yellow sides.

2 After rolling a colour, a player can do one of the following: add a stepping stone of that colour anywhere on the board; remove any unoccupied stone of that colour; or move their minifigure onto any stone of that colour that is next to its current position.

3 If a player chooses to move, they can cross more than one stone if the stones form a line of the colour rolled. However, they cannot land on or step over a stone occupied by another minifigure.

4 The winner is the first player to reach the opposite bank.

BRICKS AND STONES
Building the river with jumper plates and tiles makes it easier to add and remove the stepping stones, and makes it clear exactly where each stone should go.

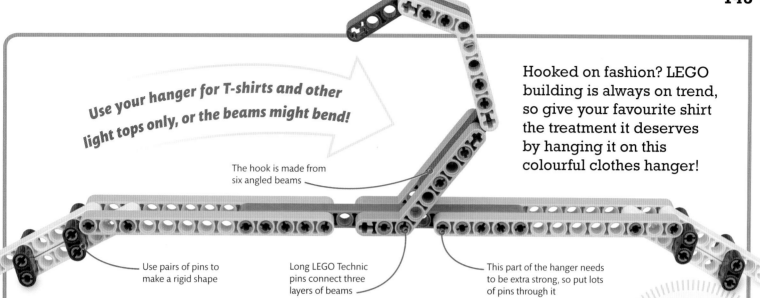

Use your hanger for T-shirts and other light tops only, or the beams might bend!

The hook is made from six angled beams

Hooked on fashion? LEGO building is always on trend, so give your favourite shirt the treatment it deserves by hanging it on this colourful clothes hanger!

Use pairs of pins to make a rigid shape

Long LEGO Technic pins connect three layers of beams

This part of the hanger needs to be extra strong, so put lots of pins through it

Construct a cool clothes hanger

196

These minifigures are on a trip to London

QUICK! WE NEED TO FIND SOMEWHERE TO HIDE!

Why not add your own picture captions?

Pose your minifigures to tell a funny story

BUILDER'S TIP

Hold a LEGO minifigure close to the camera with a scene behind to make a minifigure photobomb!

Minifigures love exploring the world. Take yours on a trip and catch their adventures on camera! Before long you will have a great gallery of all the amazing places they have been to.

Take your minifigures on a photo tour

197

BUILDER'S TIP

Use big, bold shapes and don't worry about the details – these monsters are all about first impressions!

Turn a small build into a mega monster by holding a torch behind it to cast a giant shadow! It doesn't matter what colours you use – just mix and match your most monstrous shapes to make super-scary shadows!

199

Use smooth pieces and pieces with studs – anything goes!

Each family member has a row for activities

Choose minifigures that look like your family

Dragon wings create extra-creepy shadows

Ball and socket joints make a segmented body

Make models that stand upright to keep your hands free for the torch.

Big bug eye is a magnifying glass

Row of creepy teeth is a LEGO Technic gear rack

Legs are stacked cone pieces

SHADOW PLAY

To cast a really good shadow, hold a powerful torch behind your monster and shine it onto a bare white wall. Learn how to twist and turn your monster to make the shadow change shape – and then sneak up on someone to give them a scare!

198 Cast a creepy monster shadow

Keep track with a weekly planner

Make a column for each day of the week, plus one for minifigures of your family.

IT FEELS LIKE WE'VE BEEN HERE ALL WEEK!

Printed number tiles show appointment times

Use pieces that represent activities – an easel is used to show Monday's art class

Coloured plates represent days of the week

Never miss a piano lesson again with a planner that spans the whole week! From Mum's Monday art class to Sunday football practice, all the important dates and times are marked out with minifigures and LEGO pieces.

Hold the torch near the monster's feet to make a really long shadow.

EEEK! WHAT'S THAT? OH, IT'S ME.

Simple, clear shapes make a big impact

The short legs look much longer as shadows!

BUILDER'S TIP

If you don't have number tiles, use rows of small round plates, such as three round plates for 3 o'clock.

200 Make an amazing drawing machine

You can make all kinds of patterns with this magnificent machine – all you have to do is turn the handle! The gear wheels move the pen and the paper, and swirling shapes begin to appear before your eyes!

Experiment with different gear combinations – what happens when a big gear turns a small gear?

Use a marker for the best results

These grey beams move the pen in an oval shape

Turn this handle to work the mechanism

Pins with ball ends stop the rubber band from coming off

The drawing board must have a smooth tiled surface

Panels make sides for the drawing board

Four plates with pins underneath connect a large gear wheel to the bottom of the drawing board

The drawing board turns on this pin

Two rubber bands hold a square of paper in place

A rubber band pulls these two beams together to hold the pen

Pins and angle beams hold the frame together

CHANGING GEAR

The machine works because the gear wheels move the pen in one direction, while the drawing board turns the other way. Using different combinations of gears, or changing where the pen arm connects to, would create a different pattern. Try overlaying different patterns on the same piece of paper, using different-coloured pens.

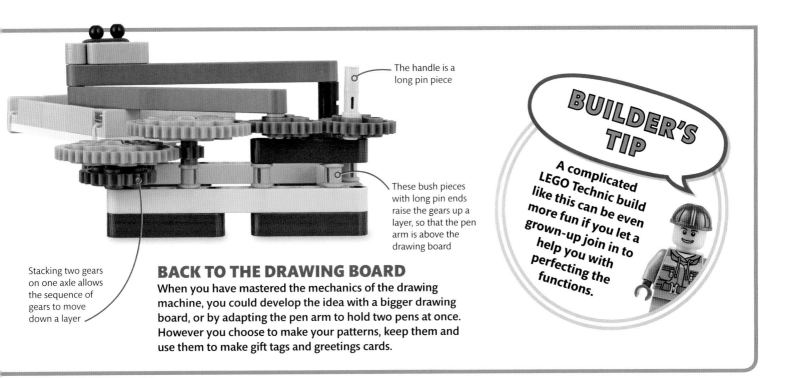

The handle is a long pin piece

These bush pieces with long pin ends raise the gears up a layer, so that the pen arm is above the drawing board

Stacking two gears on one axle allows the sequence of gears to move down a layer

BACK TO THE DRAWING BOARD

When you have mastered the mechanics of the drawing machine, you could develop the idea with a bigger drawing board, or by adapting the pen arm to hold two pens at once. However you choose to make your patterns, keep them and use them to make gift tags and greetings cards.

BUILDER'S TIP

A complicated LEGO Technic build like this can be even more fun if you let a grown-up join in to help you with perfecting the functions.

Take the five-by-five challenge

201

Grab five lots of five different types of brick, then see what you can build using all 25 bricks in five minutes! These models are made using five 1x1 round plates, five 1x1 bricks, five 1x2 bricks, five 2x3 bricks and five 2x4 bricks.

Don't worry about what colour the bricks are

Give a friend the same mix of bricks to make a two-player game.

BUILDER'S TIP

Don't be afraid to change your build into something else halfway through. Five minutes is a long time!

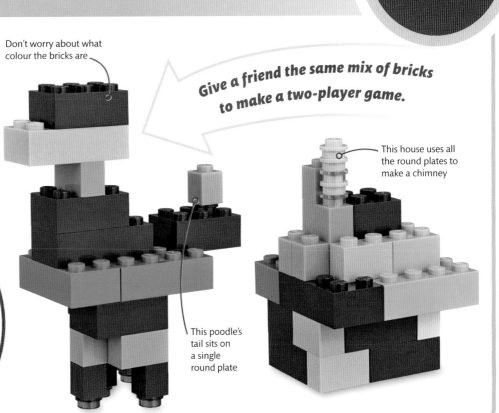

This house uses all the round plates to make a chimney

This poodle's tail sits on a single round plate

202 Keep the kitchen clean

Create a build that's not only bright and attractive, but really useful too! This practical kitchen towel dispenser is a quick and convenient way to keep on top of kitchen mess, and the LEGO frame itself is easy to clean with a little warm water.

Thinner end sections slot into the sides

A single-stud connection makes it easy to change the roll

Eight layers of long overlapping plates make a strong rail

DISPENSING ADVICE
Build your dispenser with a rail that slots into the sides from above, rather than sitting on top of them. That way, it will lift out easily when you want to change the roll, but won't come off when the towels are pulled forward. Build it with a broad base, so that it doesn't tip over when pulled.

You could use colours to match the decor in your kitchen

Make sure your build is tall enough to hold a full roll of towels

OOPS! I SPILT MILK AGAIN!

BUILDER'S TIP

Measure the length of a roll of towels before you build – your rail should be slightly longer than the roll.

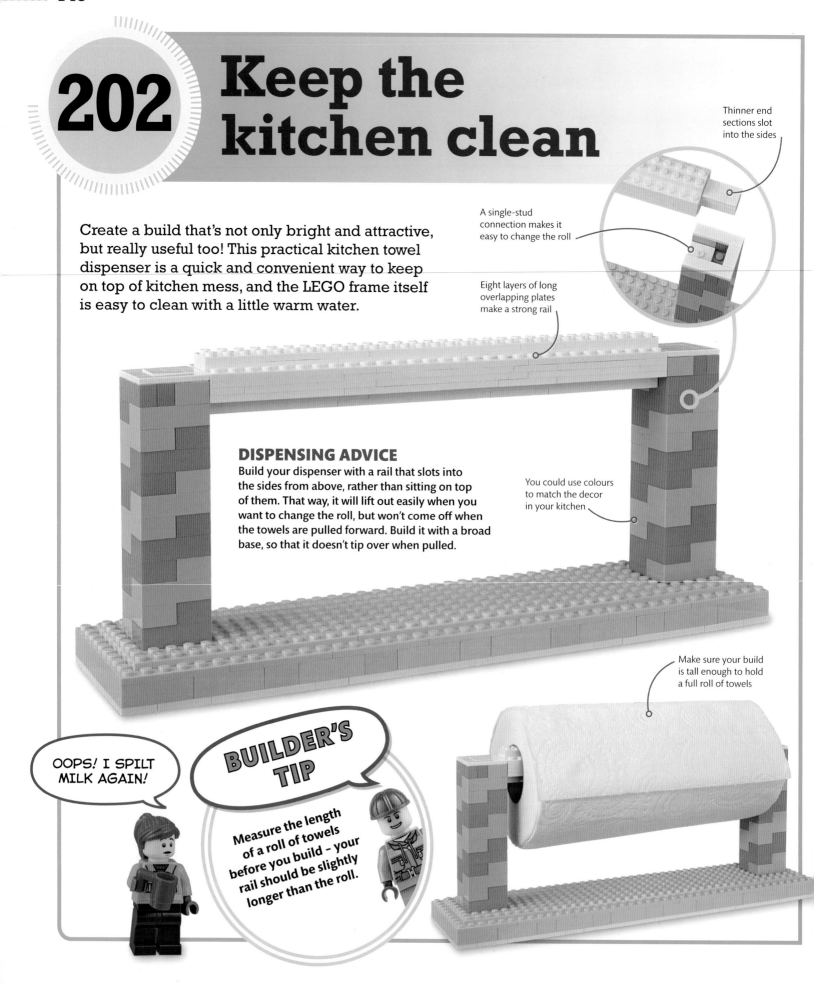

Pull a building idea out of a hat

203

Someone came up with an idea to build a lobster!

LOOK WHAT I BUILT!

I'M RUNNING OUT OF TIME!

Have a random selection of bricks on hand

Play a game that is great for getting ideas and sharing inspiration with your friends! Ask players to write five building ideas on pieces of paper and fold them up. Place them in a bag and get everyone to select one at random – without showing it to the other players. Give everyone five minutes to build the idea they picked. When the time is up, see if you can all guess what everyone has built!

204

Try a pair of calipers for size

Make a tool that will help you get the measure of your LEGO bricks! These calipers will tell you how many plates it takes to span any brick, which is especially useful for sideways building.

Build the moving part separately and slide it on from the bottom.

This round brick is nine plates across

Bricks with side studs hold the tiles in place

Units of five are marked with a bigger black plate

The sides of the moving part are long tiles

Measure up with a ruler on page 242.

205 Play Knight-Wizard-Blacksmith

The wizard stands lower so the weight of his hat doesn't pull him forward

Build the game with details to match the minifigures you choose

This game works just like Rock-Paper-Scissors. Both players have a model with the same three minifigures facing downwards on flippers. On the count of three, both players flip one minifigure up, based on which one they think their opponent will choose. Knight beats blacksmith, but blacksmith beats wizard, and wizard beats knight!

FLIP THE THEME

Your game doesn't have to have a medieval theme. You could play Bat-Tiger-Mammoth with competing LEGO® Legends of Chima™ tribes. Try any combination of minifigures! The game will always work so long as each minifigure wins in battle with one opponent, but loses when pitted against the other.

Each flipper pivots on Technic pins within 2x2 plates with rings

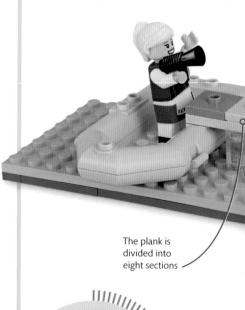

The plank is divided into eight sections

Press down to reveal your choice of minifigure

WHERE DID EVERYONE GO?

Minifigure stands on an angle plate

206

207

Make a home for your remotes

Never lose control of your gadgets again with this handy container for all your remote controls! This model has room for three different-sized channel-changers, but you can stack it as high as you need.

For a smooth finish, cover studs with tiles and slopes

Bands of raised tiles stop remotes slipping out

Long arch bricks span the front and back

Play a remote control prank – flip to page 163.

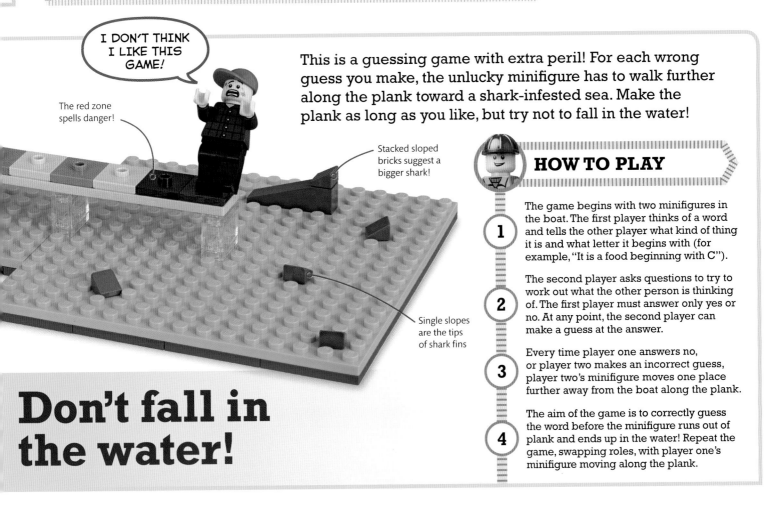

I DON'T THINK I LIKE THIS GAME!

The red zone spells danger!

Stacked sloped bricks suggest a bigger shark!

Single slopes are the tips of shark fins

Don't fall in the water!

This is a guessing game with extra peril! For each wrong guess you make, the unlucky minifigure has to walk further along the plank toward a shark-infested sea. Make the plank as long as you like, but try not to fall in the water!

HOW TO PLAY

1 The game begins with two minifigures in the boat. The first player thinks of a word and tells the other player what kind of thing it is and what letter it begins with (for example, "It is a food beginning with C").

2 The second player asks questions to try to work out what the other person is thinking of. The first player must answer only yes or no. At any point, the second player can make a guess at the answer.

3 Every time player one answers no, or player two makes an incorrect guess, player two's minifigure moves one place further away from the boat along the plank.

4 The aim of the game is to correctly guess the word before the minifigure runs out of plank and ends up in the water! Repeat the game, swapping roles, with player one's minifigure moving along the plank.

208 Build a fun photo frame

Add a favourite photo to a fairytale castle to make a decoration you can also play with! This frame has a tower with two rooms inside, and a parapet walkway that lifts to let you change the picture inside. The whole build will fit easily onto a shelf, so it is perfect for displaying or playing!

Removing the photo reveals a grid of black bricks behind

Climbing roses are made from red flower pieces on green branches

Gold flags give the castle a regal touch

The base is very wide, but just six studs deep

The walkway tilts on four hinge bricks

The front of the walkway rests on smooth tiles

PICTURE THIS
You can build a photo frame to suit any theme. A LEGO City frame might display the photo on the side of a truck, while an outer space design could feature your picture as a giant computer screen in a mission control room.

Put your photo here

A row of plates holds the photo in place at the bottom

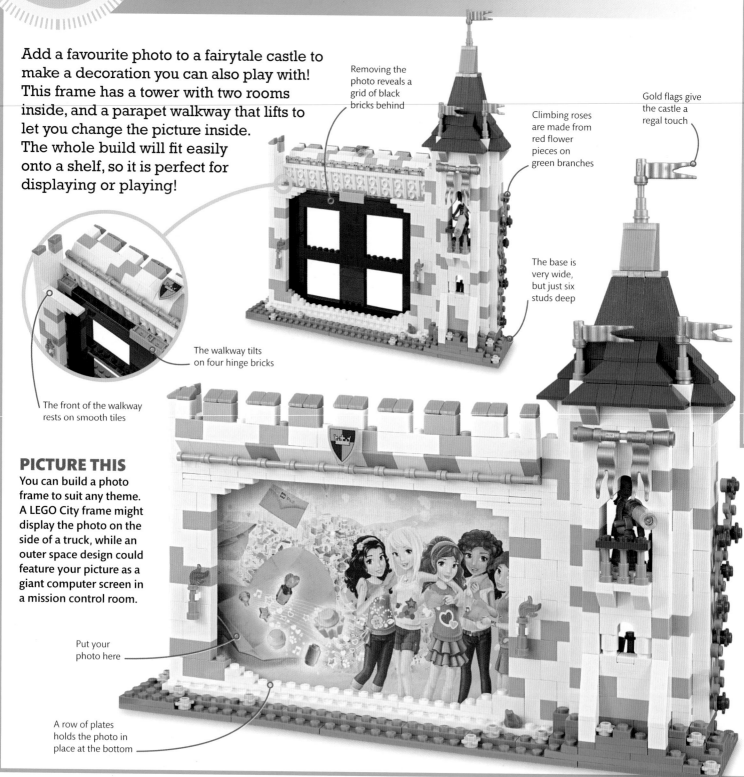

Make a train for mealtimes on page 96.

Make a monorail racetrack

209

Push these miniature trains along their smooth tile tracks. With a friend, race the futuristic bullet train against the old-style steam engine and see which one makes it to the end of the line first!

A handlebar makes a pantograph, which electric trains use to collect power

Smokestack is a small round brick

Small round plates keep the train on the track

Both trains are built with a slot for the rail

Plates with side rings look like wheels

The rail is one stud wide

Each rail is a row of tiles on a row of bricks

Tilt the tracks to build up speed, and make them as long as you can!

The black bricks strengthen the build and protect the back of the photo

The shield on the front slots into this brick with cross hole

LEGO Friends mini-dolls can explore inside the tower

Both rooms are filled with interesting details

THE SPECIAL BRICK

Hinge bricks have tops that tilt, so their studs can face upwards, sideways or anywhere in between!

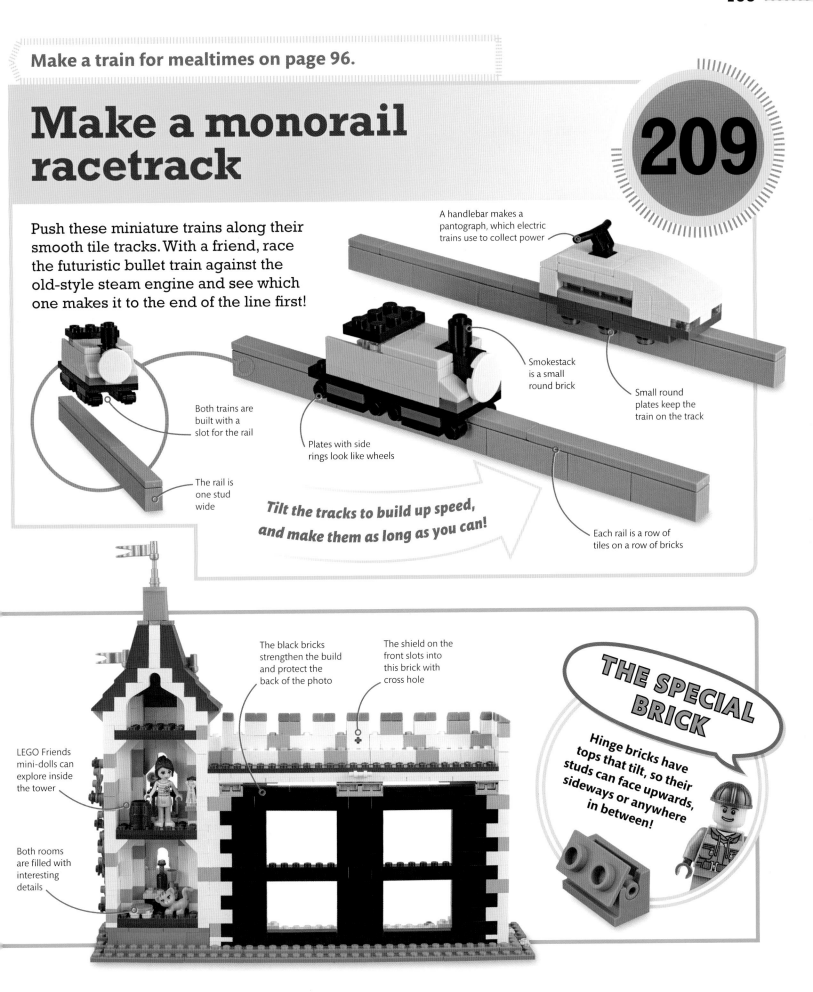

Make a modular pony

This conical horn slots into a cone brick

Swap distinctive features, such as the pony's head, feet and tail.

Slope bricks create a multicoloured mane

The tail is made from the same parts in different colours

The body is built using bricks with holes

Side studs on the legs plug into the bricks with holes on the body

The cheeks are tiles attached to bricks with side studs

Make a build with modular sections and you can easily change everything about it! This pony is built with body parts you can swap in just a few seconds, which means it can magically transform into a rainbow unicorn!

210

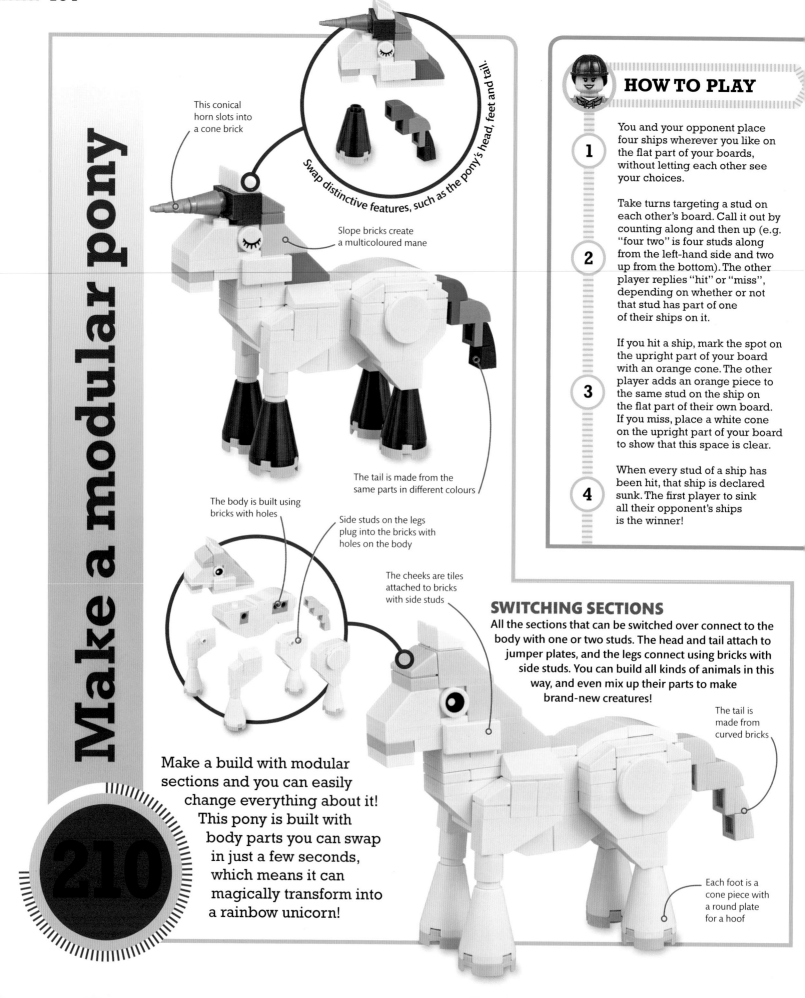

HOW TO PLAY

1. You and your opponent place four ships wherever you like on the flat part of your boards, without letting each other see your choices.

2. Take turns targeting a stud on each other's board. Call it out by counting along and then up (e.g. "four two" is four studs along from the left-hand side and two up from the bottom). The other player replies "hit" or "miss", depending on whether or not that stud has part of one of their ships on it.

3. If you hit a ship, mark the spot on the upright part of your board with an orange cone. The other player adds an orange piece to the same stud on the ship on the flat part of their own board. If you miss, place a white cone on the upright part of your board to show that this space is clear.

4. When every stud of a ship has been hit, that ship is declared sunk. The first player to sink all their opponent's ships is the winner!

SWITCHING SECTIONS

All the sections that can be switched over connect to the body with one or two studs. The head and tail attach to jumper plates, and the legs connect using bricks with side studs. You can build all kinds of animals in this way, and even mix up their parts to make brand-new creatures!

The tail is made from curved bricks

Each foot is a cone piece with a round plate for a hoof

Play a game of sinking ships

Build two hinged boards and race to sink your opponent's ships before they sink yours in this tactical game! Take aim and try to work out where the enemy vessels are hiding, using a process of elimination and a little bit of luck!

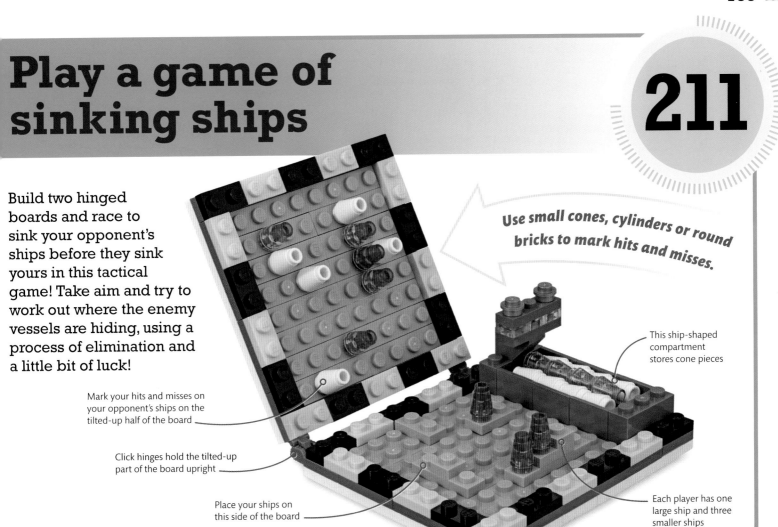

Use small cones, cylinders or round bricks to mark hits and misses.

This ship-shaped compartment stores cone pieces

Mark your hits and misses on your opponent's ships on the tilted-up half of the board

Click hinges hold the tilted-up part of the board upright

Place your ships on this side of the board

Each player has one large ship and three smaller ships

How many memories can you fit in a box? Hundreds, if they are on a digital memory card! These little boxes can hold data cards packed full of photos, and make a wonderful gift.

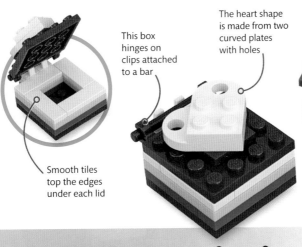

This box hinges on clips attached to a bar

Smooth tiles top the edges under each lid

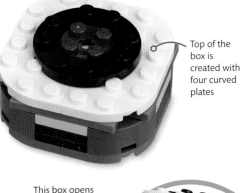

The heart shape is made from two curved plates with holes

Top of the box is created with four curved plates

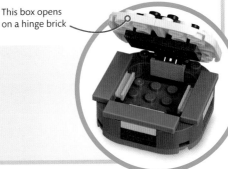

This box opens on a hinge brick

212 Build a mini memory box

Hang up a mobile

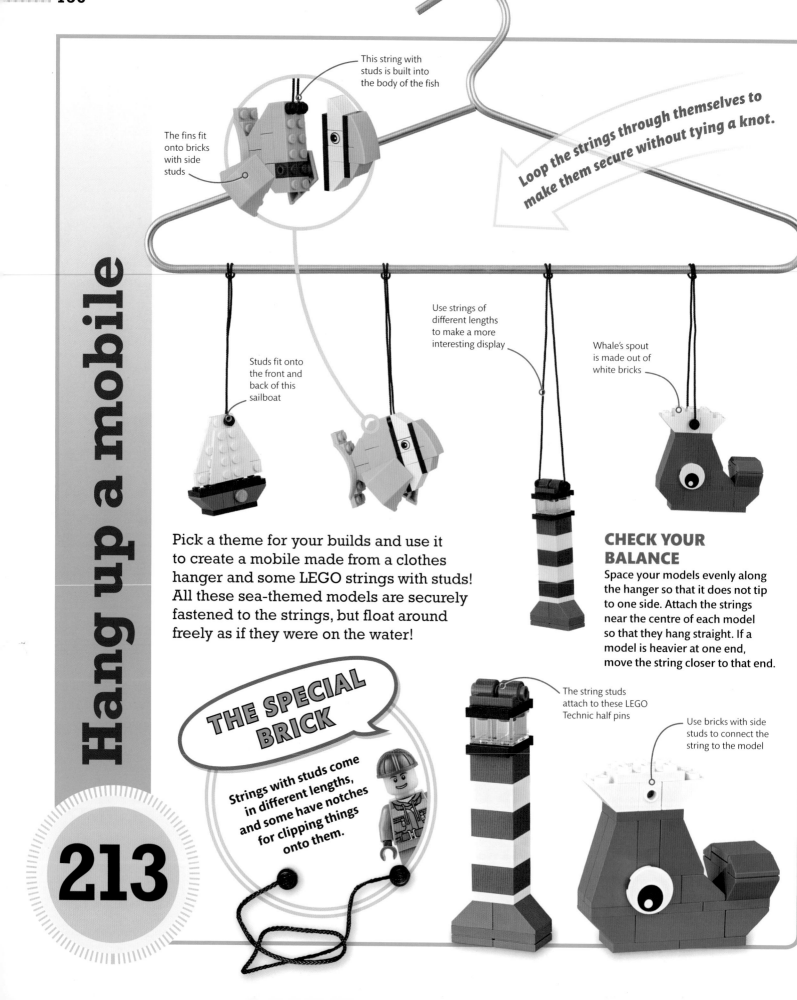

This string with studs is built into the body of the fish

The fins fit onto bricks with side studs

Loop the strings through themselves to make them secure without tying a knot.

Studs fit onto the front and back of this sailboat

Use strings of different lengths to make a more interesting display

Whale's spout is made out of white bricks

Pick a theme for your builds and use it to create a mobile made from a clothes hanger and some LEGO strings with studs! All these sea-themed models are securely fastened to the strings, but float around freely as if they were on the water!

CHECK YOUR BALANCE

Space your models evenly along the hanger so that it does not tip to one side. Attach the strings near the centre of each model so that they hang straight. If a model is heavier at one end, move the string closer to that end.

213

THE SPECIAL BRICK

Strings with studs come in different lengths, and some have notches for clipping things onto them.

The string studs attach to these LEGO Technic half pins

Use bricks with side studs to connect the string to the model

214 Form a line for a game of Fivers

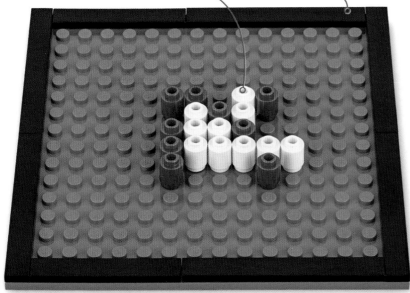

The player with white pegs has won this game after 10 turns

Smooth tiles make a border for the base plate

This game is easy to build but much harder to win! All you really need is a large square plate and lots of small round bricks – but it also helps to have a good eye and the ability to think ahead!

HOW TO PLAY

1 Player one uses white pegs and player two uses red pegs. The players take turns placing pegs of their colour anywhere on the board.

2 The object of the game is to make an unbroken row of five pegs in your colour – either vertically, horizontally or diagonally – and to stop your opponent from doing so by placing your pegs to block their progress.

3 The first player to make a row of five is the winner.

Make a music video

215

Cymbals are radar dishes

Make your favourite band or pop group out of minifigures and record your own music video! You could use stop-motion animation or lots of cool and moody-looking still images, all designed to go with your favourite song!

The neck of each guitar is a bar attached to a plate with a top clip

The body of the guitar is a plate with a side ring and two small slopes

The bass drum is built sideways and clips onto tap parts

Discover how to create a stop-motion video on page 140.

216 Tackle a tower-building puzzle

This brain-teasing tower has been puzzling people for more than 100 years! The aim is to move all five pieces of the tower from the left-hand side of the board to the right-hand side, one piece at a time. It sounds easy, but there are rules to follow! The fewest number of moves you need to solve it is 31. How many will it take you?

Each piece – apart from the top one – has a tiled top with a plate in the middle

All five pieces start on the yellow "X"

The board is topped with smooth tiles with a plate in the centre of each square

The aim is to rebuild the tower on the red "X"

217 Make two faces at once

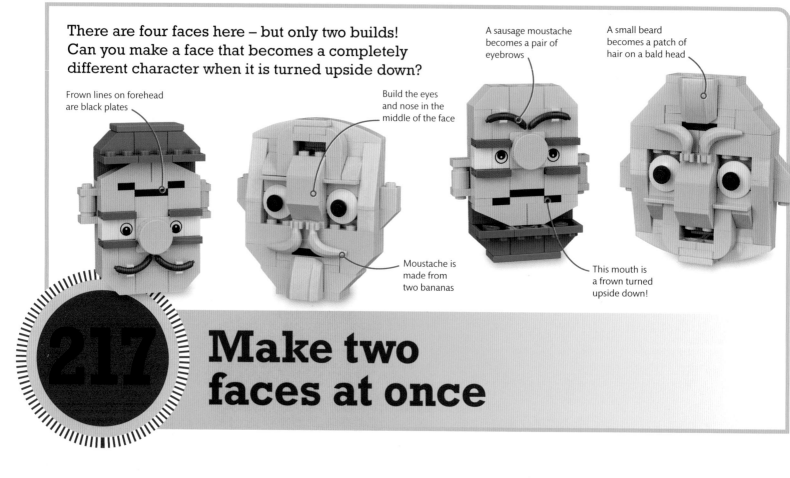

There are four faces here – but only two builds! Can you make a face that becomes a completely different character when it is turned upside down?

Frown lines on forehead are black plates

Build the eyes and nose in the middle of the face

A sausage moustache becomes a pair of eyebrows

A small beard becomes a patch of hair on a bald head

Moustache is made from two bananas

This mouth is a frown turned upside down!

HOW TO PLAY

1 Begin the puzzle with all five pieces stacked on the yellow "X".

2 The pieces can be stacked onto any larger piece – but not on top of a smaller piece. You can move the pieces to any of the three spaces on the board.

3 A piece can only be moved if it is the top piece of a stack.

4 The puzzle ends when the tower is built in the same formation in the section with the red "X".

Sound off with a shaker on page 84.

Some LEGO bricks are louder than others! Find out which ones make the best noises by building them into musical instruments. When you have found some cool new sounds to make tunes with, you can start your very own band!

Thread a long LEGO Technic axle through the entire length of the instrument

Handle is made from LEGO Technic axle connectors

Rubbing these chain pieces against the textured round bricks makes a rasping sound

SOUND ADVICE

Percussion instruments make different sounds depending on their size and shape, and what you use to drum against them. A large half-cylinder piece will make a deeper sound than a smaller one, and a beater made from a LEGO Technic axle will make more noise with a round brick on the end. Touching a brick while you strike it will dull its sound, so build your instruments with handles.

The half cylinders attach to grey angle plates

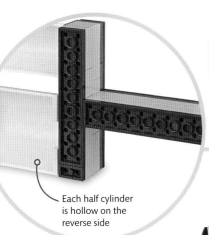

Each half cylinder is hollow on the reverse side

Mallet for striking the half cylinders is made from round pieces and a LEGO Technic pin

218 Build a LEGO brick band

219 Roll up for a raffle

Write numbers on matching squares of paper to fill the drum.

Fill this drum with numbers on pieces of paper and you can run your own raffle or bingo game! Cranking the handle turns the tumbler and mixes up all the numbers to make the game fun and fair. Open the hatch to draw the numbers and call them out for your friends to check against their just-for-fun tickets or bingo cards!

The left-hand axle is slotted through bricks with holes, and a handle is attached to the end

A round brick secures the drum at this end

Windows let you see the contents of the drum turning

The cradle needs to be sturdy to support the weight of the drum

Long plates hold the base of the cradle together

LEGO Technic pins attach these long beams to the top and bottom of the cradle

PUTTING IT ALL TOGETHER
A bingo drum is a complex build, so give yourself plenty of time to get it right. Construct it in sections, as shown on the right, then add large radar dishes to complete the ends. Thread the long axles at both ends into bricks with holes and build these onto the cradle in which the drum sits. Use bricks with holes for the base of the cradle, too, so that you can strengthen the sides with LEGO Technic beams.

THE SPECIAL BRICK
Axles with end stops have a built-in barrier at one end, so they won't pass all the way through bricks with holes.

Play minifigure charades

If you were a minifigure, who would you be? In this game, you get to act out your favourite minifigure characters while other players try to guess who you are. You can't use any words, so you have to mime, and the others have just one minute to guess correctly!

Make a line-up of minifigures for people to choose from.

HOW DO YOU MIME A SNAKE?

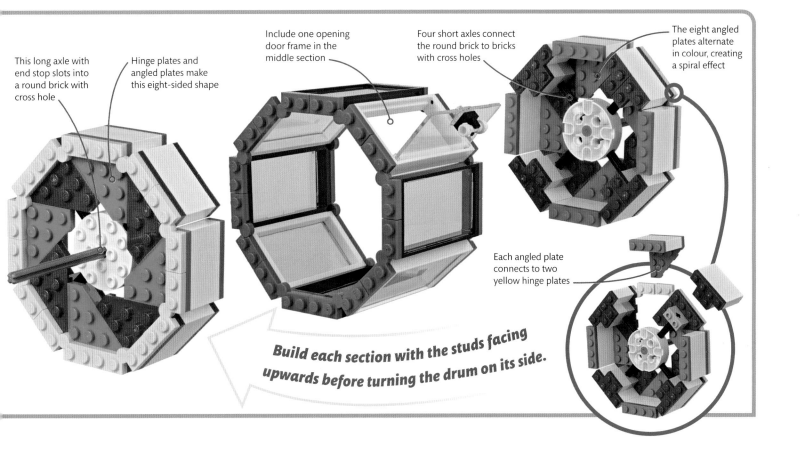

This long axle with end stop slots into a round brick with cross hole

Hinge plates and angled plates make this eight-sided shape

Include one opening door frame in the middle section

Four short axles connect the round brick to bricks with cross holes

The eight angled plates alternate in colour, creating a spiral effect

Each angled plate connects to two yellow hinge plates

Build each section with the studs facing upwards before turning the drum on its side.

221 Climb to the castle

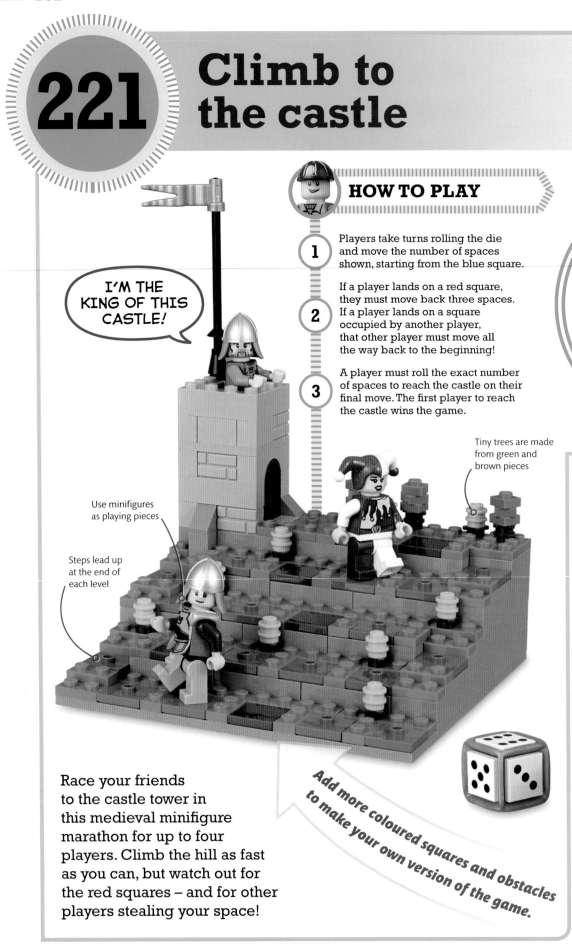

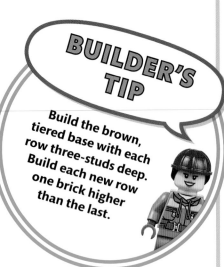

HOW TO PLAY

1. Players take turns rolling the die and move the number of spaces shown, starting from the blue square.

2. If a player lands on a red square, they must move back three spaces. If a player lands on a square occupied by another player, that other player must move all the way back to the beginning!

3. A player must roll the exact number of spaces to reach the castle on their final move. The first player to reach the castle wins the game.

BUILDER'S TIP

Build the brown, tiered base with each row three-studs deep. Build each new row one brick higher than the last.

I'M THE KING OF THIS CASTLE!

Tiny trees are made from green and brown pieces

Use minifigures as playing pieces

Steps lead up at the end of each level

Remember important numbers with a coded LEGO pattern that no one else will spot! Use the studs on each brick to represent individual digits, then line them all up to make a longer number. You could keep a piece separate from the rest of the sequence to make it extra secure!

Race your friends to the castle tower in this medieval minifigure marathon for up to four players. Climb the hill as fast as you can, but watch out for the red squares – and for other players stealing your space!

Add more coloured squares and obstacles to make your own version of the game.

222

223 Lay a trail for a treasure hunt

THE HUNT IS ON!

This first clue leads to a bedroom

A couch was found under the bookcase

This clue was found under a sofa cushion – and leads to the bathroom, where the next clue will be found!

Make a treasure hunt by hiding small builds around your home and ask your friends to find them. Each build should give a clue about where the next one will be found, until the intrepid treasure hunter finally reaches a well-earned prize!

Never forget a number

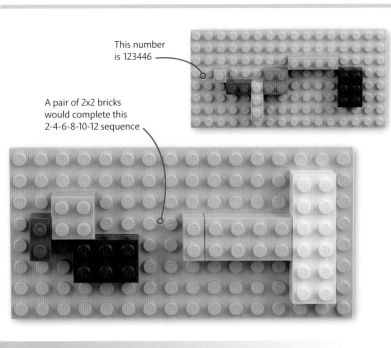

This number is 123446

A pair of 2x2 bricks would complete this 2-4-6-8-10-12 sequence

224 Play a TV remote prank

Play a harmless prank by swapping a real TV remote with a realistic LEGO replica! Make the switch while everyone's eyes are on the screen, and then wait until somebody tries to change the channel!

Use your smallest pieces to make your build look as much like your real remote as possible

MUST BE THE BATTERIES!

Craft a candlestick

BUILDER'S TIP

Slot a LEGO Technic axle into a stack of round bricks to stop it from breaking apart. This will make your candle models stronger.

The flame is an orange tooth piece

A bar connects the candle to the stick

CANDLE TRICK

For an extra touch of realism, make the white candle part shorter over time, so it looks as if it is slowly melting. If you can do it without people seeing you, they will be very confused!

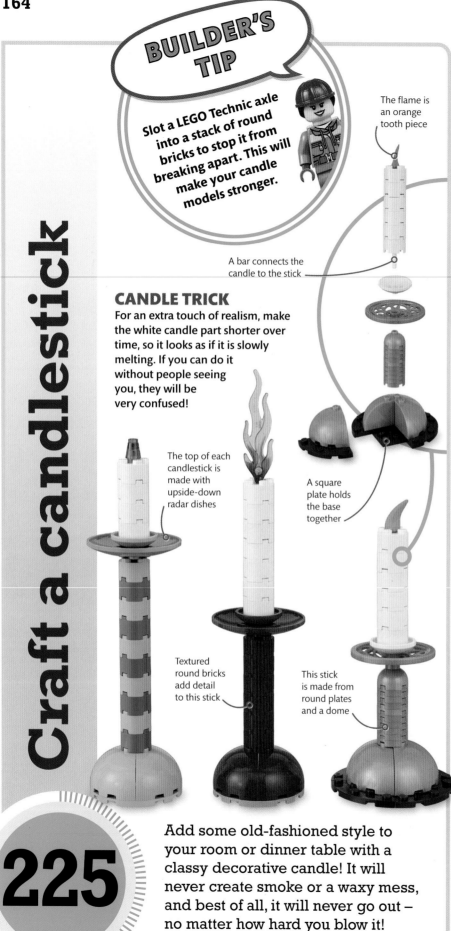

The top of each candlestick is made with upside-down radar dishes

A square plate holds the base together

Textured round bricks add detail to this stick

This stick is made from round plates and a dome

226

HOW TO PLAY

1. All 28 tiles are placed face down. The players take seven tiles each and position them so that they cannot see each other's selection.

2. After the first player places one tile face up, players take it in turns to add one tile at a time by touching matching numbers or colours together in a line. Players can add tiles to either end of the line.

3. If a player lays a double (a tile with the same number or colour at both ends), it is placed sideways. Players may branch off from a double by placing a tile at any of its free sides.

4. If a player cannot lay a tile, they pass their turn and must pick up an extra tile. The winner is the first player to use up all their tiles.

225

Add some old-fashioned style to your room or dinner table with a classy decorative candle! It will never create smoke or a waxy mess, and best of all, it will never go out – no matter how hard you blow it!

227

Keep your secrets safe with a code made from LEGO pieces! Share the code with your best friend and then spell out secret messages that no one else will be able to read! Create your secret code using your smallest pieces in lots of different colours.

Build a box of dominoes

The box opens and closes using hinge plates

The box top has a domino pattern made with round tiles

The domino set fits inside the box perfectly

The inside of the box has a smooth tiled bottom

Each tile is built on a 2x4 plate

Use printed number tiles, coloured tiles, or a mix of both

Make a set of dominoes with their own stylish carry case and you will be spotted wherever you go! A standard set features 28 tiles – one for every combination of the numbers 1–6 and blanks – but if you don't have numbered tiles, coloured ones will work just as well. You could even invent your own version of the game with a mix of both!

Send a secret message

A	B	C	D	E	F	G
H	I	J	K	L	M	N
O	P	Q	R	S	T	U
V	W	X	Y	Z		

Use a different LEGO colour for every letter of the alphabet

Can you work out what this message says?

228 Reach for a star

The five tiles (numbered 1-5) are arranged at three different levels

1 2 3 4 5

1

4 2 5

Tiles 4 and 5 stay where they are

3

Tile 3 is bent down, and tiles 2 and 1 are bent up

1 2 4 5

3

Tile 5 is built highest and folds down, over the top of the star

These stellar decorations are not made from stardust, but sprinkle them around a room and they will add a little out-of-this-world magic! They are built using just a handful of pieces, which means you can make lots of them to create a LEGO starscape!

Hinge plates link each corner of the star

Make a cool coaster

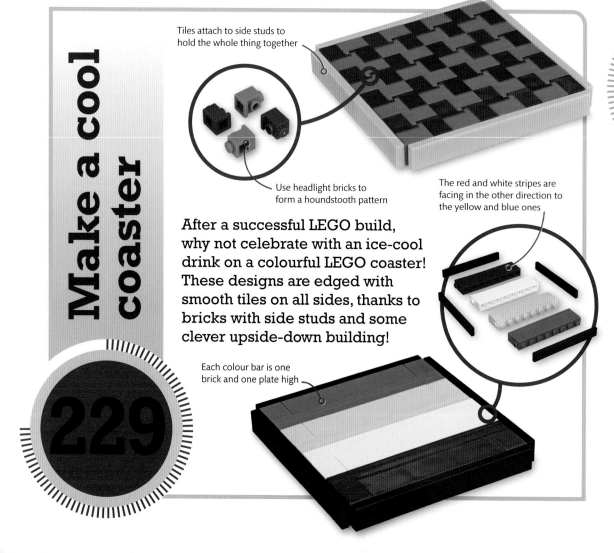

Tiles attach to side studs to hold the whole thing together

Use headlight bricks to form a houndstooth pattern

The red and white stripes are facing in the other direction to the yellow and blue ones

After a successful LEGO build, why not celebrate with an ice-cool drink on a colourful LEGO coaster! These designs are edged with smooth tiles on all sides, thanks to bricks with side studs and some clever upside-down building!

Each colour bar is one brick and one plate high

229

230

Give your minifigures an adrenaline rush with a cool (make that ice-cold!) LEGO ski slope. Build it at an angle with a smooth tiled surface, and send the skiers skimming over the snow in search of a new speed record! You could even add an upward curve at the end of the slope to make a jump and watch your skiers fly!

This star is topped with glow-in-the-dark tiles

STAR SYSTEMS
The top of the red star is made with 1x8 tiles. The key to making it is to build the tiles up at different levels with small plates on top of the hinges. Each side of the glow-in-the-dark star is 11-studs long. All of its spokes are built on the same level, with two-stud gaps where the pieces cross.

Find the fastest builder

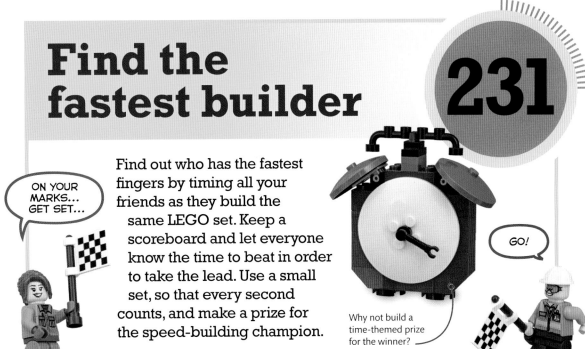

ON YOUR MARKS... GET SET...

Find out who has the fastest fingers by timing all your friends as they build the same LEGO set. Keep a scoreboard and let everyone know the time to beat in order to take the lead. Use a small set, so that every second counts, and make a prize for the speed-building champion.

GO!

Why not build a time-themed prize for the winner?

Tally up the results with a scoreboard on page 182.

Build a ski slope

Use slopes and curved slopes to give the skiers a bumpy ride!

Overhanging snow and ice is created with white tooth plates

Grille pieces make ski marks in the snow

If you don't have minifigure skis, build a pair!

The whole build leans forward on stilts of different lengths

SKIING ON STILTS!
Build a stable slope by adding stilts in the middle that are half the height of the ones at the back, with none at all at the front. That way, the slope will be supported at the front, middle and back. Don't make your ski slope too steep, or the skiers will simply fall off!

All the crayons can be taken out, just like the real thing!

The lid opens on a row of hinge bricks

Put your building skills to the test by making life-sized replicas of things around your home. Choose small objects that won't use up all of your bricks, and try to include as many details as possible. When you are finished, put your build beside the real thing and see if anyone can spot the difference!

Match a minifigure to their perfect park with a scene that is small enough to carry with you. It doesn't have to be realistic – you could make an antigravity garden for a spaceman, or a pizza park for a chef!

Stack round bricks and a cone to make a crayon

THE SPECIAL BRICK

Panel pieces have thin sides and no studs and are great for making realistic-looking walls and side details.

I COULD PAINT MY HOUSE WITH THIS!

WORKS OF ART

This painting set and box of crayons are just the same size as the real-life versions, but much less messy! Both were built by looking closely at the real things and keeping them close at hand all through the building process.

The tip of the brush is a broom piece

An extra row of panel pieces makes a space for the brush

Corner panels join up the sides in all four corners

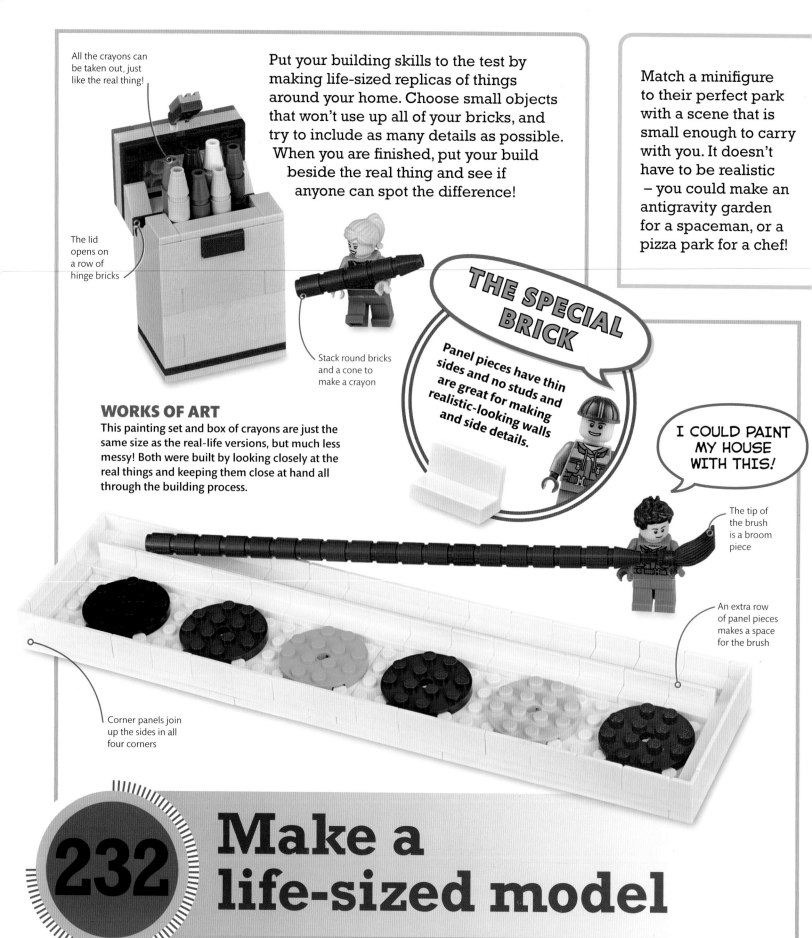

232 Make a life-sized model

233 Build a pocket park

A small tile makes a perfect table

The flowers attach to a brown brick with side studs

I WONDER IF I'M ALLOWED ON THE GRASS?

White flower pieces look like cherry blossom

Zen gardens feature pretty rocks and sculptures

Small fountain is an inverted dome

Paved path is made with sideways textured bricks

Start with a base of sideways bricks with a few side studs for adding detail.

Play a game of grab-a-brick

234

For this game, scatter some bricks on the floor – in an area away from any breakables! With your friends, take turns throwing a LEGO ball in the air, and then grab as many bricks as you can before the ball lands.

Use a ping-pong ball if you don't have a LEGO ball

Invent your own scoring system for bricks of different colours.

Choose a minifigure to represent you

Decorate a shield with accessories that represent your favourite things and create a coat of arms worthy of a noble knight! You could add pieces that portray your hobbies, favourite people or food.

This stripe sits diagonally on a jumper plate

This coat of arms belongs to a fan of cars, nature and Ninja!

The knight attaches to an angle plate

Create your coat of arms

A pizza-loving swordfighter made this shield!

235

236 # Spruce up your dining table

Each round petal clips on to a plate with a ring of bars

Make a different kind of flower for each dinner guest.

Make your guests feel special with a themed LEGO napkin ring beside every plate at the dinner table. It only takes a handful of bricks to build a simple napkin holder, which should make it easier if you need to make several for a large party!

Leaf is an angled plate

Fabric napkins will take up more space than paper ones

237 Escape from a LEGO maze

Learn how to make your way through the maze and then try it with your eyes closed!

Set a timer to see how quickly you can get a ball through a LEGO maze just by tilting the base plate from side to side! Moving one or two bricks can create a whole new maze.

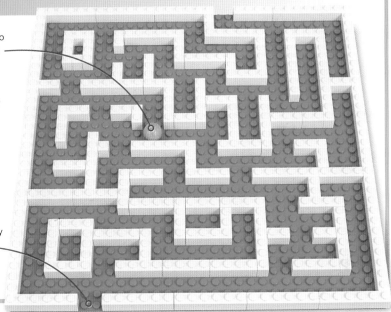

This LEGO ball will fit into passages two studs wide

Leave spaces for a way in and a way out

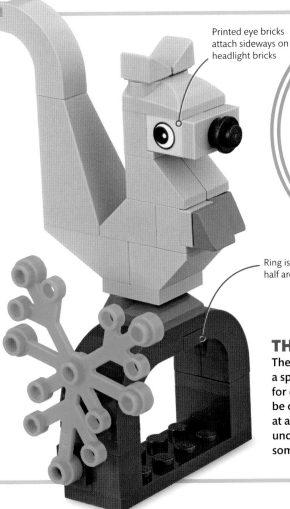

Printed eye bricks attach sideways on headlight bricks

Ring is made from half arch bricks

BUILDER'S TIP

Don't make your napkin rings too tight, or they might break apart when people take out the napkins.

Arch brick is used to create the napkin slot

This would be a great decoration for an underwater-themed party

THINGS ON RINGS

Theme your napkin rings around a special event or personalise them for each guest. The squirrel could be one of several woodland animals at an animal-lover's party, and the underwater scene could be for someone who likes to go diving.

238 Catch a ball in a cup

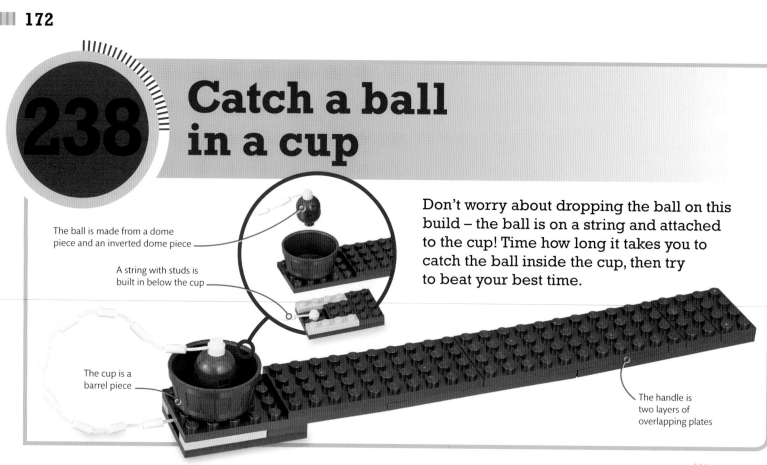

The ball is made from a dome piece and an inverted dome piece

A string with studs is built in below the cup

The cup is a barrel piece

The handle is two layers of overlapping plates

Don't worry about dropping the ball on this build – the ball is on a string and attached to the cup! Time how long it takes you to catch the ball inside the cup, then try to beat your best time.

Make a minifigure display case

239

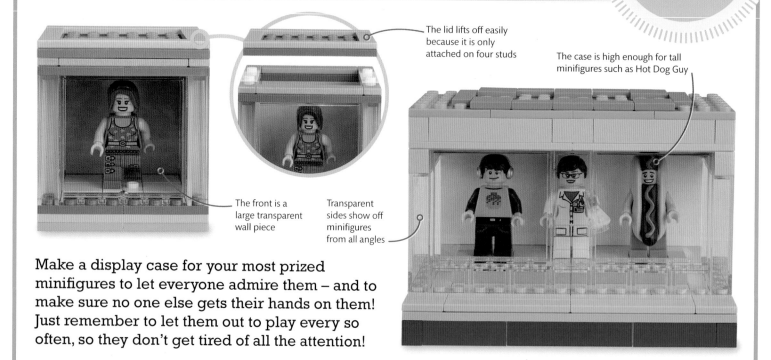

The lid lifts off easily because it is only attached on four studs

The case is high enough for tall minifigures such as Hot Dog Guy

The front is a large transparent wall piece

Transparent sides show off minifigures from all angles

Make a display case for your most prized minifigures to let everyone admire them – and to make sure no one else gets their hands on them! Just remember to let them out to play every so often, so they don't get tired of all the attention!

240

Ruffled rooster feathers are slopes

ONE GOOD TURN DESERVES ANOTHER!

See the wind in action with a working weather vane! When a gust blows, the arrow turns and points to the direction the wind is coming from. A rooster is a traditional shape for a weather vane, but you could make yours in any shape.

EASY BREEZY
To use the weather vane, position the red pointer facing north (so green is east, blue is south and yellow is west). The arrow will turn to face the direction the wind is blowing from.

To catch a lighter wind, make the back of the vane larger than the front

Tiles with holes allow the vane to spin easily

Smooth round tile with hole tops the middle section of the column

A long LEGO Technic axle threads through the column

The compass points do not move

Colours indicate the four points of the compass

Round bricks above and below the grid hide a LEGO Technic axle that helps to steady the structure

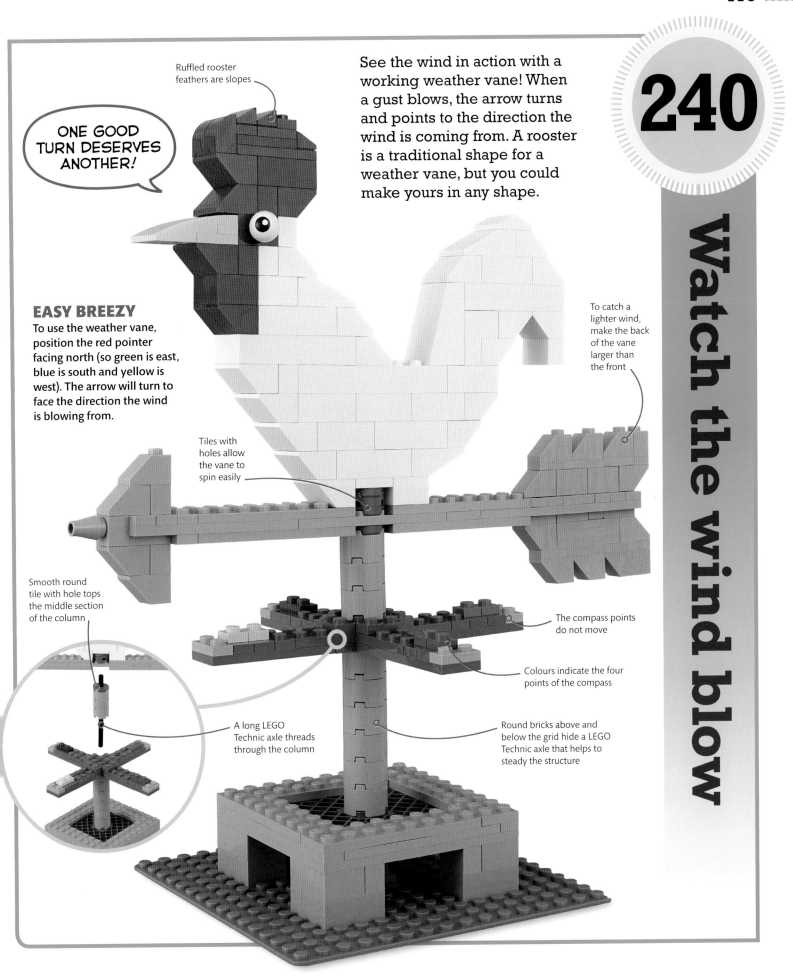

241 Build a lock

Keep your treasures safe with a working LEGO lock and key! Build it into a box with a door, or make it on its own just to see how a lock works on the inside!

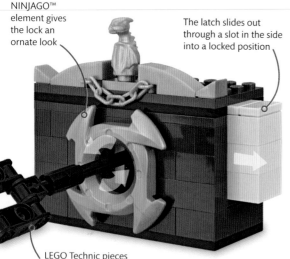

This LEGO® NINJAGO™ element gives the lock an ornate look

The latch slides out through a slot in the side into a locked position

LEGO Technic pieces make a strong key handle

Smooth tiles run along the top of the latch

This arch is off-centre so the bigger section can slide out of the box

The latch slides along on a layer of tiles

Turning the key to the side pushes the yellow latch in and out

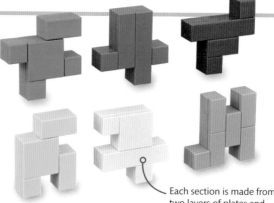

The tip of the key fits into this plate with rings

KEY INFORMATION

The key is built entirely from LEGO Technic pieces. The half beams at the end of the key need to be short enough to fit into the lock in an upright position, but long enough to move it when turned.

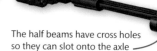

The half beams are placed one stud away from the end

The half beams have cross holes so they can slot onto the axle

It might not look like it at first, but these six shapes slot together to make a cube! Copy the shapes exactly as shown and then try to fit them all together without looking at the picture. Time yourself and then see if anyone can beat your record!

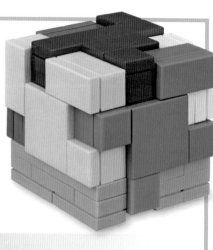

Each section is made from two layers of plates and a top layer of tiles

242 Put together a puzzle cube

243 Go places with a picture postcard

Wish you were here? Make a picture postcard out of LEGO bricks and you will feel like you are on holiday without even leaving home! Build your scene flat on a base plate and then put it on display for everyone to enjoy.

Make your postcards bigger than real ones so you can add more detail.

Use white round plates for clouds

Angled plate fits on top of smooth tiles

Sun is a yellow round plate

Sun attaches to a corner plate

White tiles create a waterfall

244 Make a colourful still life

Follow in the footsteps of famous artists with some still life studies of different fruit! Make them flat or in 3-D, and arrange them on a plate for all to see.

Fruit can look most interesting when cut in half

Layers of different-sized plates create a cross-section effect

Stone at the heart of this avocado is a round plate

Two strings with studs link to make a cherry stalk

Two small round plates make apple pips

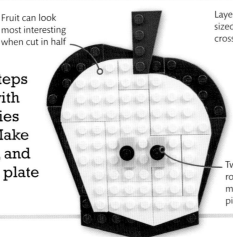

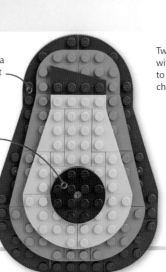

Cherries are made from dome parts

245 Build a fabulous fish tank

Make the fish swim around and play together in this amazingly lifelike aquarium! With long handles to move both fish from above, it is like a puppet theatre. You can use it to act out all sorts of adventures for these fishy friends!

Handle for moving the fish is made from a stack of round bricks

The shape of the tank is made with long LEGO Technic axles and axle connectors

THIS LOOKS VERY FISHY TO ME...

Axles slot into round bricks at the base

A wall of plant pieces makes a realistic background

A short LEGO Technic axle with a stud end fits into a sideways headlight brick

This fish is built sideways

The headlight brick fits into the back of another headlight brick

This stack of round bricks looks like a water filter

SCALE MODELS

Fish come in as many colours and shapes as LEGO bricks, so there is no end to the different types you could make! Use unusual parts such as flags for the tails, and small transparent parts to make shimmering scales. Build your fish flat, sideways or even upside down!

Play a game of Tanglefingers

246

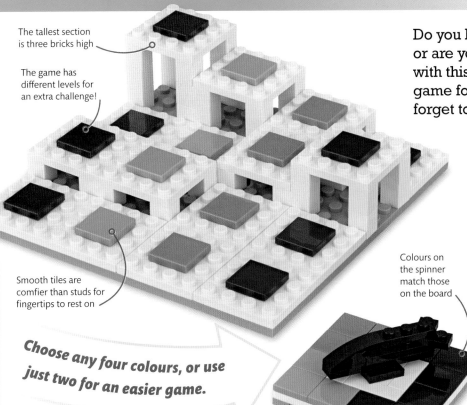

The tallest section is three bricks high

The game has different levels for an extra challenge!

Smooth tiles are comfier than studs for fingertips to rest on

Choose any four colours, or use just two for an easier game.

Colours on the spinner match those on the board

Do you have flexible fingers, or are you all thumbs? Find out with this fantastic finger-twisting game for two to four players. Don't forget to give the winner a big hand!

HOW TO PLAY

1 The first player flicks the spinner with one hand. They must then place any one finger of the other hand on the board, on a square of the colour shown.

2 Players take it in turns repeating step one, all keeping their fingers on the board as the game progresses.

3 When a player has placed all four fingers and their thumb, they can move any one of their digits to an empty square of the colour shown on their next move.

4 Players are knocked out if they cannot place a finger on the colour shown, or if their fingers come off the tiles. The last player left in the game is the winner.

Share your feelings with a friend

247

Two separate builds make one complete heart

Give one whole side of your heart over to your best friend, then put the two halves together whenever you meet. It will show that you are going to be best friends forever.

Each half is built on a square plate so they can stand apart

Smooth tiles allow the sections to slot together

Give a heart-shaped gift on page 20.

248 Try your luck on Treasure Island

THE SPECIAL BRICK

A LEGO Technic axle with a stud at one end can fit onto bricks and plates, unlike other axles.

The tree trunk is a stack of round bricks

The colours show grass, a beach and the sea around the island

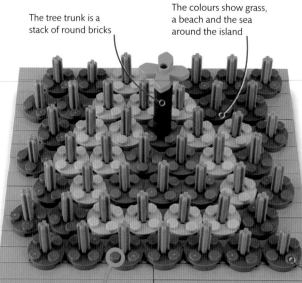

Join the hunt for buried treasure in this fun game of chance for lots of players. First, ask someone not playing the game to place the segments. Players then take it in turns removing segments from the island layout, in search of the bounty. The treasure is marked by a single red tile! Will you be the first to find it?

The treasure could be underneath any one of the segments!

EXPLORING THE ISLAND

The island is made up of 49 segments all built the same way, including the one with the tree on top. They all slot loosely into the playing board, which is built on a large plate. There are seven rows, which are each divided into seven sections. The sections are created with 1x1 round bricks with grey 1x1 round tiles on top.

Each segment is a round plate and a small bush on an axle with a stud at the end

All but one of the segments has a white 1x1 tile underneath

Just one segment has a red tile underneath

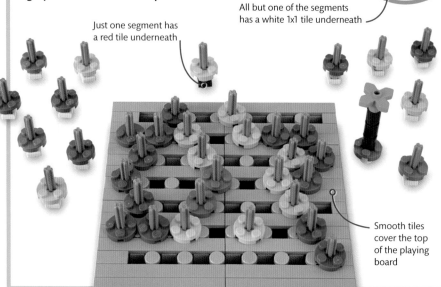

Smooth tiles cover the top of the playing board

BUILDER'S TIP

Leave a large gap between the front and back tyres. This will help the ship to move in a straight line.

HOW FAST CAN YOU FAN?

Race two ships inside using fans, hairdryers, or by flapping large pieces of cardboard! Try to make your ship as light as possible so it will be easier and faster to move. A large table or room with a smooth floor make the best racetracks.

Race a sailboat

249

Harness the power of air and create a rolling LEGO ship! This vessel has a large fabric sail that catches gusts of air, which help push it forward, just like a life-sized sailing ship. Unlike other ships, it cruises along on dry land instead of waves. Challenge your friends to build their own ships and race them to see whose is the fastest!

Use a sail from a LEGO pirate ship or make your own out of paper.

All ships need a flag!

The bigger the sail, the more air it will be able to catch

Plates with ball joints secure the top corners of the sail

Mast is a tall column piece with round bricks on top

This long cable is attached to the ship by plates with clips

Decorate your boat with a fierce face to intimidate other racers!

Use small wheels, spaced far apart

250 Build a lucky spinning wheel

Land on the star to win

Spin the wheel, round it goes, where it stops, nobody knows! This spectacular spinner adds an element of chance to your day. You could use it to decide who picks your next activity, who goes first in a game or to pick someone to complete a silly forfeit. Give it a whirl to try your luck!

Tooth pieces clip on around the edge of the wheel

The round shape is made by linking bricks with click hinges

The wheel is supported by LEGO Technic beams

Large feet on both sides keep the wheel from tipping over

This pointer shows where the wheel has stopped

251 Supersize your LEGO collection

Curved bricks wrap around a round brick to make a giant stud

This stud is made from three stacked round plates

A 1x1 plate is 6x6 studs across when supersized

A supersized model of a 1x1 brick looks huge in comparison to a real one

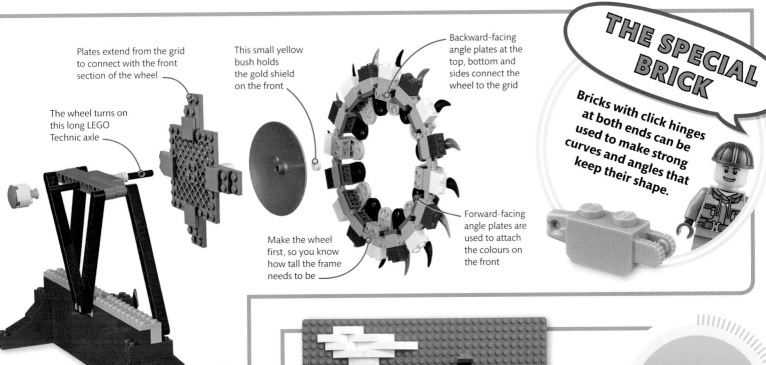

Plates extend from the grid to connect with the front section of the wheel

This small yellow bush holds the gold shield on the front

Backward-facing angle plates at the top, bottom and sides connect the wheel to the grid

The wheel turns on this long LEGO Technic axle

Make the wheel first, so you know how tall the frame needs to be

Forward-facing angle plates are used to attach the colours on the front

ANY COLOUR YOU LIKE

Make your wheel with lots of colours, including one or two special "jackpot" spaces, marked with gold or star-shaped pieces. You could even add a piece that people must try to avoid. The more you use the same colour, the more likely it is to come up when you spin.

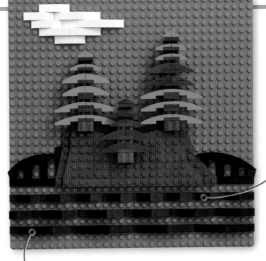

This logo is for a city with pretty trees and lakes

A logo should be a bold, simple image, more like a symbol than a picture

This area has a famous bridge across a canyon

252

Make a logo for where you live

Turn lots of LEGO bricks into a handful of giant pieces – for someone with very big hands! Make them hollow to see if you can fit them together like the real thing, and challenge yourself to make an unusually shaped piece supersize!

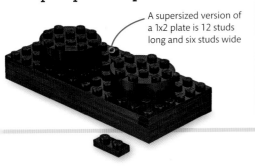

A supersized version of a 1x2 plate is 12 studs long and six studs wide

Give your hometown its own emblem, based on what you like best about it. It could be an image of a favourite part of town, or something the area is famous for. Ask other people what makes them proud to live there to get ideas for a logo that everyone will love!

Make a number display screen

BUILDER'S TIP

You can use any colours to make the numbers, so long as they stand out clearly from the background.

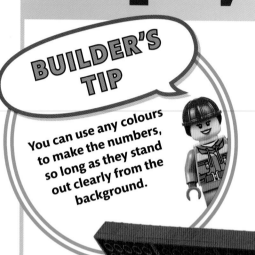

It is easy to change the numbers on this display, so you can use it as a scoreboard in games with two teams, make it into a desk calendar that shows the day and the month, or even set it to show the time and play a fun prank on your friends by pretending it is a real clock!

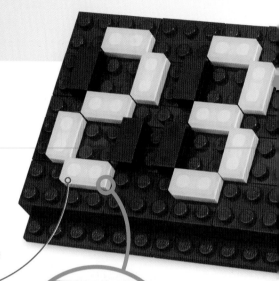

Each number is made using a mix of seven light and dark pieces

The board is held at an angle on two rows of hinge bricks

Each slot has a smooth tiled base so the numbers can be changed easily

The board is built with slots for the bricks that make up each number

---

Make a long line of LEGO dominoes, then give the first one a tap to see them all topple in sequence! Create a line as long and curvy as you can, snaking around corners and table legs – or even branching off into two separate lines!

Space out your dominoes at two-stud intervals on a flat surface.

Use 2x4 plates with tiles on top to make your dominoes

Make each domino two layers deep so you can stand them up easily

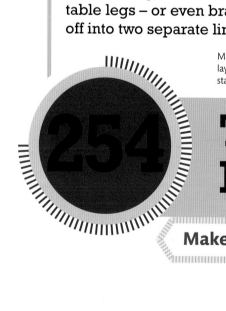

254

Topple a trail of LEGO dominoes

Make a set of LEGO dominoes on page 165.

253

The numbers 23 and 59 could be two competing scores, or they could indicate one minute to midnight

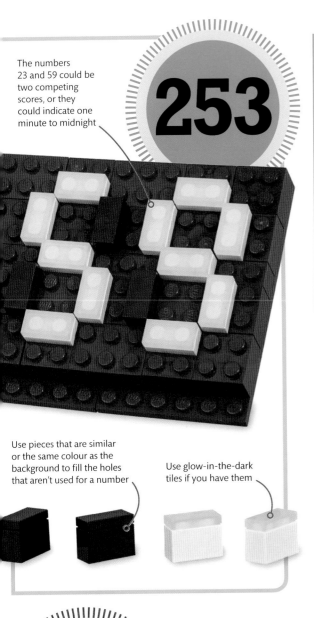

Use pieces that are similar or the same colour as the background to fill the holes that aren't used for a number

Use glow-in-the-dark tiles if you have them

256

Build a single-colour scene

Put your building skills to the test by making a model using just one colour. Use your favourite shade, or one where you have lots of interestingly shaped pieces. Use natural-looking colours such as greys and browns and the results can look like they have been carved from a single block of stone or wood!

This white build looks like a marble sculpture

I'M FEELING A LITTLE PALE

Minifigure head pieces come in lots of colours

255

Run a cable-car cruise

Give your minifigures a bird's-eye view of your bedroom with a scenic cruise in a cable car! Make a gentle slope with a length of string and watch the cable car slide along it. Be sure to give the passengers a guided tour and point out the key sights on the journey!

The cable car hangs on a LEGO Technic triangle beam

This single pin connection makes the car stay level on a sloping string

Thread the string under, then over, then under the wheels

Keep the string tight, or the car will stop

Lift off the roof to place minifigures inside

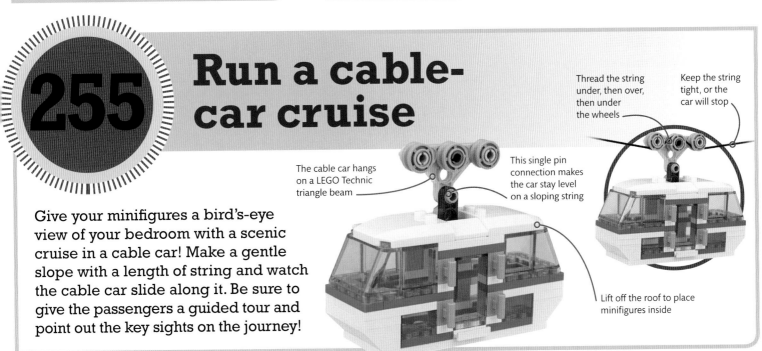

Make a model from memory

257

THOSE BRICKS LOOK FAMILIAR!

Blocks of bright colours will be harder to forget!

Show a friend a simple model and give them one minute to study it. Next, give them the bricks they will need to build the model from memory. See how closely they can match the original in just five minutes!

Use simple shapes to make a build people will be able to remember

Give your friend precisely the same bricks you used for your model

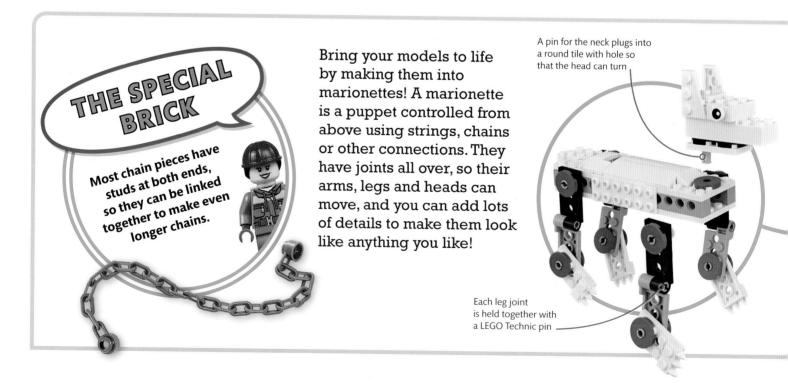

THE SPECIAL BRICK

Most chain pieces have studs at both ends, so they can be linked together to make even longer chains.

Bring your models to life by making them into marionettes! A marionette is a puppet controlled from above using strings, chains or other connections. They have joints all over, so their arms, legs and heads can move, and you can add lots of details to make them look like anything you like!

A pin for the neck plugs into a round tile with hole so that the head can turn

Each leg joint is held together with a LEGO Technic pin

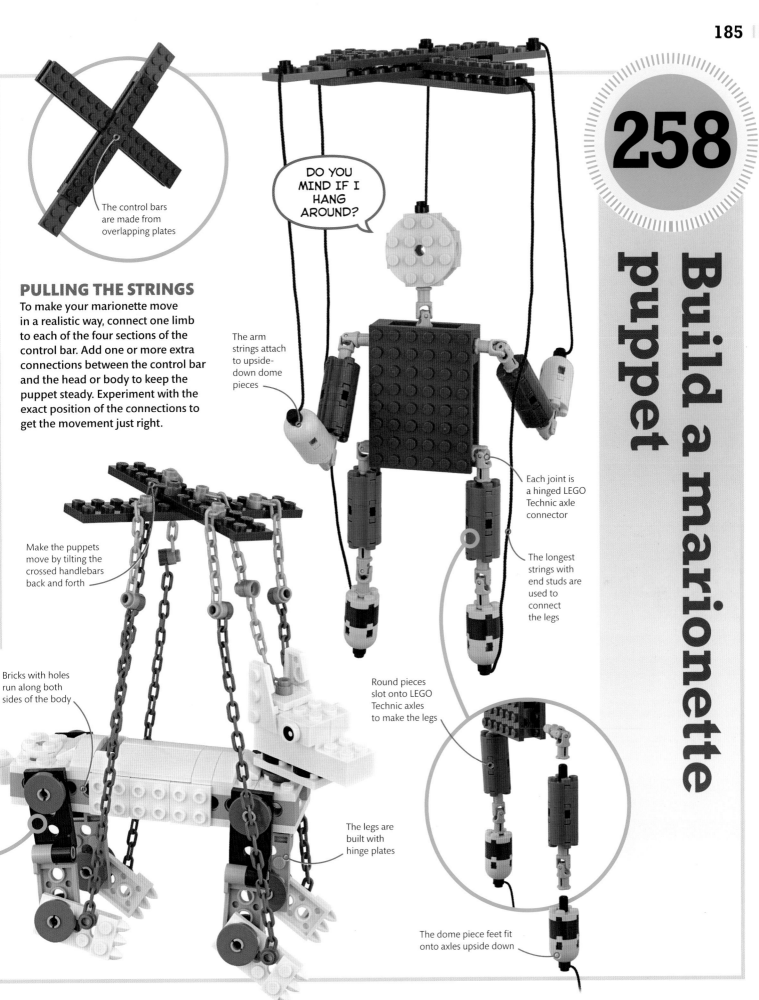

258 Build a marionette puppet

The control bars are made from overlapping plates

PULLING THE STRINGS

To make your marionette move in a realistic way, connect one limb to each of the four sections of the control bar. Add one or more extra connections between the control bar and the head or body to keep the puppet steady. Experiment with the exact position of the connections to get the movement just right.

DO YOU MIND IF I HANG AROUND?

The arm strings attach to upside-down dome pieces

Make the puppets move by tilting the crossed handlebars back and forth

Bricks with holes run along both sides of the body

The legs are built with hinge plates

Each joint is a hinged LEGO Technic axle connector

The longest strings with end studs are used to connect the legs

Round pieces slot onto LEGO Technic axles to make the legs

The dome piece feet fit onto axles upside down

259 Take a turntable for a spin

Different sizes of angled plate make the rounded edge

The centre of the disc is a large plate

Plates extend outward from all sides of the central plate

This round plate connects to the turntable in the centre of the base plate

Smooth tiles on the base plate support the sides of the disc

Make a small turntable into a giant one, simply by building out from it! This one starts with a 4x4 turntable at its centre, but extends to be 28-studs across! It makes a great revolving stand for displaying models, such as these beautiful LEGO cakes!

Create cool light effects

260

Build a model with just one window to create an arty photo with dramatic lighting. Shine light in from different directions and distances to make different effects, and experiment with the shape, size and location of the window.

The roof keeps excess light out

Keep your pens and pencils in a LEGO brick box to give them a home as colourful as they are! It is perfect for your paintbrushes and other art gear too. Take it with you wherever you go, so you can paint and draw whenever inspiration strikes you. Just don't forget to take a pad of paper with you as well!

Shining a lamp from further away makes a softer-edged pattern

This fence piece creates the diamond pattern

Shining a lamp from above casts light down on the minifigure

I REALLY NEED TO BUY SOME CURTAINS!

261

Play a game of tiddlywinks

262

To play tiddlywinks, all you need is a target and some discs to jump into it! Use round tiles as your discs, and press down on their edges to make them jump. Play against a friend or against the clock to see how many times you can hit the target!

Make your target using a single piece like this, or a frame made from several plates

Press down with a plate piece to make your tiles jump

If playing against a friend, each of you should choose a colour for your tiles

Smooth tiles line the inside for the lid to slide along

Use lots of different colours to inspire your art!

Smooth tiles run around the lid where it slides beneath the top plates

Pull on this curved plate to open the box

The overhanging plates are placed on bricks that are one-stud thick

A layer of overhanging plates around three of the edges holds the lid in place

STRONG BOX
Find your favourite pencils first of all, to work out how big your box needs to be. Make the base and the lid from two layers of plates each for extra strength, and the sides all two-studs thick – except for where the lid slides on at the top.

Build an art box

263 Start a skiffle band

Ridged slope bricks top this skiffle board

Wide ridges will make a deeper sound

The feet are round bricks

Plates with top clips hold these ladders in place

Smooth tiles allow the ladders to lie flat

The strummer is a round brick with a slide plate on the end

Handle is made from LEGO Technic axles inside axle connectors

Rub a round brick along these musical instruments to make a rattling rhythm! Their up-and-down surfaces produce a rasping sound – just like the chirping of a cricket or the washboards that skiffle bands use to make music.

What's the scariest face you can make? Yikes, that's scary – now try making it with LEGO bricks! These spooky, kooky faces would make great decorations for a haunted house party!

Vampire hair is made from black slope bricks

Vampire's eyes are transparent-red satellite dishes

Build a layer of black behind the eyes of the skull

Scary eyebrows are purple angled plates

Fangs are angled tooth plates

Teeth are white cone pieces

Red plates form a creepy clown mouth

264 Make a set of scary faces

CAN YOU TURN IT UP A BIT?

DIFFERENT STROKES

There are lots of other ways to make LEGO skiffle boards. Antennae, LEGO Technic axles or simply the studs on top of a plate or brick will all make different sounds, as will a different design of strummer to rub along them.

Hold both chopsticks in one hand

The chopsticks are made from two layers of plates with a layer of smooth tiles on top

Start with a pile of differently sized bricks

Make a new pile with the bricks you pick up

Make a pair of LEGO chopsticks and see how many bricks you can pick up with them in just two minutes! Build two pairs to play this game with a friend, or simply try to beat your best score.

AH! I'M NOT A BRICK!

Take a chopstick challenge

265

Make a paperweight decoration on page 129.

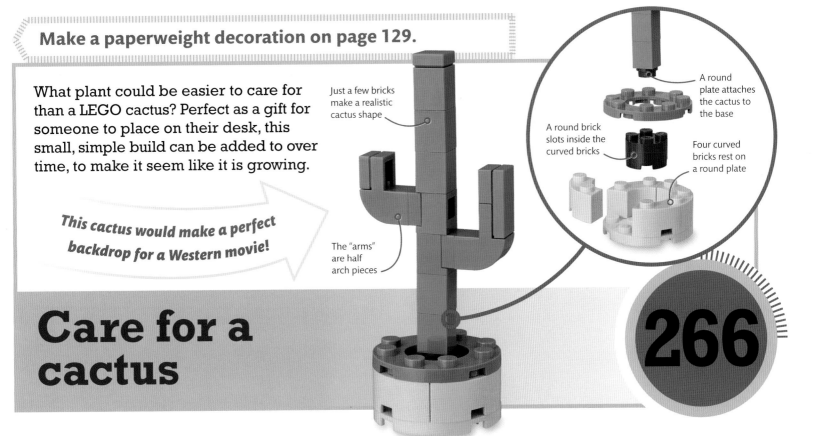

What plant could be easier to care for than a LEGO cactus? Perfect as a gift for someone to place on their desk, this small, simple build can be added to over time, to make it seem like it is growing.

This cactus would make a perfect backdrop for a Western movie!

Just a few bricks make a realistic cactus shape

The "arms" are half arch pieces

A round plate attaches the cactus to the base

A round brick slots inside the curved bricks

Four curved bricks rest on a round plate

Care for a cactus

266

Design your bedroom

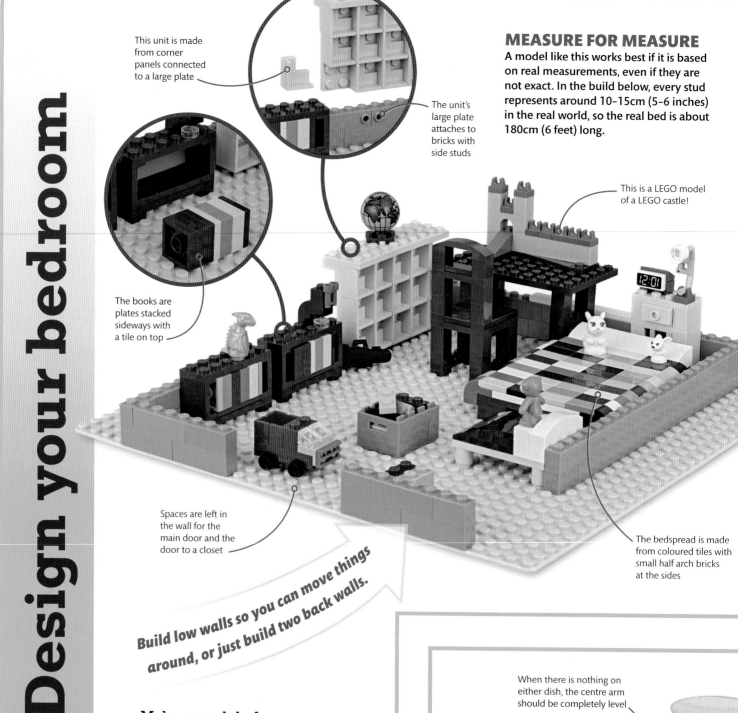

This unit is made from corner panels connected to a large plate

The unit's large plate attaches to bricks with side studs

MEASURE FOR MEASURE
A model like this works best if it is based on real measurements, even if they are not exact. In the build below, every stud represents around 10–15cm (5–6 inches) in the real world, so the real bed is about 180cm (6 feet) long.

This is a LEGO model of a LEGO castle!

The books are plates stacked sideways with a tile on top

Spaces are left in the wall for the main door and the door to a closet

The bedspread is made from coloured tiles with small half arch bricks at the sides

Build low walls so you can move things around, or just build two back walls.

267

Make a model of your own room and you can rearrange the furniture – without any heavy lifting! If you are moving to a new home, it is also a great way to remember your old room, or to work out where your things will go in the new one!

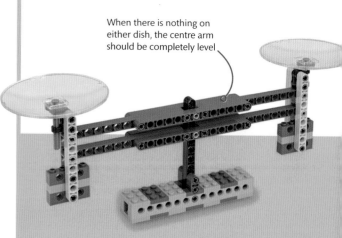

When there is nothing on either dish, the centre arm should be completely level

Make yourself into a minifigure

How would you look if you were a minifigure? Find the face, hair and clothes that most closely match your appearance, and make a mini you! Take a photo and you can use it as your profile picture online!

If you can't find the right hair, wear a hat!

You might find a minifigure that looks just like you, otherwise mix and match different pieces

Play a minifigure mixing game on page 43.

Make a working pair of scales to find out what things weigh in LEGO bricks! Try to guess how many bricks it will take to balance an item before you weigh it, and make a game of it by getting your friends to guess too.

MY DIET WORKED!

BUILDER'S TIP

Make the balance with a broad base so that it does not tip over, and use it to weigh small items only.

Long LEGO Technic pins connect all the beams

Each dish attaches to a LEGO Technic axle and an upside-down round plate

The balance pivots on an upright beam in the very centre

BALANCING ACT

To use the balance, place the item you want to weigh onto one of the dishes. Then add bricks to the other dish until both are level, and the centre arm does not tilt in either direction. Now you know the weight of your item in LEGO bricks!

Build a balance

270 Store your watch in style

Keep a classy wristwatch in tip-top condition by storing it inside a special box. This one has a drawer that slides out of the front, and a detailed model watch on top. Build it for your own watch, or give it as a gift for a family member to keep by their bedside.

The rails slot into slider bricks so they can move back and forth

Plates with rails are built into both sides of the pull-out drawer

The inside of the drawer is lined with smooth tiles

Four curved bricks form the body of the watch

The hands are spanners connected to a plate with pin

The watch strap is made from caterpillar tracks

The handle sides plug into bricks with holes

The handle is made from cylinders linked by LEGO Technic pins

WATCH CLOSELY

Build the box with your watch close by so you can check that it fits inside, and to help you make the model on top look like the real thing. Look after your watch by keeping the box flat when it is in use.

Tiles on the base plate help the drawer slide smoothly

Build a model musical instrument to give as a gift to a music lover. With its smooth lines and cool colours, this xylophone makes a striking decoration!

You could try building some other model instruments, like a keyboard or a tambourine.

271

Plan your perfect playground

272

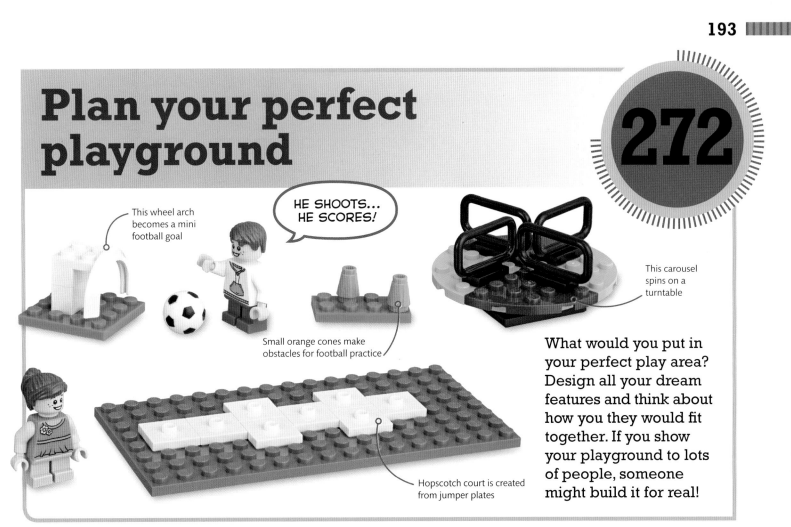

This wheel arch becomes a mini football goal

HE SHOOTS... HE SCORES!

This carousel spins on a turntable

Small orange cones make obstacles for football practice

Hopscotch court is created from jumper plates

What would you put in your perfect play area? Design all your dream features and think about how you they would fit together. If you show your playground to lots of people, someone might build it for real!

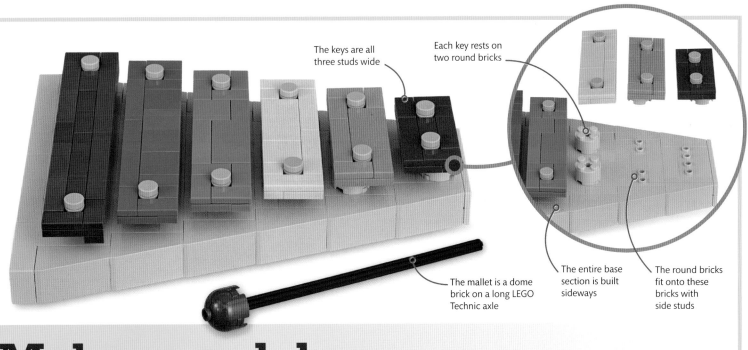

The keys are all three studs wide

Each key rests on two round bricks

The mallet is a dome brick on a long LEGO Technic axle

The entire base section is built sideways

The round bricks fit onto these bricks with side studs

Make a model xylophone

Make your own name

Here is a way to really make a name for yourself! These cool nameplates make a great decoration for your home, and lets everyone know who lives there! Make your full name, your nickname or just your initials. Why not build someone else's name and give it to them as a gift too?

Long tile forms the top of the "M"

Bricks with holes have special studs that make this part of the build work

Jumper plates allow the dark-grey bricks to be positioned half a stud back to make the letters appear engraved

LEGO Technic pins slot into bricks with holes to connect the towers to the nameplate

Slider bricks make the fancy details at the tops and bottoms of the letters

Make your name really stand out with bright colours on a black background.

The dot of the "i" connects to a black angle plate

The bricks at the top of the "n" sit on a plate below

A mix of different bricks and colours make the towers look old and interesting

Alternating 1x2 and 2x2 bricks builds the letters into the background

273

INS AND OUTS

There are endless ways to build your name, and different letter shapes call for different techniques. In the "Simon" build above, the letters stick out from the background. For "Maria", the name is set into the bricks – as if it has been carved into stone!

The base is made from LEGO® Minifigures display stands

M-A-R-I-A...
I'M A SPELLING BEE!

Add your favourite minifigures on top

Smooth tiles on top complete the carved stone look

Light-grey plates and bricks stick out from the middle of the letters

Stack up some good deeds

274

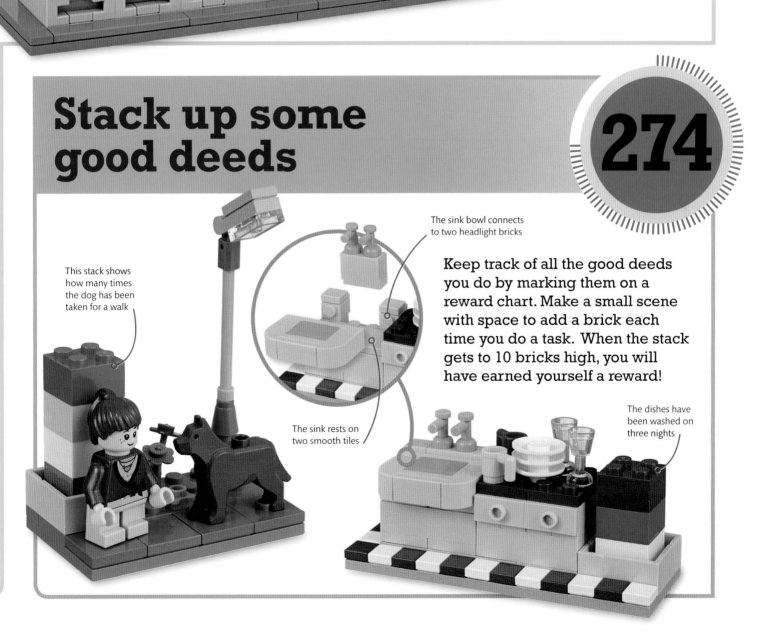

This stack shows how many times the dog has been taken for a walk

The sink bowl connects to two headlight bricks

The sink rests on two smooth tiles

Keep track of all the good deeds you do by marking them on a reward chart. Make a small scene with space to add a brick each time you do a task. When the stack gets to 10 bricks high, you will have earned yourself a reward!

The dishes have been washed on three nights

Recreate a local landmark

275

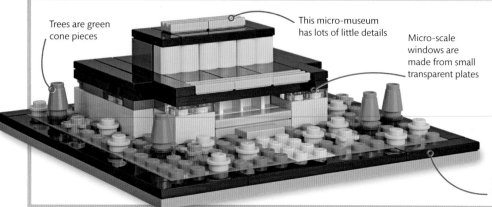

Trees are green cone pieces

This micro-museum has lots of little details

Micro-scale windows are made from small transparent plates

Put your neighbourhood on the map by building a local landmark in the style of a LEGO® Architecture set! Whether it is your school, a museum, a skyscraper or a mansion, use small parts to make it in micro-scale.

LEGO Architecture sets all have black tiled borders

Build a floral buttonhole

Look the part at a fancy event with a LEGO flower to wear in your jacket. Give it a long, thin stem so it will slot into your pocket, and big, bold petals to make it eye-catching. If you don't have a special occasion coming up, why not invent one and invite your friends?

The green clips attach to a round plate with a ring of bars

Each petal is a tile on a plate with clip

OH NO, I FORGOT MY BUTTONHOLE!

The stem is a long LEGO Technic axle

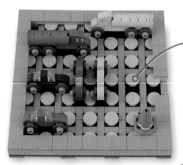

276

Create a whole bunch of flowers on page 126.

PARKING POSITIONS

This game has lots of different solutions, depending on where you position the obstacles. Two starting layouts are shown here. Try to come up with the toughest arrangements you can and challenge your family and friends to solve them.

The round tiles are raised higher than the grey tiles to create the grooves for the vehicles to move in

Starting layout 2

A row of transparent-red tiles marks out the exit route

The board

277

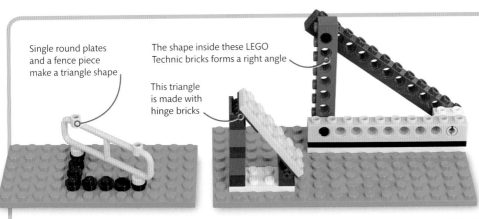

Single round plates and a fence piece make a triangle shape

This triangle is made with hinge bricks

The shape inside these LEGO Technic bricks forms a right angle

How many ways can you make a LEGO triangle? Take a random selection of bricks and see how many three-sided shapes you can build in three minutes. Challenge your friends to do the same, then decide whose triangles are the best!

278

Test yourself with triangles

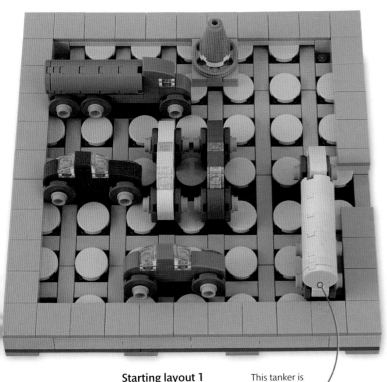

Starting layout 1

This tanker is blocking the exit

Beep beep! The red car needs to get out of this car park! It should be easy – drive in a straight line through the exit on the side. But there are lots of other vehicles in the way! You can slide them around to make a clear route for the red car, but you can't move the traffic cone, and you can't lift vehicles off the board!

Round tiles with holes fit onto bricks with side studs to make the wheels

These round bricks slot onto an axle with a stud end

A plate under each car lifts the wheels clear of the round tiles on the board

Traffic cone is built with a cross shape underneath so that it can't slide

Play the gridlock game

Grow a jewellery tree

Make a beautiful LEGO tree to help you organise your or a family member's jewellery. This tree has lots of places to store necklaces, bracelets and earrings, and it looks pretty even when there is nothing hanging from it!

Use cone pieces for a topmost branch that can also hold rings.

This plate fits onto the middle of a jumper plate and secures the branch at the top

Round plate with hole slots into centre of green plate above

Jewels in the leaves add a touch of sparkle

Upper branches are ideal for hanging necklaces

Half arch brick connects to jumper plate below

The pink branches fit onto green jumper plates

Green plates lock the pink branches in place

Lower branches can support bracelets

Slope bricks form bottom of trunk

BRANCHING OUT
A tall tree like this needs a broad base and a sturdy trunk so that it doesn't fall over. Be sure to add branches on all sides so that the weight is spread around equally, and to lock the branches in place with bricks above and below, especially at the top.

Earrings can hang from these plates with bars

Broad base for extra stability

279

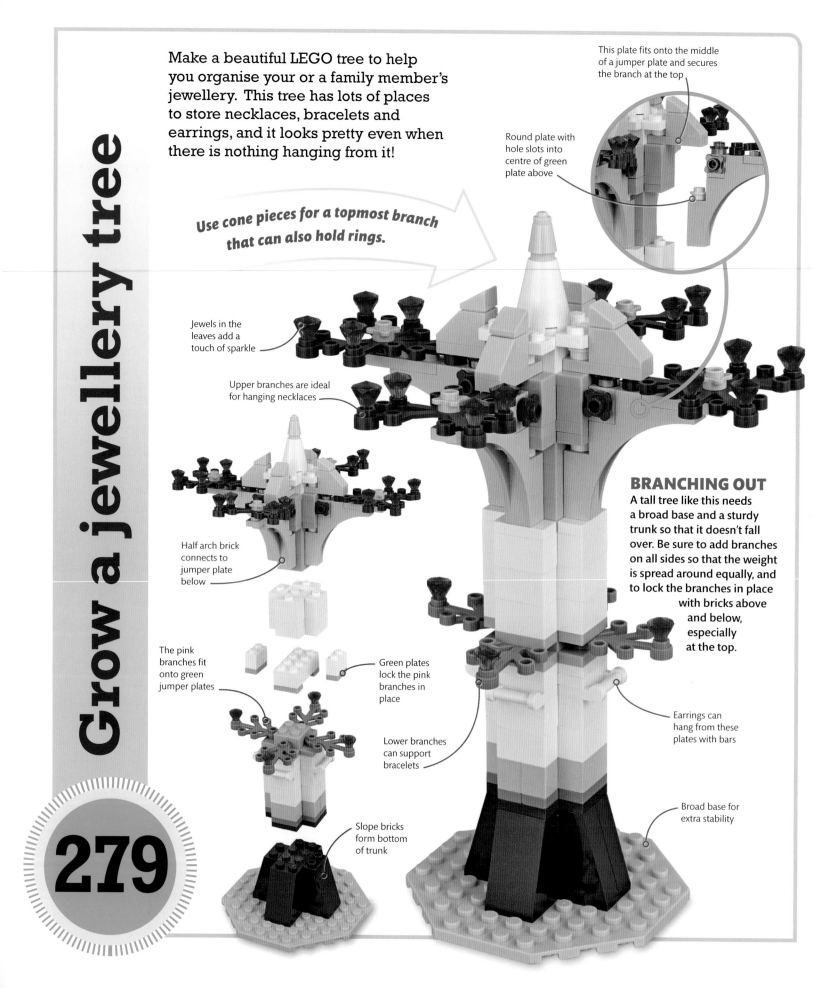

280 Balance a bird

Eyes are made from sideways studs

A plate with bar and a plate with clip connect the shorter, red tail feather

Create a beautiful bird of paradise that can balance on just two tiny talons! Its amazing tail is not just for display – it also acts as a counterweight for its body.

Body is built sideways with studs facing the front

Feet are banana pieces!

Long tail feathers start with a click hinge

Balance your bird on a shelf edge or on your fingertip!

THE SPECIAL BRICK

Plates with click hinges are designed to stay in a fixed position until moved, making them ideal for this kind of precision build.

The end of the tail needs some weight to balance out the body

Click hinge

BALANCING ACT

You'll need to experiment with the angle of the tail to get the balancing act just right, adjusting the click hinges as you go. It should reach further forward than the body above it – but not too far!

See how many minifigures you can stack before they topple over! Minifigures can fit together in all kinds of ingenious ways. For a more difficult challenge, try stacking them against the clock!

Staff slots into diver's flipper

ALL THIS TO CHANGE A LIGHTBULB?

The smaller the base, the tougher the challenge

Stack a minifigure

281

282 Beat the bandits

The game breaks down into 15 sections

This central platform is built as two sections

Blast these bandits in their hideout with this great demolition game! Each section rests on smooth pieces or attaches to a single stud, so a well-placed cannon shot will leave the bad guys with nowhere to hide! How many shots will it take you to bring the whole thing tumbling down?

Try to knock over as many sections as you can with each shot!

The roof is built as a single section

The roof section rests on panel pieces

BUILD IT UP AGAIN
Knocking down the hideout is just half the fun! Finding ways to build it up without making it too strong is a game all by itself. You will need a steady hand to balance the loose sections on the smooth tiles. You should also assemble the model where you plan to knock it down, so you won't have to move it!

Each column stands on a jumper plate – this holds it steady but makes it easy to knock over

The missile has a rubber tip

This cannon is a spring-loaded element

Give yourself one point for each section that you blast away!

The treasure rests on smooth tiles, but is held in place by a single stud

Balancing minifigures on one leg will make them easier to knock over!

283 Never lose your glasses

Can't find your glasses? Try looking on the end of your nose! This funny face is perfect for hanging your spectacles on at night, so you always know where to find them in the morning! If you don't wear glasses, make it as a gift for somebody who does.

Why not make the face look like the person you are building it for?

The eyes are built on white round plates

The glasses arms fit into this rest at the back

Glasses rest on the bridge of the nose

A big moustache adds character to the face

This shaft is a single tower piece

A wide base stops the build from tipping over

Become a zookeeper on page 108.

Build a micro-safari

Make the world's biggest animals with just a few bricks when you build in micro-scale! Set yourself a challenge to see just how small you can make them, and then show off your micro-safari to see if your friends can identify them all!

This giraffe is mostly made from round plates

ARE THESE ANIMALS SMALL, OR AM I VERY BIG?

The elephant's trunk is built on a minifigure neck bracket

This camel is made from just eight pieces!

The rhino's horn is held by a plate with clip

284

285 Make a map of the stars

Brown and yellow pieces look like a fancy frame

The stars are glow-in-the-dark bricks

SPACE SHAPES

Put grey plates between the stars to make the shapes that give the constellations their names. Taurus resembles the horns of a bull, while Scorpio has the curling tail of a scorpion. It can sometimes be difficult to spot the shapes – Sagittarius is supposed to look like an archer, but some people see its top-right area as a teapot!

In the dark, only the stars can be seen

Taurus

Scorpio

Sagittarius

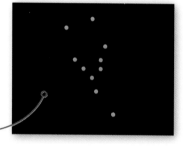

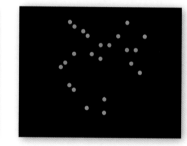

Start a brick toss tournament

286

Take three plastic storage tubs and spread them out as targets for a game of brick-toss! Make each tub worth a different number of points, and give each player their own colour of bricks so you can count up the scores. Everyone has 30 seconds to toss as many LEGO pieces as they can!

The farthest tub is worth the most points

Line your tubs up or spread them out

All players should stay behind a marker line

Raise your eyes to the skies and search for different stars with help from these LEGO constellations! Use books and websites to find the names and shapes of different patterns of stars, then build glow-in-the-dark LEGO versions that you can use when you are looking for the real thing!

Build a stylish pot

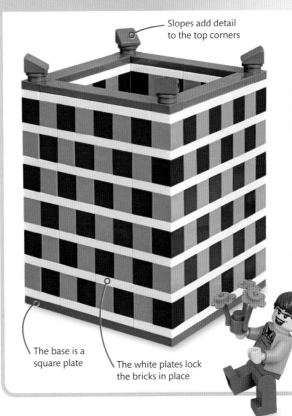

Slopes add detail to the top corners

The base is a square plate

The white plates lock the bricks in place

287

It is always useful to have a pot handy – you can put anything you like in it! To make it stylish as well as useful, build it with a simple but striking repeating pattern. This one has blue chequers made from small bricks, with stripes built out of white plates to hold it all together.

I THINK THIS VASE IS A LITTLE TOO BIG!

Turn your whole room into a LEGO racetrack by making obstacles for your cars out of furniture, shoes and whatever else you can find! Build a start and finish line, a pit stop and a winners' podium. Mark out areas that don't have any obstacles using cones and long bricks as crash barriers.

White and black bricks create a chequered flag effect

This starting line has lights and loudspeakers

Include some minifigures to be the pit crew

Pit stops have tools, air tanks, fuel and spare parts

Mark out areas with cone bricks

MY JOB IS VERY TIRING!

Turn a room into a racetrack

288

289

Make a working winch

An axle connector matches the width of the reel on the other side

The thread is tied through the ball at the top of the hook

This strong A-frame is all one piece

The end of the thread is tied onto this reel

The reel slots onto this LEGO Technic axle

Why bend over to pick things up, when you can use a LEGO winch instead? This cool crane mechanism makes a great desktop toy, and is a fun way to tidy up! It can also be used to lower minifigures into exciting adventures – and to hoist them back up again in the nick of time!

Turn these small gears on either end to work the winch

The A-frame can be put in several positions, thanks to these click hinge cylinders

Make your crane with a broad, flat base

Flip up the brake to stop any items falling

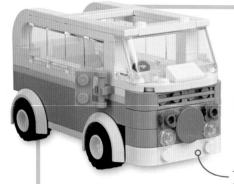

Swapping the flower pieces for round tiles fits the LEGO City style

Use bold colours to rebuild a LEGO Friends set to look like it comes from LEGO City.

This LEGO Friends minibus is part of the Summer Riding Camp set (3185)

Give your favourite LEGO set a makeover by rebuilding it in your favourite colours! Follow the original instruction booklet as closely as you can using your new colour scheme, and be creative when it comes to any parts that you don't have in those colours.

This LEGO City sports car is built all in red

Make your model as colourful as you like!

Give a set a colour change

290

Go to the movies

291

With a tablet in place, the show can begin

This top bar holds the front and back of the frame together

Slide a tablet computer into the frame to watch a movie.

I LOVE A GOOD BRICK FLICK!

THE BIG SCREEN

Start your cinema by measuring the height of your tablet in bricks, and its width and depth in studs. Check that the tablet fits into your build as you go along, and that your build is strong and stable enough to hold it upright securely. Get permission to use the tablet if it doesn't belong to you.

Tall slope bricks at the front and back of the frame make sturdy feet to hold it in place

Side pillars go in front of and behind the tablet

The seating is built onto a broad base of overlapping plates to make the whole build stable

The long edge of the tablet rests on a row of smooth tiles

Take your minifigures to the movies with this working cinema screen! It is built to hold a tablet computer, so you can watch real movies in its brick-built frame. All you need to do is grab some popcorn, take a seat behind the minifigures, then sit back and enjoy the show!

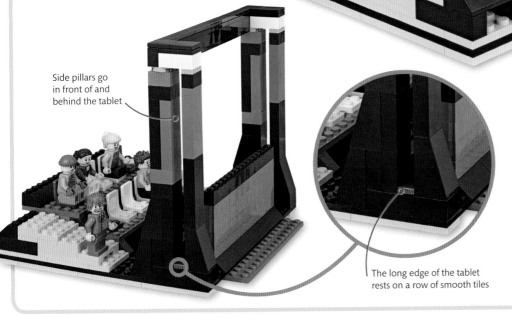

205

292 Build a LEGO pinwheel

Put this pinwheel on a flat surface and watch as the breeze spins it round and round! Build a simple pattern on the blades and see it become a blur when a strong breeze really gets going!

Make more pinwheels with different parts to see which ones spin fastest.

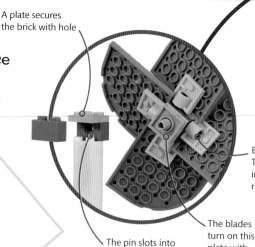

A plate secures the brick with hole

Black LEGO Technic pins slot into plates with rings beneath

The pin slots into a brick with hole

The blades turn on this plate with pin below

Angle the blades to catch the breeze

This tall column is all one piece

Make a winter wonderland

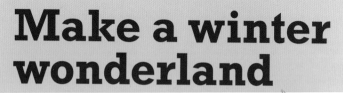

I SEE YOU'VE DRESSED UP AS WELL

293

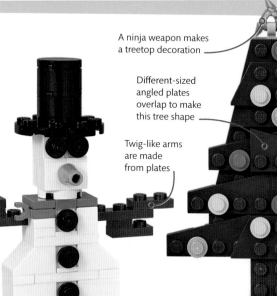

A ninja weapon makes a treetop decoration

Different-sized angled plates overlap to make this tree shape

Twig-like arms are made from plates

Start with a long brown plate and build the green sides onto it

These penguins look similar, but use lots of different parts

Warm up for winter by filling your home with seasonal decorations! It doesn't matter what time of year it is – a few builds themed around snow and celebrations can inspire festive feelings all year round!

Discover decorations for springtime on pages 74–75.

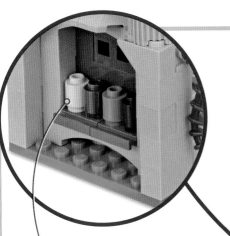

The secret colour code sits on a shelf built into the back of the gate

Can you beat the gatekeeper and find the secret code to enter the castle? You have eight chances as you cross the drawbridge, and the gatekeeper will tell you if you are right or wrong. If you guess correctly, you become the gatekeeper, and can challenge another player!

294

Beat the gatekeeper

Making a longer drawbridge will mean the adventurer can have more guesses!

HOW TO PLAY

1 One player is the gatekeeper and sits behind the doors at the end of the drawbridge. The other player is the adventurer, who must try to guess the secret entry code before they reach the doors.

2 The gatekeeper lines up four different-coloured round bricks behind the gate without the adventurer seeing. The adventurer then has eight chances to guess the sequence of colours.

3 Guesses are made by setting out a sequence of round bricks on the drawbridge. The gatekeeper lets the adventurer know whether they are right or wrong by placing round tiles on both sides of the water on the same row.

4 A green plate indicates a round brick of the right colour, but in the wrong place in the sequence. A red plate means a brick of the right colour is also in the right place. No plates mean there are no matches.

5 The gatekeeper wins if the sequence is not guessed on the eighth go, when the adventurer runs out of drawbridge. The adventurer wins if they guess the sequence correctly.

It took this player five tries to find the right sequence

The order of the plates in the water should match the order of the guesses

These chests are for storing the round bricks

On the first go, the player guessed three colours correctly, but only one in the correct position

Make a photo mosaic

BUILDER'S TIP

Experiment with the brightness and contrast settings on a digital photo for an image that will be clear in LEGO form.

Build an amazing mosaic by copying a photo from your computer. Decide how wide you want your mosaic to be, then resize your photo to that number of pixels across. The photo will turn into a grid of squares, just like LEGO bricks, which you can copy using the real thing!

Choose a photo with clear light and shade and not many small details.

This photo of builder Drew was the starting point for the mosaic

A mosaic like this can be built with bricks or plates

Use large pieces for areas of solid colour

If you can't see the face straightaway, try squinting!

PIXEL PERFECT

This mosaic has been built on a 32x32 base plate, copied from a square photo resized on a computer to be 32 pixels across. Editing software was also used to make the photo have just four colours. If you don't have a computer, you can also break a picture down into squares by using a ruler to draw a grid on a copy of it.

295

Uncover a magical mosaic on page 56.

296

Circular pieces are a single LEGO element

Use small pieces to record your number of wins

Play a minifigure guessing game

297

Make a mystery box and play a guessing game with your friends by hiding a minifigure inside. See how quickly they can guess the identity of your chosen minifigure by asking questions that can only be answered with "yes" or "no"!

DO I HAVE WINGS? YES!

Tiles line the top of the box

The question mark is made from plates and 1x1 bricks

Corner plates hold the box together at the top

The plain sides of the box are large wall pieces

Build a noughts-and-crosses board

Build a LEGO game of noughts and crosses using Xs and Os, or anything you like! It could be LEGO Friends pets versus flowers, or LEGO® NEXO KNIGHTS™ heroes versus monsters! Make a grid to match your theme and challenge your friends to a thrilling game!

Spikes make a border of trees

Make five pieces for each player

This board is built like a garden with spaces for flowers and animals

Jumper plates help secure the playing pieces

HOW TO PLAY

1 Two players take turns placing one of their markers in any of the spaces on the board.

2 The game is won when a player gets three of their markers in a row – horizontally, vertically or diagonally.

298 Design a dreamcatcher

Hang a LEGO dreamcatcher above your bed and enjoy sweet dreams all through the night! Start with a wheel or other round shape, then add strings of beads made from round bricks, plant pieces and lengths of thread. According to legend, bad dreams will be caught in the beads before they reach you and disappear by morning!

BUILDER'S TIP

Packing the bricks tightly onto short strings will enable you to bend them into curving shapes.

Tying the thread can be fiddly! Ask an adult to help you.

Tie each thread onto the cartwheel

Small LEGO Technic pieces add variety

Use pieces with holes for the thread to run through

Race through the ruins

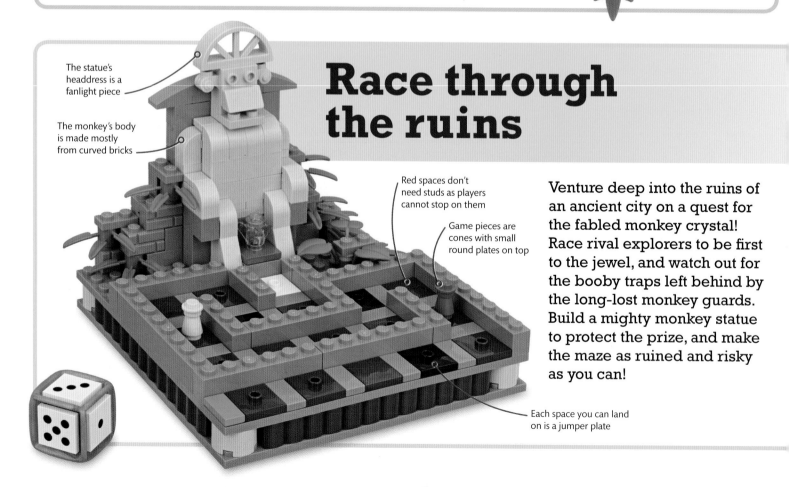

The statue's headdress is a fanlight piece

The monkey's body is made mostly from curved bricks

Red spaces don't need studs as players cannot stop on them

Game pieces are cones with small round plates on top

Each space you can land on is a jumper plate

Venture deep into the ruins of an ancient city on a quest for the fabled monkey crystal! Race rival explorers to be first to the jewel, and watch out for the booby traps left behind by the long-lost monkey guards. Build a mighty monkey statue to protect the prize, and make the maze as ruined and risky as you can!

Say it with a sign

300

A hinged handle can be used to pull the advert out of the frame

The handle disappears into the frame when not in use

Lights can tilt on hinges to shine on the billboard at night

Make an advertising billboard for your LEGO City scenes – or simply to get your message across! You can build any image or slogan to go inside this billboard frame – from a call for more surprise parties to a campaign in favour of fewer trips to the dentist!

WHY DO I KEEP BUYING GIFTS?!

The message of this advert is that minifigures should buy gifts for each other

The advert has smooth tiles on the top

The platform gives a minifigure worker somewhere to stand when the poster needs to be changed

299

HOW TO PLAY

1. Players start at the turquoise line and take turns rolling the die, moving forward the number of spaces indicated.

2. If you land on a red square, you must move back one space. If you land on a black square, miss a turn. If you land on the other player, they must move back one space.

3. To win, roll the right number on the die to reach the white square to claim the treasure! If you miss, try again on your next turn.

CHANGE OF SCENE

The advert is built separately from the frame, so that it can be swapped for another image. The frame has a row of smooth tiles inside to help the adverts to slide in and out easily. The advert image is built up using lots of small plates, but you could also draw an advert on paper or card and slide that into the frame.

Make a neon sign that really shines on page 109.

Play a pencil prank

Play a fun trick on your friends with these incredibly realistic-looking LEGO pencils. Build your pencil using the tips below, place it in your friend's pencil case, then sit back and watch…

Make sure all the side slots face the same way, so that they are easy to hide.

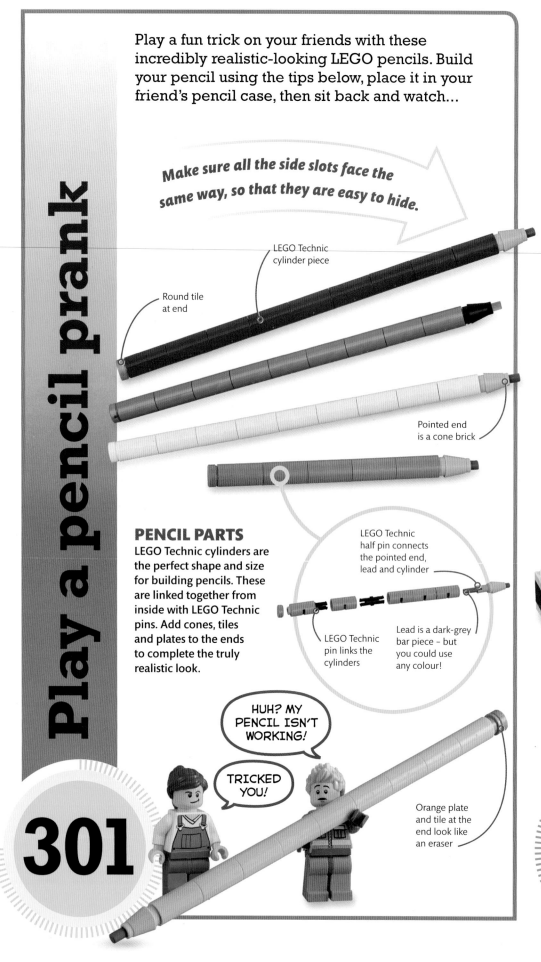

LEGO Technic cylinder piece

Round tile at end

Pointed end is a cone brick

PENCIL PARTS

LEGO Technic cylinders are the perfect shape and size for building pencils. These are linked together from inside with LEGO Technic pins. Add cones, tiles and plates to the ends to complete the truly realistic look.

LEGO Technic half pin connects the pointed end, lead and cylinder

LEGO Technic pin links the cylinders

Lead is a dark-grey bar piece – but you could use any colour!

HUH? MY PENCIL ISN'T WORKING!

TRICKED YOU!

Orange plate and tile at the end look like an eraser

301

Here's a game of skill and steely nerves for any number of players. The aim of the game is to remove the blocks without tipping the tower over – but you don't get to choose which colour of block you have to remove!

HOW TO PLAY

1 The first player spins the colour picker and has to remove a block of the selected colour from the tower, using only one hand.

2 Each player repeats step one in turn, keeping each block they remove.

3 The game ends when a player causes one or more blocks to fall from the tower! The winner is the player who removed the most blocks from the tower before it fell.

Turntable piece allows the colour picker's arm to spin

302

This central column of bricks is built into the base

Loose blocks are arranged around the column

Build a skeleton

Corner slope brick for front of forehead

Make a skeleton that can be posed in lots of different ways. Place it against a dark background and it takes on a spookier look – all the joints seem to disappear!

Grey round plates between white plates form the vertebrae and ribcage

Turntables allow the hips and skull to rotate.

Make large feet so your skeleton can stand up.

Ball-and-socket plates are used for the knees, ankles, shoulders, elbows and wrists

This solid layer of black bricks adds weight to the base

Column fits onto four exposed studs in the centre of the base.

STRAIGHT DOWN THE MIDDLE

Only the white central column of the tower is secured with studs. This should be the tallest part of the game, and should be built onto a broad, stable base. Build a smooth layer of tiles for the bottom layer of game blocks.

Take on a tumbling tower

Each block is a brick with a tile on top

304 Make a model of your home

Find out more about your own home by building it out of LEGO bricks. Look at a photo of the outside as you build, and recreate details you may never have noticed before. Add objects in all the windows and don't forget to include yourself and your family in minifigure form!

This micro-scale house is just five bricks high!

Try to get the shape right and don't worry about having the perfect colours

If you don't have transparent bricks, leave open spaces for the windows

Each room is packed with little details

Inverted slope bricks make curtains behind this window

This home even has a mouse beneath the floorboards!

I'M MOVING IN STRAIGHT AWAY!

CUSTOM-BUILT HOMES
There are lots of ways to build your home with LEGO bricks. You could make a complete model with rooms inside, or you could just build the front as it looks from outside. You could even make a flat floor plan, marking out the walls with plates, and then adding furniture to all the rooms.

Design your bedroom on page 190.

Recreate a build with your eyes closed

305

Let your fingers do the work by building a model without looking at it! Take a simple build, break it apart, and then put it back together by touch alone. To stop yourself from peeking, wear a scarf as a blindfold.

Make sure any identical parts are all the same colour

Tusks fit onto plates with clips

DON'T WORRY – I WON'T BITE!

Try to memorise the shape of your model before you try to rebuild it

1x4 bricks are used here, so that they are not confused with the 2x4 brown bricks above

306

Build the strongest bridge

What's the longest, strongest bridge you can build with a set number of bricks? Try to span a short distance by using the same type and number of pieces in different ways and see which bridges stay up and which ones bend and break!

Tightly packed bricks are strong but don't go far

This bridge blends the best parts of the other two

This bridge is long but not very strong

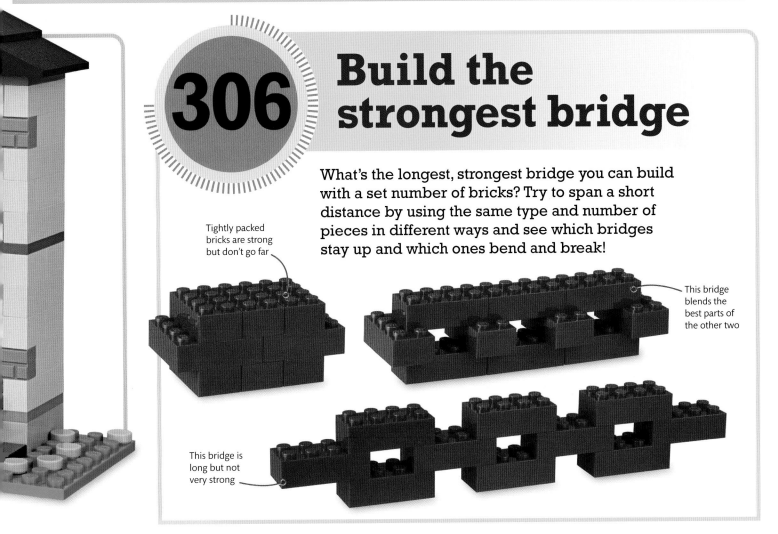

307 Take the 2x2 challenge

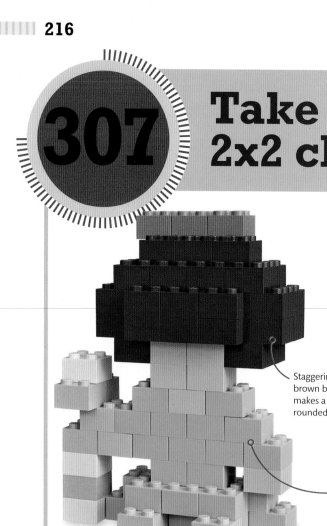

What can you build using only 2x2 bricks? Anything, if you put your mind to it! Gather together all the 2x2 bricks you can find, and build something big, blocky and bold! Don't be put off by not having any curved or flat shapes – this girl's curly hair and the long, flat sword are both made with nothing but 2x2s!

Staggering the brown bricks makes a rounded shape

Don't try for lots of detail - a few simple shapes make a cool model.

Each green brick overlaps the ones below it to bond them all together

Centre bricks at the top and bottom of the sword to lock it together

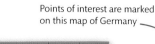

Points of interest are marked on this map of Germany

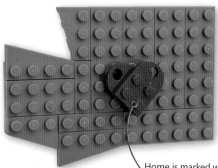

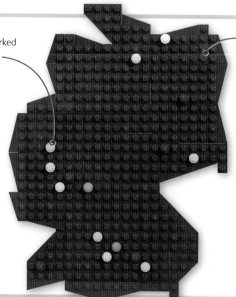

Different angled plates are used to make the shape of the country

Build a model map of your city, state, country or continent, and you can use it to mark all the places you have been, and the places where you would like to go. Make models of lots of different countries to find out about their shapes and sizes, and you will be on your way to a map of the world!

Home is marked with a heart shape on this model of Washington state, USA

308 Mark your territory on a LEGO map

Express yourself in a funny face race

309

Take a big pile of bricks and build as many funny faces as you can in just five minutes! Keep them small and simple so you have time to make lots of different ones. Get your friends to join in, and you can compare funny faces when the time is up.

I'M A HEAD OF THE PACK! GEDDIT?

These heads would be a great starting point for some funny robots!

Give each face eyes and a mouth

BUILDER'S TIP

Build the double helix flat, and then twist it gently into a spiral. Display it standing upright on its feet.

See the molecule that makes us all by building a DNA double helix! There is DNA inside every living thing, but it is so small that it can only be seen with a special microscope. Making a scaled-up model lets you see its pretty spiral shape and the chemical pairs (called base pairs) that make you who you are!

Each 2x2 plate represents a chemical in the DNA strand

Each chemical forms a pair with a chemical on the other strand

Strands on both sides are made from ball-and-socket plates

The plates are linked by cylinders, held in place with LEGO Technic pins

These plates make feet for the spiral to stand on

There are three billion base pairs like this in every human being!

310 Build a DNA double helix

Build a flappy bird

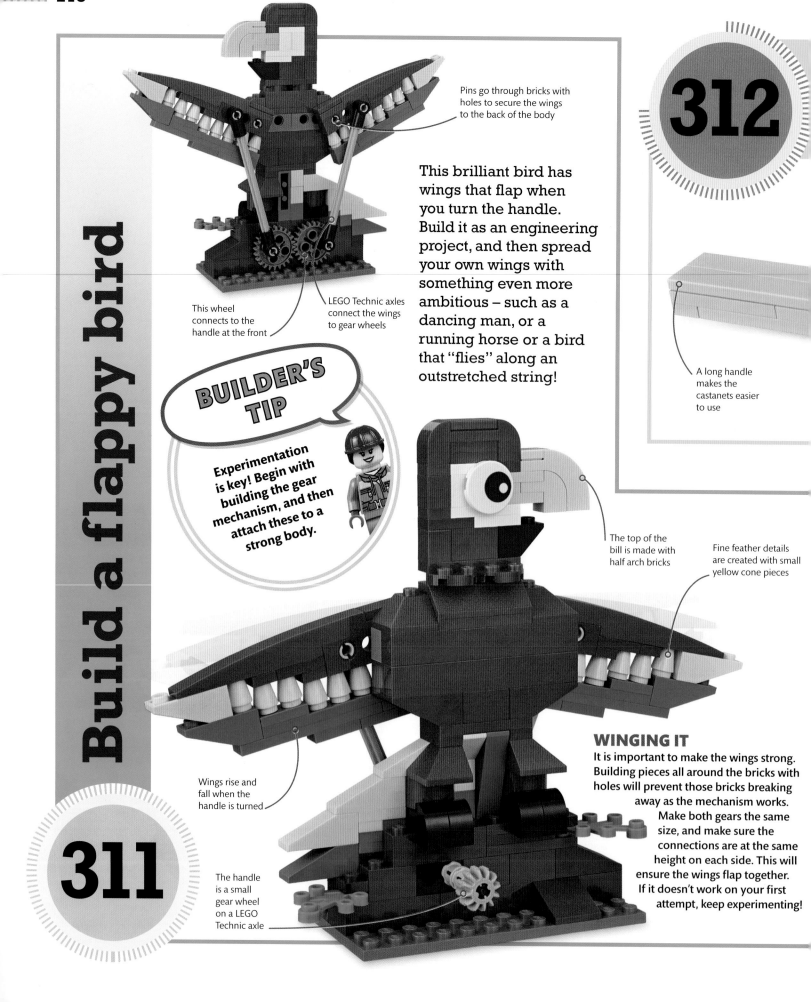

Pins go through bricks with holes to secure the wings to the back of the body

312

This brilliant bird has wings that flap when you turn the handle. Build it as an engineering project, and then spread your own wings with something even more ambitious – such as a dancing man, or a running horse or a bird that "flies" along an outstretched string!

This wheel connects to the handle at the front

LEGO Technic axles connect the wings to gear wheels

A long handle makes the castanets easier to use

BUILDER'S TIP

Experimentation is key! Begin with building the gear mechanism, and then attach these to a strong body.

The top of the bill is made with half arch bricks

Fine feather details are created with small yellow cone pieces

Wings rise and fall when the handle is turned

WINGING IT
It is important to make the wings strong. Building pieces all around the bricks with holes will prevent those bricks breaking away as the mechanism works. Make both gears the same size, and make sure the connections are at the same height on each side. This will ensure the wings flap together. If it doesn't work on your first attempt, keep experimenting!

311

The handle is a small gear wheel on a LEGO Technic axle

Create a new sound

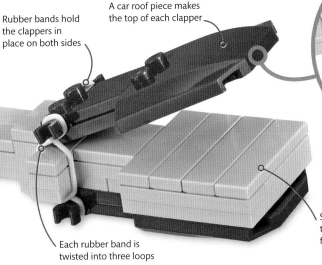

Rubber bands hold the clappers in place on both sides

A car roof piece makes the top of each clapper

Each rubber band is twisted into three loops

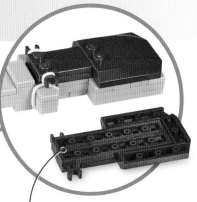

The bottom clapper attaches upside down

Smooth tiles stop the top clapper from getting stuck

THE SPECIAL BRICK

Bricks are not the only useful LEGO pieces! Some LEGO Technic sets come with rubber bands that are just the right size and strength for LEGO building.

Rattle out a rhythm with some clicking castanets. Shake them as fast as you can – and add an awesome new noise to your LEGO band!

Make more musical instruments on page 188.

Balance a plate pyramid

313

Try making towers with longer plates and shorter ones to see which work best.

Can you make a pyramid just by balancing LEGO plates? You will need a steady hand and lots of patience! See how high you can stack your plates in a triangle tower – then try to beat your best height against the clock!

Use plates that are all the same size

BUILDER'S TIP

You could build your tower on a LEGO base plate – its studs will help to stabilise the bottom layer.

314 Transform a box of tissues

The hole in the top is made with four angled plates

Two layers of plates form a strong top

Make a boring box of tissues into a dazzling decoration with a covering of LEGO bricks! This brightly coloured build has different designs on all four sides, and is open at the bottom so it can slip over the top of a regular box of tissues.

A heart makes a simple but striking decoration

Add your initial to one side of the box

Bricks with side studs hold the curved slopes in place

The apples on this tree fit onto bricks with side studs

This curving pattern is made from sideways curved slopes held together by plates

Look through your LEGO windows and be inspired to decorate your buildings in new ways. Try adding interesting pieces to standard LEGO windows or design frames from scratch – then create the buildings that you think they should belong to!

Have a look at some real buildings, then try to recreate their windows using LEGO bricks!

315

SOMETHING TO SNEEZE AT

Different brands of tissue come in differently shaped boxes, so start your build by getting hold of a box and working out how big your LEGO cover needs to be. Decide how you want to decorate each side before you begin, so you can build them all up together.

316 Take on a farmyard building challenge

Lock horns with the rest of your herd in this udderly amazing building challenge! Begin by sitting with your friends around a big pile of LEGO pieces. Set a timer to 10 minutes, and then start building. See who can build the funniest farm animal before the time runs out!

You could try using other themes for this challenge – why not build cars or scary monsters instead?

THIS REALLY GETS MY GOAT!

The goat's horns are robot claws on tap pieces

Slot a head and tail on with LEGO Technic pins

To build animals like these, use bricks with holes at both ends of the animal's body

All the animals' legs are small round bricks, with small round plates for feet

Horns are held on by clips with plates

Add head details to a sideways brick with side studs

Build a fancy floor on page 128.

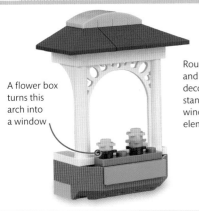

A flower box turns this arch into a window

Round pieces and slopes decorate this standard window element

Four window pieces behind special half arch bricks make this interesting shape

A wheel arch creates a canopy over this window

Sideways transparent plates give a pebbled glass effect

Open up a world of windows

This end has a smooth tiled "top"

The plates fit on side studs at one end only

317 Build a memory box

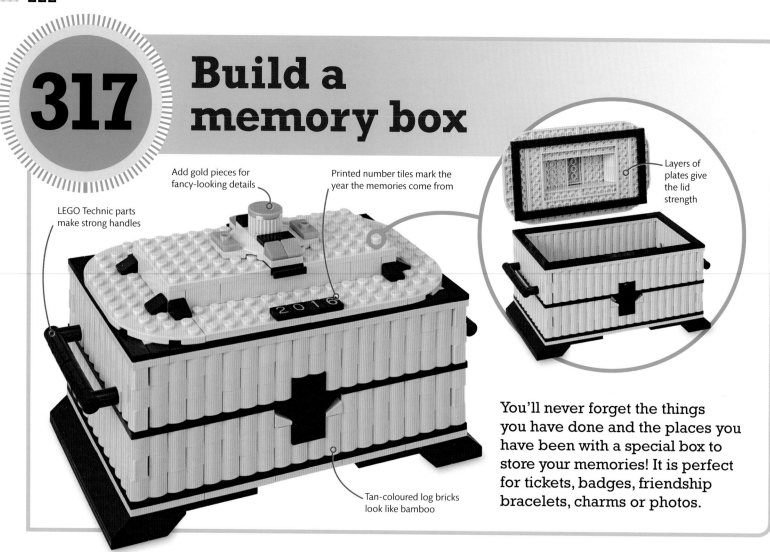

LEGO Technic parts make strong handles

Add gold pieces for fancy-looking details

Printed number tiles mark the year the memories come from

Layers of plates give the lid strength

Tan-coloured log bricks look like bamboo

You'll never forget the things you have done and the places you have been with a special box to store your memories! It is perfect for tickets, badges, friendship bracelets, charms or photos.

318 Let it snow, let it snow!

Build some beautiful snowflakes and hang them around your home as a winter decoration. No two snowflakes are ever alike, so make each one in a different way! These snowflakes are very different, but all have six-way symmetry.

A hexagonal LEGO Technic piece is the starting point for this snowflake

Flag pieces make delicate ends

Transparent plates add an icy sparkle

Six connected hinge plates create a hexagonal shape

Pick a colour and play Reversi

319

Try and think two steps ahead of your opponent, or risk losing all your pieces in the blink of an eye! The aim of the game is to fill the board with your colour – black or white – but the counters are double-sided and keep getting turned over!

Try and predict your opponent's next move – and block it!

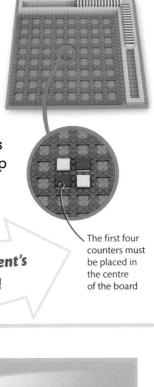

The first four counters must be placed in the centre of the board

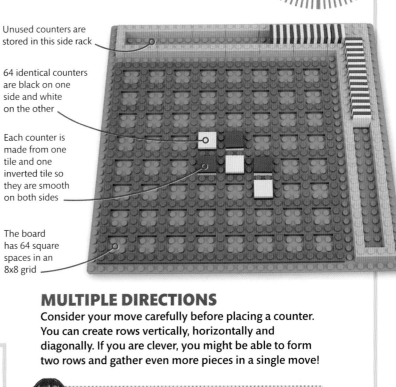

Unused counters are stored in this side rack

64 identical counters are black on one side and white on the other

Each counter is made from one tile and one inverted tile so they are smooth on both sides

The board has 64 square spaces in an 8x8 grid

MULTIPLE DIRECTIONS

Consider your move carefully before placing a counter. You can create rows vertically, horizontally and diagonally. If you are clever, you might be able to form two rows and gather even more pieces in a single move!

HOW TO PLAY

1. Each player plays as one of the two colours, black and white. The players take turns laying counters with their colour face up. For the first four moves, both players must play their counters in the four centre squares of the board. Black is first to play.

2. On the fifth move, black must place a counter so that a white piece is in between two black counters. The white counter is then turned over to become black and the move ends.

3. Play continues in this way, with each player trapping one or more counters of the other colour on each move. Any counters caught in a straight line between two of the opposite colour are turned over. Lines can be formed horizontally, vertically or diagonally.

4. If a player cannot move because there is no way to trap one of their opponent's pieces, the turn passes back to the other player. If a move is possible, you must play it.

5. Play continues until the board is full, or until neither player can move. The winner is the player whose colour is facing up on the most squares.

Overlap hinge plates to make the centre rings and petal shapes of these flakes.

Slope bricks attach to bricks with side studs underneath the grey plates

320 Build a bedside lamp

This bright idea is just the thing if you have a lightbulb moment in the night! Keep it by your bedside and its special LEGO light brick will bring a glow to your room while you write down your latest brilliant building plans!

Stacked transparent plates make the domed top

The light brick is fitted sideways between a brick with side studs and two headlight bricks

The light shines through transparent bricks on all four sides

A slot in the side lets you see the switch in action

Push this switch to turn the light on and off

A thick column of bricks keeps the lamp steady

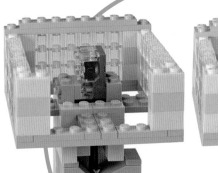

The light is off when the axle is between these two slope bricks

Pushing the switch makes the axle move upwards, switching on the light

The base is the same width as the top of the lamp

THE SPECIAL BRICK

Light bricks have an LED light inside, and a cross-hole in the back, for adding a LEGO Technic axle as a switch.

LIGHT AND SHADE
You don't need this many transparent pieces to make a LEGO lamp. A top built with standard plates will act as a shade, directing the glow through the clear bricks at the sides and the open spaces below the light brick.

Start a friendship chain

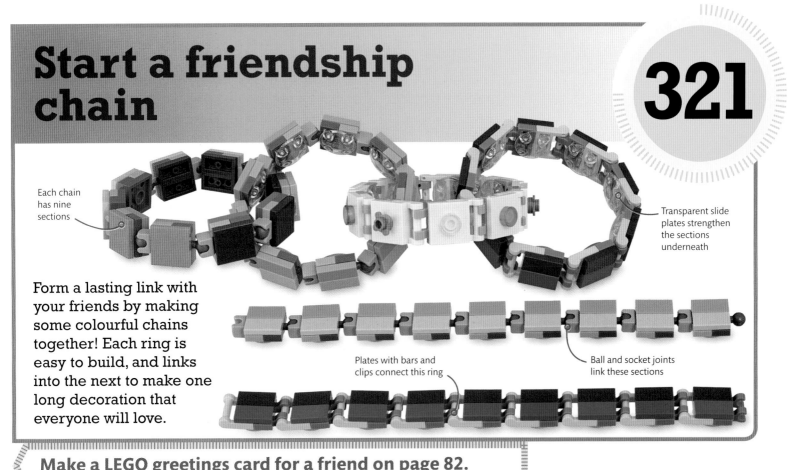

Each chain has nine sections

Transparent slide plates strengthen the sections underneath

Form a lasting link with your friends by making some colourful chains together! Each ring is easy to build, and links into the next to make one long decoration that everyone will love.

Plates with bars and clips connect this ring

Ball and socket joints link these sections

Make a LEGO greetings card for a friend on page 82.

WHERE ARE THE REINS ON THIS THING?!

The rocket's nose is a slope brick

The engines attach to plates on the rocket's side

Jet engine pieces make great rocket parts!

Give your favourite minifigures a twist by mixing them with the most unlikely modes of transportation. Build a spaceship for a sheriff, make a jet ski for a jester or simply put a spaceman on a horse!

ONWARD, FAITHFUL STEED!

Have you ever seen a knight riding a moped?

Mix up your minifigure transportation

323 Build a brigade of bugs

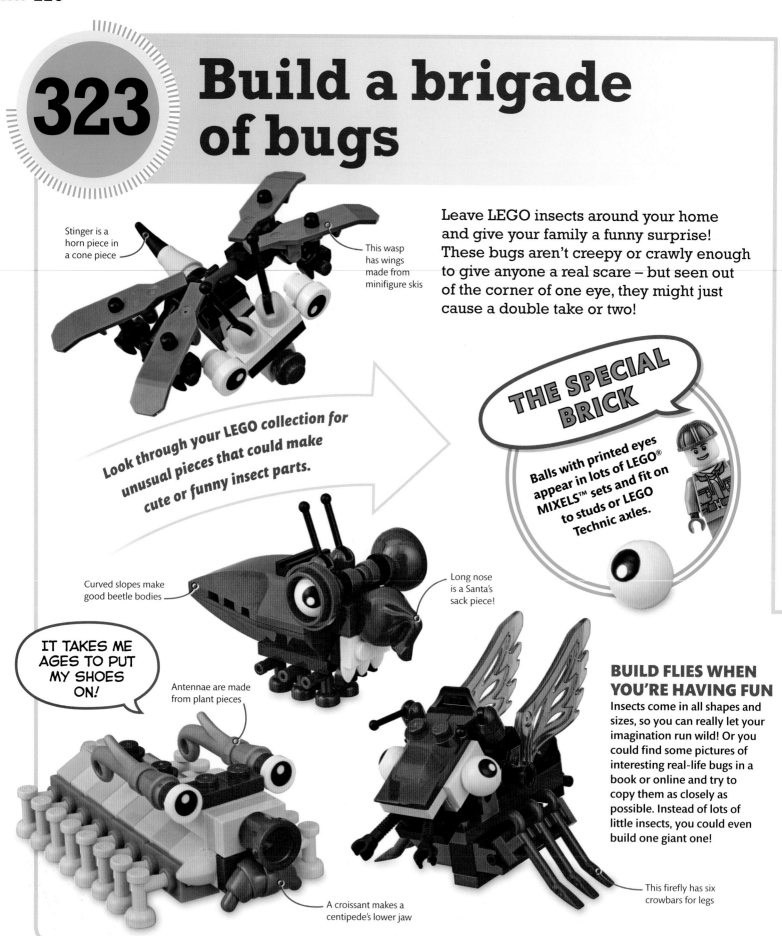

Stinger is a horn piece in a cone piece

This wasp has wings made from minifigure skis

Leave LEGO insects around your home and give your family a funny surprise! These bugs aren't creepy or crawly enough to give anyone a real scare – but seen out of the corner of one eye, they might just cause a double take or two!

Look through your LEGO collection for unusual pieces that could make cute or funny insect parts.

THE SPECIAL BRICK

Balls with printed eyes appear in lots of LEGO® MIXELS™ sets and fit on to studs or LEGO Technic axles.

Curved slopes make good beetle bodies

Long nose is a Santa's sack piece!

IT TAKES ME AGES TO PUT MY SHOES ON!

Antennae are made from plant pieces

BUILD FLIES WHEN YOU'RE HAVING FUN

Insects come in all shapes and sizes, so you can really let your imagination run wild! Or you could find some pictures of interesting real-life bugs in a book or online and try to copy them as closely as possible. Instead of lots of little insects, you could even build one giant one!

A croissant makes a centipede's lower jaw

This firefly has six crowbars for legs

266

324 Play a game of super pairs!

The lids have plates underneath to stop them sliding around

Each lid is a plate with a brick for a handle

Make the handles brightly coloured so they stand out

Choose distinctive pieces so that they are easier to remember

"Dangerous" dynamite piece

Once you have placed the items, you should spin the board a few times so that no one can cheat!

The walls of the board are topped with smooth tiles, so that the lids lift off easily

Super pairs is a tricky game that tests your memory to its limits! The board is full of pairs of objects, and the aim of the game is to remember which square each object is in, so that you can find its pair. Be warned, though, as making the wrong choice can have very serious consequences!

The eyes slot onto a short axle that fits into a plate with ring above

Slugs and grubs are easy to build with just a few pieces

Antennae attach to a brick with side studs

I'M SLEEPY! WHERE'S MY CATER-PILLOW?

This caterpillar has a small arch brick for a body

HOW TO PLAY

1. Each player takes it in turns to remove two lids. If the two pieces underneath the lids match, then the player gets to keep the pieces. The player then puts the lids back on the board.

2. If a player uncovers only one of the dangerous dynamite pieces, then their opponent gets two turns. If a player uncovers both dynamite pieces, then they get two turns (and they keep the two dynamite pieces, too)!

3. The player with the most pairs once they've all been found wins the game.

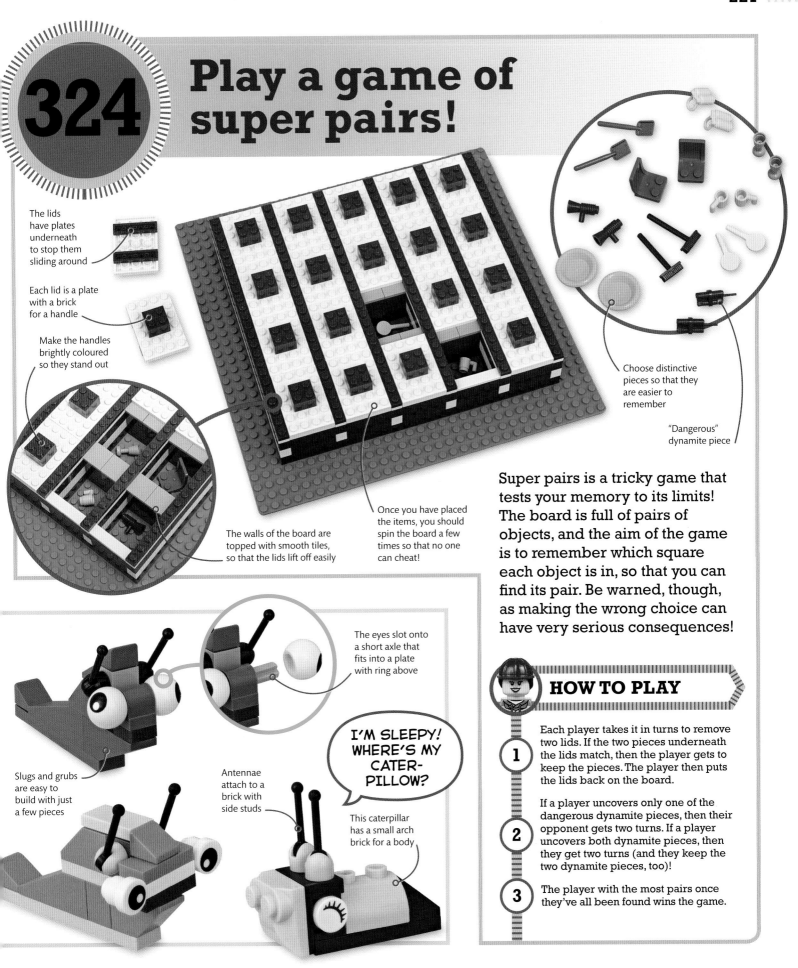

325 Play croquet

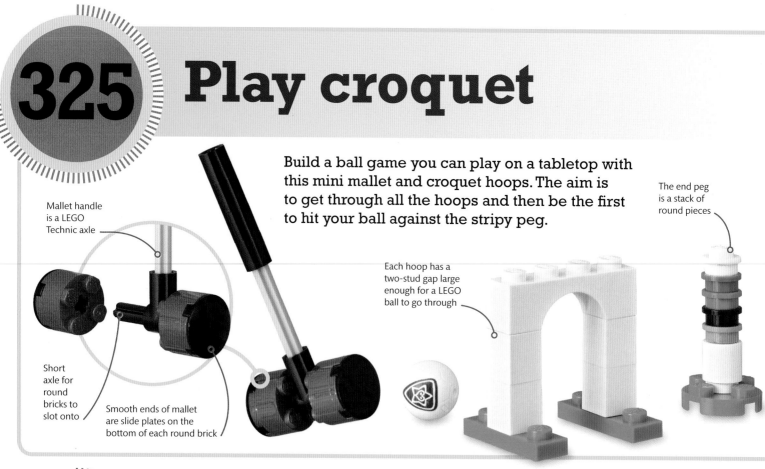

Build a ball game you can play on a tabletop with this mini mallet and croquet hoops. The aim is to get through all the hoops and then be the first to hit your ball against the stripy peg.

Mallet handle is a LEGO Technic axle

Short axle for round bricks to slot onto

Smooth ends of mallet are slide plates on the bottom of each round brick

Each hoop has a two-stud gap large enough for a LEGO ball to go through

The end peg is a stack of round pieces

326 Build a LEGO bookmark

I'M GOING TO NEED A BIGGER BOOK!

Magnifying glass and map detail sit above the top of the book

You'll never lose your place in a story with this colourful LEGO bookmark. Slim pieces slip easily between the pages of a book. Larger pieces can be added to the top to poke out of the book – you could even add your favourite minifigure!

Tile joins two long rotor blade pieces

This simple wreath is made from two layers of plates

Ribbon ties are small curved slopes

327

Find out how to make LEGO bookends on page 87.

LAY OUT YOUR LAWN

Space out six hoops to make a full croquet lawn, and decide a route that the ball must travel along. Use two balls to race with another player, or try to complete the course with the fewest strokes, and then see if you can beat your best score.

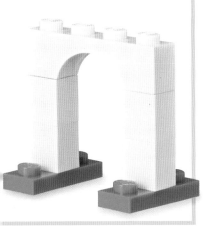

328 Make a mystery jar

Fill a jar with LEGO bricks to make a guessing game for a party or fair. Everyone writes down how many bricks they think are in the jar, and the person who comes closest to the right answer wins a LEGO prize!

Don't count the bricks until after the contest if you want to join in yourself!

A brick-built question mark adds to the sense of mystery!

Use a clear container so people can see inside

Grab some green plates and deck your hall with a festive wreath! Try swapping the green and red colours with oranges and yellows for autumn, or experiment with even more colours for summer and spring.

Instead of bows, you could add festive bells made from yellow radar dishes and dome pieces.

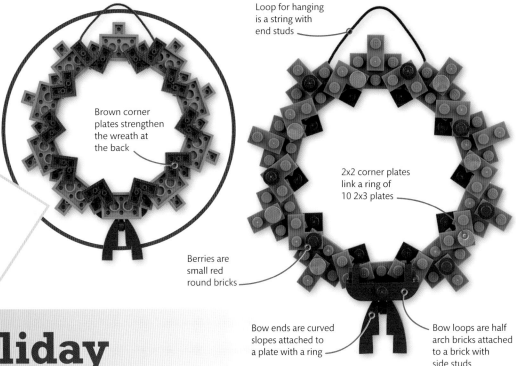

Brown corner plates strengthen the wreath at the back

Loop for hanging is a string with end studs

2x2 corner plates link a ring of 10 2x3 plates

Berries are small red round bricks

Bow ends are curved slopes attached to a plate with a ring

Bow loops are half arch bricks attached to a brick with side studs

Hang a holiday wreath

329

Sculpt a scary pumpkin

Set a spooky scene with pumpkin decorations made from LEGO bricks. It only takes a few orange pieces to make a basic pumpkin shape, but if you have more, try making the biggest pumpkin you can!

I USED TO BE CINDERELLA'S STAGECOACH!

Use leaf pieces for pumpkin tops

You could leave gaps where the black parts are, and shine a light from behind

A smiling pumpkin is less scary than a scowling one!

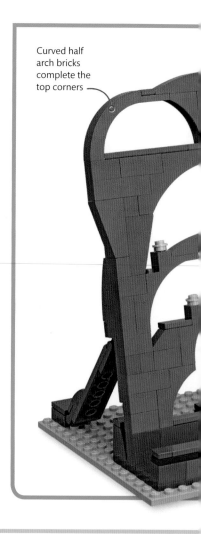

Curved half arch bricks complete the top corners

330

Create a cool comic strip

Use a camera and a photo-editing app to make great picture strip stories with your favourite minifigures. Add your own speech bubbles and special effects, and then print out your stories to make your very own comic!

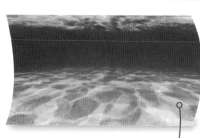

Print out a picture for the background and curve the paper around the minifigures to make it look like they are part of the scene

Use different faces to show a minifigure's changing moods

Make props to tell your story before you start taking photos

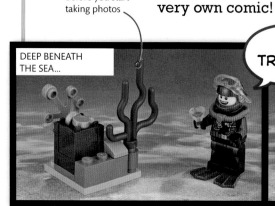

DEEP BENEATH THE SEA...

WOW, TREASURE!

AND IT'S ALL MINE!

THAT'S WHAT YOU THINK!

Make a display stand

Two small half arch bricks make this pointed arch shape

AS IT STANDS
Build the main section of the stand first, then the base and supports. The stand doesn't connect to the base at the front – it simply rests in the channel made by two rows of bricks. It leans back on three struts made from plates, which connect to the base using clips and bars.

Put your instruction booklet on the stand the next time you build a LEGO set.

Curved slopes create these smooth arch tops

Add a row of bricks at the front to stop the stand from sliding forward

Whether you are a budding musician or a LEGO master builder, you won't want to be without this beautiful display stand! It is perfect for studying sheet music or LEGO instruction booklets, and it makes an impressive ornament when you are not using it!

Use interestingly shaped brown bricks to make a stand that looks like a wood carving.

THE SPECIAL BRICK
Half arch bricks have studs that can be built onto – unlike curved half arch bricks, which have smooth tops.

Plates with clips snap onto plates with bars at both ends of the three 2x8 plates

A row of slope bricks supports the stand at its base

332 Balance a build on just one brick

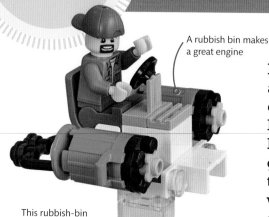

A rubbish bin makes a great engine

This rubbish-bin rocket has a 1x2 brick at its base

Perform a brilliant balancing act with a model that stands on just one brick! Make your build as big as possible, so it looks as if it is really defying gravity – but remember that the secret is to spread the weight evenly on all sides of the model.

The weight of this leg is balanced out by a broad chest in front

A single 1x3 brick is enough to support this running man

333 Make a TV photo frame

Become a star of the small screen with this realistic-looking TV photo frame! Slide a picture of yourself into the slot at the top, or give some screen time to your friends and family. Put two or three pictures in at once, then swap them around to change channels!

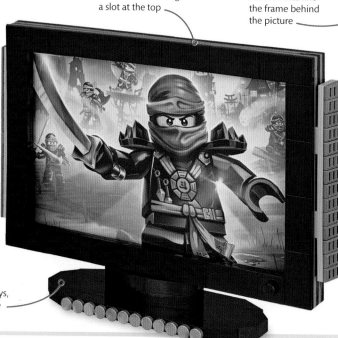

Pictures fit in through a slot at the top

Smooth tiles line the frame behind the picture

Build the whole TV sideways, starting with the brick base

NOT-SO-FLAT SCREEN
The TV is five-plates deep, with a two-layer back section, then a layer of plates around three sides where the picture goes in (don't add plates at the top of this layer). The next layer is a border of plates around all four sides at the front, and the final layer is a covering of smooth tiles.

334 Create amazing 3-D shapes

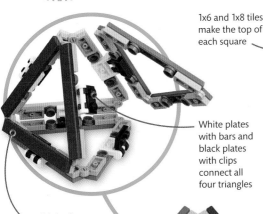

1x6 and 1x8 tiles make the top of each square

White plates with bars and black plates with clips connect all four triangles

Build the four sides flat, then fold them all together

Hinge plates create the triangle shapes

GETTING INTO SHAPES

You can make all kinds of shapes by connecting triangles, squares and pentagons. Build enough triangles and you can make an eight-sided octahedron or a 20-sided icosahedron. And with a mix of squares and triangles you can build a 14-sided cuboctahedron and a 26-sided rhombicuboctahedron!

This shape will roll like a ball, even though it has flat sides!

1x6 plates strengthen each pentagon underneath

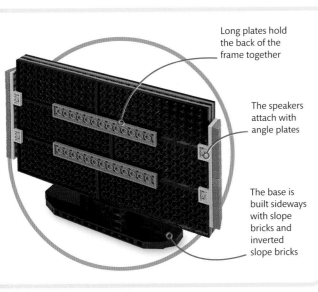

Long plates hold the back of the frame together

The speakers attach with angle plates

The base is built sideways with slope bricks and inverted slope bricks

Turn flat shapes into fabulous 3-D models – just by joining them together! The cube above is built out of six simple squares, and the pyramid is made from four triangles. The incredible dodecahedron is made using 12 identical five-sided pentagons!

335 Design a display case

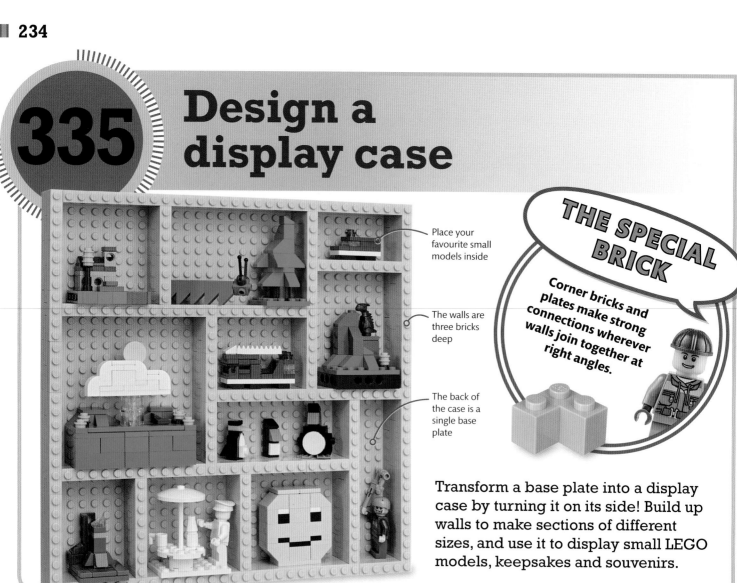

Place your favourite small models inside

The walls are three bricks deep

The back of the case is a single base plate

THE SPECIAL BRICK

Corner bricks and plates make strong connections wherever walls join together at right angles.

Transform a base plate into a display case by turning it on its side! Build up walls to make sections of different sizes, and use it to display small LEGO models, keepsakes and souvenirs.

This grey base is covered with smooth tiles

Make a square pattern where all of the colours are separate builds, and then mix them up to make a puzzle. Set a timer and see how quickly you can put the square back together. Is there more than one way to do it?

The 22 puzzle pieces can fill the grid in different ways

Each puzzle piece is made from plates with tiles on top

The frame edges are raised above the base to hold the puzzle pieces in

336 Put together a pattern puzzle

Play the post game

HOW TO PLAY

1 Every player has their own coloured door and starts the game with five letters, drawn at random from a bag.

2 Players take turns rolling a die. If you roll a 1, you must give a letter to another player. If you roll a 2, you must post a letter through another player's door.

3 Roll a 3 or a 4, and you can post one of your letters through your own door, as long as its stamp is the same colour as your door. Roll a 5 or 6, and you can post any one of your letters through your own door.

4 The winner is the player with the most post through their door when all the letters have been posted.

Keep the post moving with this door-to-door delivery game, as you compete to get the most letters through your door. Players build their own doors before the game begins – aim to impress with your fanciest designs! To play the game, put the doors in a row, or if you're feeling energetic, spread them around a room and race to each door!

Build the doors in different styles, including one that matches your own front door.

Lamps are tap pieces

This door has a key-shaped knocker

The grooves in this door are made from side-on log bricks

Each door has a postbox big enough for a letter two-plates deep

The stamps should match the colours of the doors – build five letters with each colour for each player

Use plates and tiles to create your letters

GET A HANDLE ON DOORS

Take a look at front doors in your neighbourhood and you will be surprised by how many different designs there are! Make the doors for the game as diverse as you can and make each one a different colour to match the stamps.

338 Duck back in time

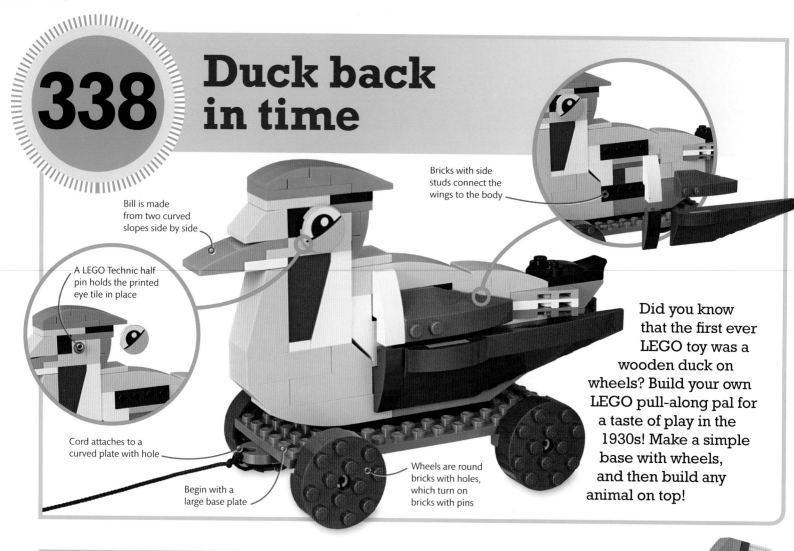

Bill is made from two curved slopes side by side

Bricks with side studs connect the wings to the body

A LEGO Technic half pin holds the printed eye tile in place

Cord attaches to a curved plate with hole

Begin with a large base plate

Wheels are round bricks with holes, which turn on bricks with pins

Did you know that the first ever LEGO toy was a wooden duck on wheels? Build your own LEGO pull-along pal for a taste of play in the 1930s! Make a simple base with wheels, and then build any animal on top!

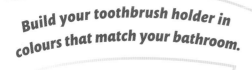

Build your toothbrush holder in colours that match your bathroom.

Put a LEGO model in your bathroom and it will bring a shiny white smile to your face every time you clean your teeth! You can create a simple container with stacked transparent plates, or make it even more impressive by adding stripes and a tube of toothpaste.

A tap piece adds to the bathroom theme

Don't try to clean your teeth with a LEGO toothbrush!

339 Build a toothbrush holder

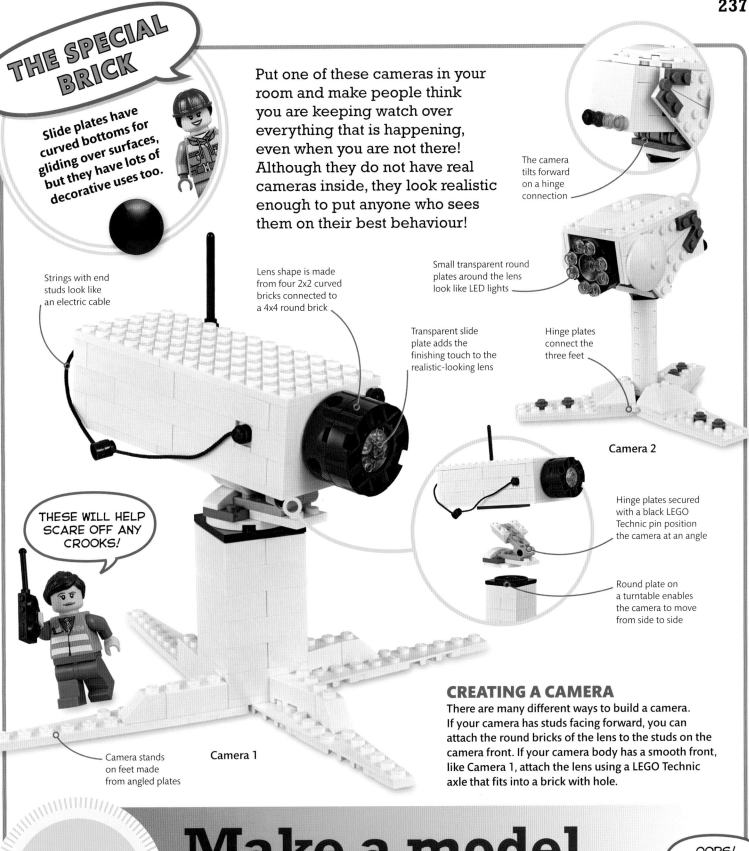

THE SPECIAL BRICK

Slide plates have curved bottoms for gliding over surfaces, but they have lots of decorative uses too.

Put one of these cameras in your room and make people think you are keeping watch over everything that is happening, even when you are not there! Although they do not have real cameras inside, they look realistic enough to put anyone who sees them on their best behaviour!

The camera tilts forward on a hinge connection

Small transparent round plates around the lens look like LED lights

Strings with end studs look like an electric cable

Lens shape is made from four 2x2 curved bricks connected to a 4x4 round brick

Transparent slide plate adds the finishing touch to the realistic-looking lens

Hinge plates connect the three feet

Camera 2

Hinge plates secured with a black LEGO Technic pin position the camera at an angle

Round plate on a turntable enables the camera to move from side to side

THESE WILL HELP SCARE OFF ANY CROOKS!

CREATING A CAMERA

There are many different ways to build a camera. If your camera has studs facing forward, you can attach the round bricks of the lens to the studs on the camera front. If your camera body has a smooth front, like Camera 1, attach the lens using a LEGO Technic axle that fits into a brick with hole.

Camera stands on feet made from angled plates

Camera 1

340 Make a model security camera

OOPS! CAUGHT ON CAMERA!

341 Play a trick with a computer mouse

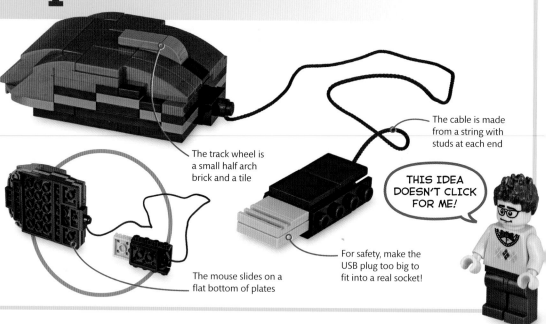

Build a mouse to match the one you use at home, then swap it with the real thing to prank whoever tries to use it! Make your mouse the same size and colour as the real one, and use curved slopes and smooth tiles so that it feels the same in your hand.

The track wheel is a small half arch brick and a tile

The cable is made from a string with studs at each end

THIS IDEA DOESN'T CLICK FOR ME!

The mouse slides on a flat bottom of plates

For safety, make the USB plug too big to fit into a real socket!

Food is passed through this serving hatch to the waiting staff

MY SPECIALITY IS BLOCK AU VIN!

If you could dine out anywhere, where would you go and what would you eat? Make a model of your dream restaurant and fill it with staff, customers, a kitchen and all of your favourite foods! Will it be a glamorous gourmet hangout, or a party spot with a wacky theme?

This giant burger is built with upside-down pieces

Fill your restaurant with happy minifigure customers!

Build in small sections so you can change your restaurant's layout.

Design your dream diner

342

Cast a creepy monster shadow on page 144.

Put on a shadow puppet show

343

Close the curtains and shine a bright light to tell a story with nothing but shadows! Build different characters with interesting outlines and then hold them in front of the light. Their shapes will appear much bigger on the walls!

BUILDER'S TIP

Use black LEGO Technic pins for the joints – these make a tighter connection than pins in other colours.

A chainsaw piece makes an aerial on the robot's head

I FEEL A LITTLE FLAT...

This gap looks like a light-up dial on the robot's chest.

I'M NOT AFRAID OF MY OWN SHADOW!

A single slope forms a nose, suggesting a man's face in profile

The man's head tilts on a LEGO Technic pin

The arm is built upside down

A long LEGO Technic beam forms the handle

The arched window piece casts a shadow that looks like an old-fashioned lamp

SHADY JOINTS

The best shadow puppets have simple shapes with a few distinct details, such as big teeth, a pointy nose or a tall hat. Remember that it doesn't matter what colours you build with, since they all cast the same shadows! Build your models with joints so you can pose them, and add long handles so you can make them move without putting your hands in the way of the light.

Try drawing ideas for your puppets first, then recreate them using LEGO pieces.

344 Build your dream job

What do you want to be when you grow up? Make a model of you doing your dream job! You could be a LEGO builder, a zookeeper or a very important person in an office in a stylish suit! Or why not let someone – such as your teacher, sports coach or parent – know what their hard works mean to you and give them a model of them doing their job.

Textured bricks make a building site for this LEGO builder

Small radar dish forms the base of a swivel chair

Keep count on an abacus

345

An abacus is a build you can always count on when you need to check your sums! This one has four rows with 10 moving beads on each. Slide the beads back and forth to do adding up and taking away!

Long LEGO Technic axles slot into bricks with cross holes

The centre of each bead is a brick with hole

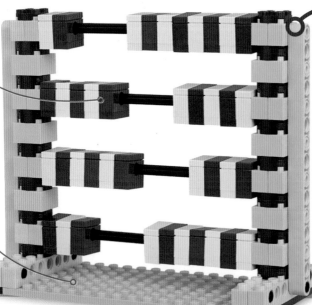

LEGO Technic beams add strength to the sides

A large plate holds the two sides together at the base

IT ALL ADDS UP...

You can use this abacus for adding and subtracting numbers all the way up to 9,999! If you want to know the answer to 9,876 – 5,432, simply slide the beads to one side to make the first number: nine on the top row, eight on the next, then seven, then six. Then slide five, four, three, and two beads back again to leave you with the answer: 4,444!

346 Play a game of chance

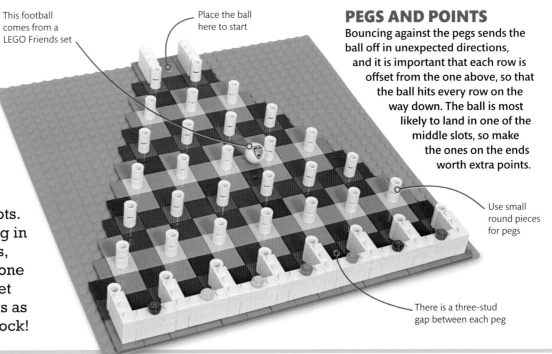

This football comes from a LEGO Friends set

Place the ball here to start

Build this fun rolling ball game on a LEGO base plate and prop it up to play. Place a ball in the top and watch it bounce through the pegs into one of the slots. Score points for landing in different coloured slots, or for guessing which one you will hit. Or try to get balls into all seven slots as you race against the clock!

PEGS AND POINTS
Bouncing against the pegs sends the ball off in unexpected directions, and it is important that each row is offset from the one above, so that the ball hits every row on the way down. The ball is most likely to land in one of the middle slots, so make the ones on the ends worth extra points.

Use small round pieces for pegs

There is a three-stud gap between each peg

Step up to the podium 347

The flagpoles fit onto bricks with clips

Add numbers to the podium using small red plates

Give a winner the glory they deserve, with a place on top of a LEGO podium! This model makes a great prize for a star performance or as an ever-changing league table in an ongoing tournament. You could even make the minifigures look like the real players!

348 Build a hatching egg

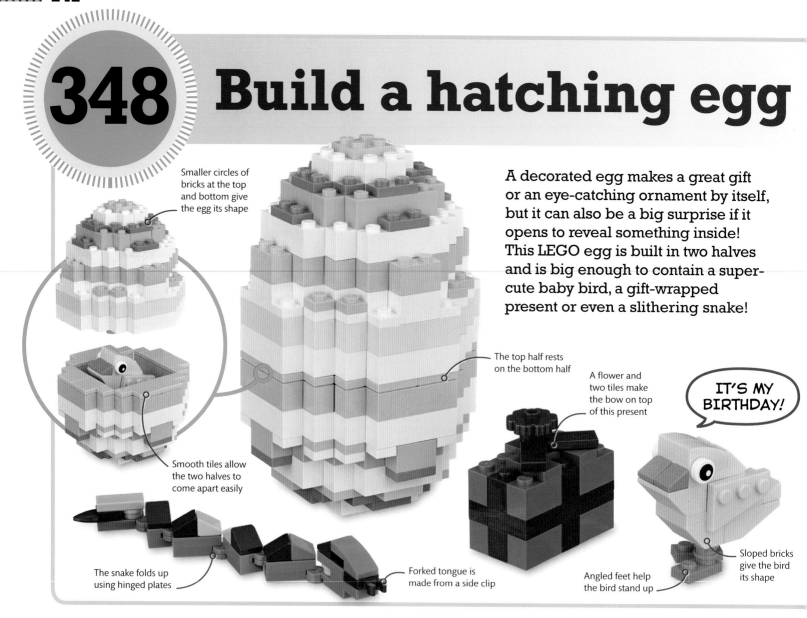

Smaller circles of bricks at the top and bottom give the egg its shape

Smooth tiles allow the two halves to come apart easily

A decorated egg makes a great gift or an eye-catching ornament by itself, but it can also be a big surprise if it opens to reveal something inside! This LEGO egg is built in two halves and is big enough to contain a super-cute baby bird, a gift-wrapped present or even a slithering snake!

The top half rests on the bottom half

A flower and two tiles make the bow on top of this present

IT'S MY BIRTHDAY!

The snake folds up using hinged plates

Forked tongue is made from a side clip

Angled feet help the bird stand up

Sloped bricks give the bird its shape

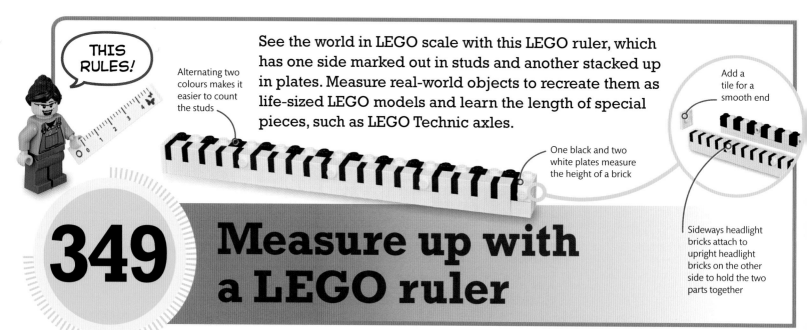

THIS RULES!

Alternating two colours makes it easier to count the studs

See the world in LEGO scale with this LEGO ruler, which has one side marked out in studs and another stacked up in plates. Measure real-world objects to recreate them as life-sized LEGO models and learn the length of special pieces, such as LEGO Technic axles.

Add a tile for a smooth end

One black and two white plates measure the height of a brick

Sideways headlight bricks attach to upright headlight bricks on the other side to hold the two parts together

349 Measure up with a LEGO ruler

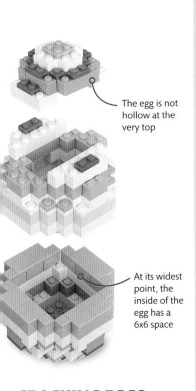

The egg is not hollow at the very top

At its widest point, the inside of the egg has a 6x6 space

CRACKING EGGS

Building a hollow egg shape uses the same circle-building basics seen on page 52. Make the base flat enough for the egg to stand upright, but build the top into more of a point. Build whatever you want to fit inside the egg first, and keep checking that it fits as you go along.

350 Play a game of draughts

Check it out! This board is perfect for a game of LEGO draughts. Two players can have hours of fun trying to outwit each other or can play against the clock for a fast-paced speed challenge!

HOW TO PLAY

1 Start with the board arranged as pictured. Players take turns moving one piece at a time. Pieces can move diagonally forward only.

2 Pieces move just one square at a time, unless a piece is able to hop over a single opposing piece in its path, in which case it moves two squares, and the opposing piece is removed from the board.

3 If a piece reaches the far side of the board, another piece of the same colour is added on top of it and it becomes a "king". A king can move and jump in any direction.

4 The winner is the player who captures all of their opponent's pieces, or boxes them in so that they cannot move.

Plates in alternating colours make up the playing area

Start with eight or 12 pieces each on the board

Make a card keeper

351

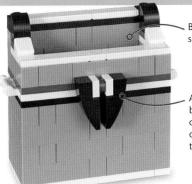

Build the box around a pack of cards, so you know that it is big enough

A multicoloured band and curved slopes decorate the box

Pick a card – any card! This box is the perfect size to hold trading cards. It would also make a great gift for a grown-up, as a colourful business card holder.

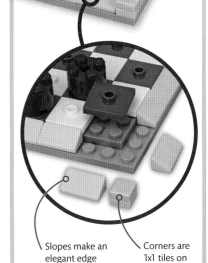

Slopes make an elegant edge for the board

Corners are 1x1 tiles on 1x1 plates

352 Make a block print picture

Experiment with all kinds of pieces to create lots of different effects.

Grille pieces are good for adding small stripes to a picture

A polka dot pattern is made with an area of exposed studs

Simple designs like this spiral make bold printed patterns

Use soft crayons that won't tear through the paper

Make a cool LEGO design last forever by covering it with paper and rubbing a wax crayon across the top! This technique is great for making LEGO themed cards or gift wrap.

Start your own sports hall of fame by building your favourite teams and players out of LEGO bricks! Build each player's outfit using their team colours, and add identifying features such as hairstyles to make your dream team as realistic as possible.

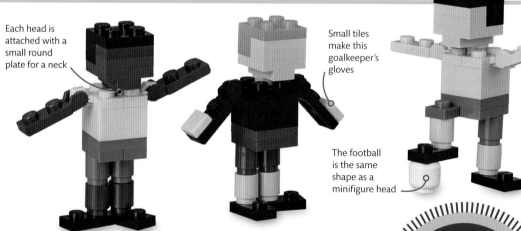

Each head is attached with a small round plate for a neck

Small tiles make this goalkeeper's gloves

The football is the same shape as a minifigure head

Build a field of sporting stars

353

354 Transform a LEGO model

What does your LEGO City need? The perfect addition to your favourite set might not exist as a LEGO model, but that doesn't mean it can't be built! Use extra bricks to add a cool new feature to an existing model, or custom-build one you've always wanted, such as this amazing air tanker. It puts out fires from above by dropping water out of its trapdoor! The minifigures of LEGO City are safe once again.

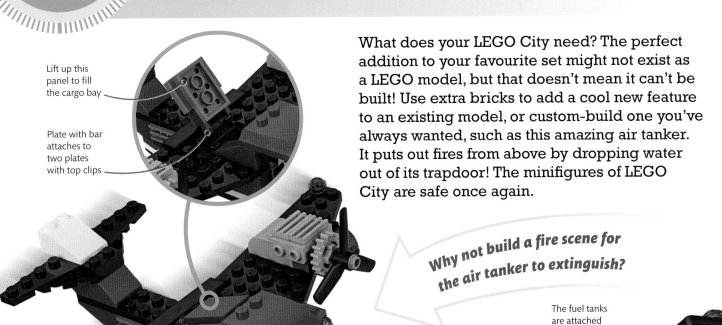

Lift up this panel to fill the cargo bay

Plate with bar attaches to two plates with top clips

Why not build a fire scene for the air tanker to extinguish?

The fuel tanks are attached using angle plates

Complex-looking engines are made with a mix of interesting grey elements

PLANE TALK
Some air tankers fill up by skimming over the surface of lakes, so you could build your cargo bay door with a scoop mechanism to catch the round plates from below. You could also make a plane with a sliding bay door – released by pulling a handle at the base of the tail – or a push-down button release made with a LEGO Technic axle running down from the top of the plane.

Slide plates have rounded bottoms that glide smoothly over surfaces

The liquid cargo is made from transparent-blue round plates

The bay door is a tile with clips attached to a plate with a bar

355 Penguin parade

How many bricks does it take to make a penguin? It can be just three or four! Use a timer and challenge yourself or your friends to make as many different penguins as possible in five minutes.

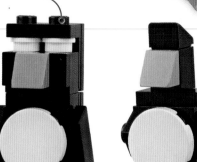

Beak is a small slope piece

An angle plate makes the top and back of this penguin's head

Tooth plates can make bellies, beaks and wings

Bring the outdoors in

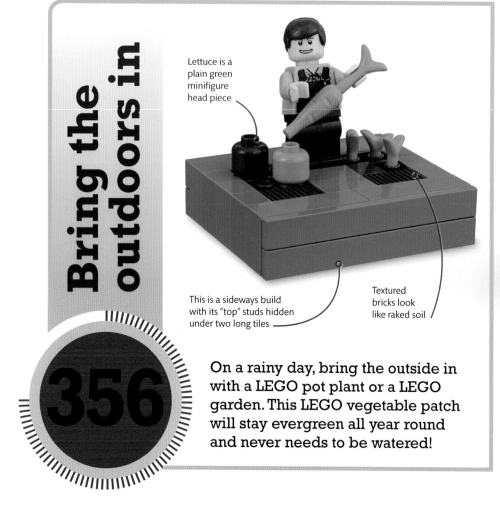

Lettuce is a plain green minifigure head piece

This is a sideways build with its "top" studs hidden under two long tiles

Textured bricks look like raked soil

356

On a rainy day, bring the outside in with a LEGO pot plant or a LEGO garden. This LEGO vegetable patch will stay evergreen all year round and never needs to be watered!

I'VE GOT SUDS IN MY STUDS!

Brush up your bricks

PENGUIN PARTS

When building a tiny LEGO penguin, think about which features would be visible on a real penguin from a distance. You would just see its general shape and colours – a black body, a white belly and a yellow or orange bill.

HAVE AN ICE DAY!

An old toothbrush is great for getting dust out from between brick studs. For a good clean, use washing-up liquid with cool water (40°C/104°F at most). Never put LEGO bricks in a washing machine or dishwasher, and always let them dry out at room temperature.

Show off your clean bricks with a bath-themed build!

357

Make a pencil pot

358

THINK OF A THEME

Your pencil pot doesn't have to be pirate-themed. Think about what you like to write about and draw before you begin. Maybe your pot will be the mouth of a monster or a cool castle tower.

Start by thinking about what needs to fit in your pot.

A clip-on lid seals the treasure chest.

Add somewhere to store your sharpener and eraser

A fierce pirate minifigure guards your things!

If you don't have a barrel piece, build a pot out of small bricks

A broad base stops the scene tipping over when your pencils are inside

Shiver me timbers – 'tis a pencil pot for a pirate! Build somewhere to stash your stationery… when you're not drawing treasure maps and writing pirate adventure stories!

Find a desk organiser for your stationery on page 37.

359 Make a micro construction site

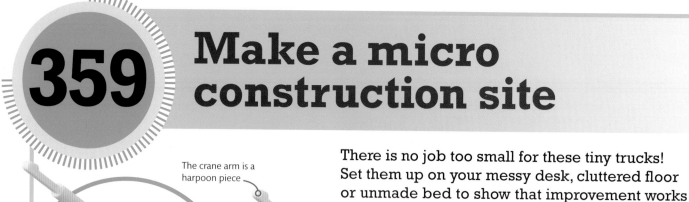

There is no job too small for these tiny trucks! Set them up on your messy desk, cluttered floor or unmade bed to show that improvement works are underway – you just haven't finished them yet!

The crane arm is a harpoon piece

The tracks fit onto bricks with side studs

Each caterpillar track is a small LEGO Technic half beam

A sideways panel piece makes a bucket for this loader

Transparent slopes look like a windscreen

360 Invent your own kooky car

Take all the parts you would normally use to make a LEGO car – and then don't use any of them apart from the wheels! This kooky car is built from all kinds of unusual parts and looks like it was made by a brilliant inventor! Can you make one that looks even weirder?

Use LEGO Technic parts for a heavy-duty, mechanical look.

I CAN FEEL THE WIND IN MY HAIR PIECE!

Transparent wall pieces form the windscreen

This big, exposed engine is powered by a crystal!

Use large half arch bricks for go-faster fins!

Two chair pieces make a wide bench seat

361 Build a box in a box in a box

A jumper plate holds the two halves of the biggest box together

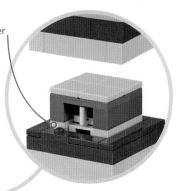

How many smaller boxes can you fit inside a big one? Start with the smallest box you can make and build another box around that – then build another around that one as well! Build each box in a different way, and see how quickly you can separate them again!

The largest box splits in two

The medium-sized box is open on one of its sides

The smallest box has a hinged door and a handle for pulling it out of the second box

Stick with a snail tape dispenser

362

The eye-stalks fit onto plates with clips

Decorate your snail's shell with some colourful details

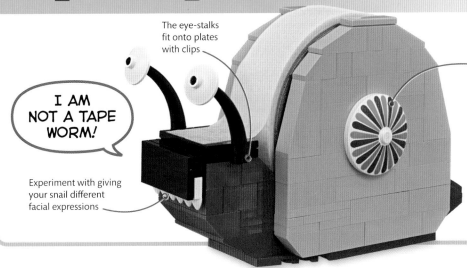

I AM NOT A TAPE WORM!

Experiment with giving your snail different facial expressions

This snail doesn't leave a sticky trail behind him – it runs out from between his eyes instead! The middle of his shell is a roll of adhesive tape, and the top of his head is a smooth tile for sticking down the end of the roll.

363 Build a big red button

Whatever you do, don't press the big red button! (Well, unless you really want to, of course!) The springy band inside allows the button to be pressed down and pop back up again. It makes a great desk toy for trainee secret agents and would-be supervillains!

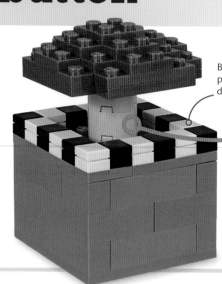

Black and yellow pieces look like a danger warning!

Build up the walls two-studs deep all around the button to keep it from wobbling

Loop small LEGO bands around plates with handled bars

A rounded slide plate stops the button from sticking to the base

364 Race to claim the pirate's treasure

HOW TO PLAY

1. One player starts on the grey path and the other player starts on the brown path. Players take turns moving by rolling the die in a race to be first to the treasure.

2. Where the paths cross over, players can choose to stay on their colour, or take the other route.

3. If a player's move ends on the first spider square, they must go back to the start of their path. If they land on one of the other spider squares, they must go back as far as the palm tree.

4. The winner is the first player to roll the right number of moves to reach the treasure. If the player overshoots, they must miss a go, and try again!

Welcome, pirates, to Spider Island! Choose one of the paths leading to the treasure, but watch where you step on your way to the booty! Scary spiders are lying in wait, and love nothing more to eat than a pirate's leg. They don't even mind if it's a wooden one!

Add more paths and obstacles for a harder game with extra players.

Use pirate minifigures as the playing pieces

The beach is made from five 8x8 plates

Make a tower with just one brick!

365

I THINK I'M DOING IT WRONG!

Spread out lots of pieces with their studs face up

You can only touch the top brick – and only with one hand!

Can you build a tower by touching only one brick? Pick up a brick and press it onto another, then another, then another. Keep going, still holding only the brick at the top of your ever-growing stack, and see how big you can make it in just one minute!

THE SPECIAL BRICK

Even LEGO spider pieces can be used for building! They fit onto studs, and have gripping clips for jaws!

NEXT YEAR, I CHOOSE OUR HOLIDAY!

Palm tree trunk is made from tall slope bricks

Each spider sits beside a printed warning tile

Rather than LEGO treasure, you could put sweets in the chest as a prize for the winner!

Corner plates hold the beach sections together

This LEGO die has printed tiles on all six sides – you can use a regular die instead

366

Invent your own LEGO® idea!

Not every year is made up of 365 days – every fourth year there are 366! Take the leap-year challenge, and come up with your very own unique LEGO® activity. It could be a **GAME**, a **BUILDING CHALLENGE**, a **TRICK** to play on a friend, a **PIECE OF ART**... absolutely **ANYTHING!**

Feeling inspired? Get creative and share your ideas with other LEGO fans. Take a photo of your idea and upload it along with a brief description, here:

www.dk.com/LEGO366idea

Terms and conditions apply. Only open to UK, Ireland and Australia.

Have fun exploring the gallery of ideas and keep a look out for exciting competitions.

Grab your bricks and get creative!

BUILDER'S TIP

A fun idea doesn't have to mean a huge model – or even a model at all! Think about how you could use your LEGO bricks in unusual ways.

Check out some amazing LEGO ideas here!

A GAME?

A TRICK?

SOMETHING FOR YOUR HOME?

WHAT WILL YOUR IDEA BE?

A CHALLENGE?

A PUZZLE?

Solutions

60 SOLVE A LEGO® SUDOKU P54

94 SOLVE THE FARMER'S PUZZLE P78-79

• The farmer and the chickens cross the river (the fox and grain are safe together). He leaves the chickens on the opposite side of the river and goes back across to the fox and grain.

• The farmer then takes the fox across the river, but because he can't leave the fox and chickens together, he brings the chickens back.

• Again, because the chickens and grain can't be left together, he leaves the chickens and he takes the grain across and leaves it with the fox.

• He then returns to pick up the chickens and heads across the river one last time.

109 SPOT THE DIFFERENCE P88

1 Different-coloured walls

2 Frying pan missing from wall

3 Different pan on cooker

4 Different-coloured cupboard door

5 Different-coloured floor pattern

6 Goblet added to row of mugs

7 Different-coloured can in corner

8 Different-coloured tap

9 Different utensil in mini-doll's hand

10 Different carton in bottom of fridge

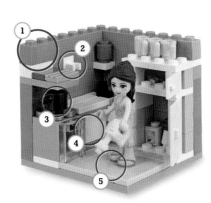

1 Different bird in tree

2 Missing brickwork detail behind tree

3 Different windowpane design

4 Pirate has different-coloured trousers

5 Different-coloured chest

6 Different-coloured flag

7 Fewer leaves on tree

8 Different item in pirate's hand

9 Extra barrel behind tree

10 Different treasure in chest

Meet the builders

Barney Main

DAY JOB
Engineering student

LEGO® SPECIALITY
Animals with crazy expressions, historical landscapes

FAVOURITE BRICK
LEGO® MIXEL™ eyes because they're great for building characters.

SIZE OF COLLECTION
30,000 bricks... maybe?

ONE OF MY FAVOURITE ACTIVITIES IN THE BOOK
134 Build a ship in a bottle (p104). This was fiddly to build, but really satisfying when I finished it. Getting a good bottle is important.

ONE DAY I'D LIKE TO BUILD...
A robot that climbs the stairs – it would be a fun challenge.

Rod Gillies

DAY JOB
Marketing for a big beer company

LEGO SPECIALITY
Steampunk (science fiction with old-fashioned machinery), micro-scale

FAVOURITE BRICK
Tough question. Probably a headlight brick or a 1x1 modified plate with clip light – it's really useful!

SIZE OF COLLECTION
Probably more than I need, but don't tell anyone I said that!

ONE OF MY FAVOURITE ACTIVITIES IN THE BOOK
145 Make a micro-scale set (p112) is my absolute favourite. I love that fire station!

ONE DAY I'D LIKE TO BUILD...
A minifigure-scale model of the Nautilus submarine from *20,000 Leagues Under the Sea*.

Alice Finch

DAY JOB
Educator, mother, chief brick stacker at Bippity Bricks (online LEGO store)

LEGO SPECIALITY
Architecture, landscapes

FAVOURITE BRICK
1x2 plate with rail – it creates interesting shadows on buildings

SIZE OF COLLECTION
2.65 million bricks (give or take a few)

ONE OF MY FAVOURITE ACTIVITIES IN THE BOOK
191 See inside a cell (p139). I like the idea of children using brick-built models for school projects. It's a cool way to do homework.

ONE DAY I'D LIKE TO BUILD...
Minas Tirith from J.R.R. Tolkien's universe

Joshua Berry

DAY JOB
Student

LEGO SPECIALITY
Architecture

FAVOURITE BRICK
2x2 tile

SIZE OF COLLECTION
Too many to count!

ONE OF MY FAVOURITE ACTIVITIES IN THE BOOK
215 Make a music video (p157) because I love the minifigure-scale band, especially the drum kit.

ONE DAY I'D LIKE TO BUILD...
I hope to build a big cathedral one day, like the Cattedrale di Santa Maria del Fiore in Florence, Italy.

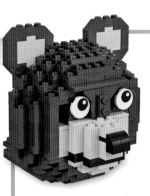

DAY JOB
LEGO artist—I design and build LEGO models and sculptures.

LEGO SPECIALITY
Miniland scale (the scale used at LEGOLAND® themeparks), castles

FAVOURITE BRICK
The classic 2x4 brick

SIZE OF COLLECTION
Around 1 million bricks

ONE OF MY FAVOURITE ACTIVITIES IN THE BOOK
43 Animate a bear (p44). I love that it is animated, which makes the model come to life.

ONE DAY I'D LIKE TO BUILD...
A life-sized room with furniture made from LEGO bricks – so I can feel like a minifigure!

Kevin Hall

DAY JOB
Electrical engineer

LEGO SPECIALITY
LEGO® Space, science fiction

FAVOURITE BRICK
A very rare translucent-yellow wedge from the classic LEGO Space era. It was only used in one set!

SIZE OF COLLECTION
Somewhere around the 2 million bricks mark!

ONE OF MY FAVOURITE ACTIVITIES IN THE BOOK
166 Put on a play (p124). Although it is quite a large model, I built it in just a few hours. I can imagine people putting on great performances with it.

ONE DAY I'D LIKE TO BUILD...
A large mansion house with intricate detailing and grand rooms.

Jason Briscoe

DAY JOB
Web developer

LEGO SPECIALITY
Collecting minifigures, small-scale models

FAVOURITE BRICK
1x1 "cheese" slope

SIZE OF COLLECTION
I have no idea!

ONE OF MY FAVOURITE ACTIVITIES IN THE BOOK
197 Take your minifigures on a photo tour (p143) because it provides opportunities for storytelling.

ONE DAY I'D LIKE TO BUILD...
A large-scale space station

Drew Maughan

DAY JOBS
Freelance LEGO builder (Naomi); Systems engineer (Stuart)

LEGO SPECIALITIES
Buildings, mathematical shapes (Naomi); Space, buildings (Stuart)

FAVOURITE BRICKS
Headlight brick (Naomi); 2x2 corner plate (Stuart)

SIZE OF COLLECTION
Over half a million bricks

ONE OF MY FAVOURITE ACTIVITIES IN THE BOOK
277 Play the gridlock game (p197) – the vehicles are really cute (Naomi); **102** Make a long-armed grabber (p83) because it works and it's so much fun to play with (Stuart).

ONE DAY I'D LIKE TO BUILD...
A micro-scale town with working trains (Naomi); a near-human-sized minifigure (Stuart).

Naomi Farr and Stuart Crawshaw

Senior Editor Helen Murray
Senior Designer Jo Connor
Editor Pamela Afram
Designers Ellie Boultwood and Rhys Thomas
Additonal editors Beth Davies, David Fentiman
and Laura Palosuo
Pre-Production Producer Siu Chan
Senior Producer Lloyd Robertson
Managing Editor Paula Regan
Design Manager Guy Harvey
Art Director Lisa Lanzarini
Publisher Julie Ferris
Publishing Director Simon Beecroft

Models built by Joshua Berry, Jason Briscoe, Stuart Crawshaw, Naomi Farr,
Alice Finch, Rod Gillies, Kevin Hall, Barney Main and Drew Maughan
Photography by Gary Ombler
Cover design by Lisa Lanzarini

Dorling Kindersley would like to thank Randi Sørensen, Paul Hansford, Martin Leighton Lindhardt,
Henk van der Does, Lisbeth Finnemann Skrumsager, Michael Madsen and Jens Rasmussen
at the LEGO Group. Thanks also to Julia March at DK for editorial assistance and
Sam Bartlett for design assistance.

Picture credits: p100 (l): Peter Wilson © Dorling Kindersley;
p100 (r) Max Alexander © Dorling Kindersley.

First published in Great Britain in 2016 by
Dorling Kindersley Limited
One Embassy Gardens, 8 Viaduct Gardens, London, SW11 7BW
A Penguin Random House Company

2020 edition published in Great Britain by
Dorling Kindersley
One Embassy Gardens, 8 Viaduct Gardens, London, SW11 7BW
A Penguin Random House Company

10 9 8 7 6 5
008–280814–Jan/2020

Page design copyright © 2020 Dorling Kindersley Limited

A CIP catalogue record for this book
is available from the British Library.

ISBN: 978-0-24142-798-9

Produced in China

A WORLD OF IDEAS:
SEE ALL THERE IS TO KNOW

www.dk.com
www.LEGO.com

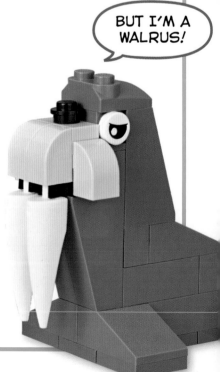

18

132

264

249

200

55

326

135

3